Also by James Naughtie:

*The Rivals: The Intimate Story of a Political Marriage*

James Naughtie presents *Today* on BBC Rad... chief political correspondent of the *Guardian*, a... *The Rivals*, an account of the relationship between ... Gordon Brown. He also presents programmes on book... on BBC radio and television. A former Laurence M. Ste... on the *Washington Post*, he has written and broadcast on Am... politics for many years.

# THE
# ACCIDENTAL
# AMERICAN

## TONY BLAIR
*and the*
## PRESIDENCY

## JAMES NAUGHTIE

PAN BOOKS

First published 2004 by Macmillan

This edition published 2013 by Pan Books
an imprint of Pan Macmillan, a division of Macmillan Publishers Limited
Pan Macmillan, 20 New Wharf Road, London N1 9RR
Basingstoke and Oxford
Associated companies throughout the world
www.panmacmillan.com

ISBN 978-1-4472-6158-2

A CIP catalogue record for this book is available from
the British Library.

Typeset by SetSystems Ltd, Saffron Walden, Essex
Printed and bound by CPI Group (UK) Ltd, Croydon, CR0 4YY

For Catherine

# CONTENTS

# ACKNOWLEDGEMENTS

I am grateful to many friends on both sides of the Atlantic for puzzling over the subjects of this book with me. It was first written for Americans, thanks to Peter Osnos in New York, and I hope it makes as much sense to those who know Tony Blair at closer quarters. I interviewed him several times for the BBC during his second term: in Washington, at the UN in New York, in airports and trains as well as in London, and I also spoke to him on the record in Downing Street in May 2004 for this book. Unless otherwise attributed, quotes from him come from those encounters. Inevitably, there are anonymous remarks quoted here—in a book involving political machinations and argument how could it be otherwise?—but I hope not so many as to be an irritation. Old comrades on the political circuit have been kind and illuminating— especially Martin Kettle, Peter Riddell, Peter Hennessy, Philip Stephens and Sidney Blumenthal. My editor at *Today* Kevin Marsh, the head of radio news at the BBC Stephen Mitchell and Gordon Corera, a companion on many a Washington expedition, have been stalwart supporters, and my agent Felicity Bryan and Georgina Morley at Macmillan as patient and persuasive as ever. Book writing is an all-consuming business and, as Andrew, Catherine and Flora can testify, my wife Ellie manages it better (and more quickly) than me. They all have my love.

# INTRODUCTION

When Tony Blair went to bed on the night of the American presidential election on 2 November 2004, he thought that George W. Bush might have been defeated. His staff were ready with a phone number for Senator John Kerry, and the Prime Minister had prepared himself to congratulate the Democrat who might have beaten his friend. But no one knew what he wanted to happen, what he wished for when he was alone with his thoughts.

He told a minister in Downing Street that day that for him it was "win-win". Either way he prospered. He'd mesh with a second Bush administration even more comfortably than he had with the first; but if Kerry were president he'd get the political benefit of an ally who would be popular in the Labour Party and across Europe. As usual, Blair saw opportunities he thought he could exploit however events turned out, and relaxed.

Around him, there was not so much relaxation as rampant (and hopelessly premature) excitement. During the afternoon in Washington, early and incomplete exit polls from across the United States were whizzing around the mobile phone networks and the internet in an orgy of gossip and speculation, persuading desperate Democrats that after a year in which their campaign had swung from optimism to troughs of pessimism their vast effort to get the vote out had won it for Kerry. In Downing Street they shared the froth and fun of those hours, hearing every rumour: Bush was sunk in gloom, record turnouts were swamping him in the swing states, Kerry's staff were already celebrating with the candidate in Boston and the place was awash with champagne.

Blair's staff, by an overwhelming majority, wanted the Massachusetts senator to win. Labour MPs felt the same. In the Foreign Office, though continuity is usually treasured there and familiarity with Bush's Washington was going to be an advantage if he stayed in office, there was a stirring of interest. Might everything change overnight? In other European capitals, there was hope that the frost that now clung to the transatlantic alliance might be about to melt. Fed by excited chatter from Washington, where Democrats were busy wondering who'd be secretary of state and national security adviser, and dreaming of the thrills of a transition and an inauguration, a surge of heady energy flowed through Downing Street.

Of course, it was all nonsense. Karl Rove, strategist and personal coach to Bush, was right when he told him that he could deliver several million extra votes in the important states to add to his total in 2000 (his popular vote increased by about 8 million). The Republican operation, using a new computer programme to target the most sensitive parts of the electorate, was the best (as well as the most expensive) that anyone had ever seen. The Democrats thought their operation in the big swing states was better, but they were wrong. By early evening the drinking at Kerry headquarters had become the preliminary to a wake.

There is a moment in one of the classic novels of American politics *The Last Hurrah*, set in Boston, when the candidate spots before anyone else a telltale little figure in the early precinct tallies that warns him of trouble. In a moment, he knows that his dreams of a landslide have died, and it is all over, even while the celebrations go on around him. For Kerry, it was just as quick. When the real votes started to be counted the early exit polls evaporated in an hour or two and were soon gone with the wind. The states began to pile up. By the early hours in London it was clear he was beaten. The Democrats refused to concede until the last votes were in from Ohio well into the next day but it was a hopeless gesture against the inevitable.

The British Embassy in Washington, however, had remained sober even when the election day fever took hold. Throughout the campaign, Sir David Manning, the closest to the Prime Minister of all his ambassadors, had believed that Bush was likely to prevail. He had spent time with Kerry and despite the puzzlement and irritation of some Democrats about Blair's closeness to Bush and his support for the Iraq war, relations were in a state to be warmed up quickly if there was a change of administration. But the betting was on the Republicans, and the calculation was right.

Blair woke to a familiar scene, and spoke to Bush. But there had been moments when his staff wondered how close he had come to hoping for a Kerry win; it would have given him a political lift. The Labour Party would have cheered, such was its disaffection with Bush, and in parts of Whitehall the departure of neo-conservatives from administration offices in Washington would have been the cause of much celebration. Blair would certainly have had a period of awkwardness with the president-elect, whom he barely knew and who resented the support he had given Bush. But the view in Downing Street and the Washington Embassy was that within a few weeks they could have been walking along the beach on Nantucket like old friends. They would have had to; there was a war on.

The prospect did attract Blair, because he would be writing on a clean sheet. He had an election to fight, and George W. Bush was an incubus on his back, a companion the electorate did not want. The cold political calculation was that Kerry would have been good news. It wouldn't even have meant a U-turn in Iraq, because the commitment of American forces could not now be undone overnight, and Blair was well aware that in his conception of "muscular diplomacy" in the post-Cold War world he and Kerry spoke the same language. Their speeches could have been swapped without anyone noticing, save in the passages referring to Bush. Some in his circle are convinced it is what he wanted; he wasn't saying.

Blair could have worked with either man, but the reason that Downing Street was so jumpy on election day, and that the gossip crackled with such life at the election night party at the American Embassy in London, was that he had become much more than just another foreign leader who would make his dispositions and hope for some favours from the White House. He was intimately involved. In his second term, he had developed from a traditional ally to a partner in war and even a kind of adopted American hero. It had been unexpected, quick and profound.

The alliance between Bush and Blair is one of the unlikeliest of our age, and one of the most potent. Its very peculiarity is responsible for much of that strength, because they have sometimes seemed so dazzled and surprised by the relationship that they have cherished it all the more. But the partnership is also one of the most divisive of modern times.

Their celebration of the pact that was fully consummated after 11 September 2001 led them to war in Iraq and gave each of them more determination to follow a policy which convulsed the Middle East, divided Europe and perpetuated in the United States the divisions that dramatized Bush's election and remained unhealed through his first term. Blair seemed a natural Democrat, so Democrats wondered why he relished Bush's company. At home, Labour asked the same question. Bush drew on the power of that mystery to sustain his own foreign policy, and the result was a transatlantic relationship that appeared to be the closest, personally, since the two countries entered into the Cold War together after the Second World War.

Blair was fascinated by the United States, and Americans by him. It was a strange affair for a prime minister who felt instinctively European, and whose premiership had as one of its principal purposes the embedding of Britain in the European Union to put an end to forty years of post-imperial dithering. Yet after 9/11 he became part of the American political scene, and it was in Washington that he found a sounding-board for his ideas about the disordered world of the new century, and a readier welcome than he did in some European capitals where ideologically he might have been expected to be more at home.

Bush, too, found he was not alone when the feeling for revenge in the "war on terror" opened up a path to Baghdad. At every turn,

Blair was with him. They had disagreements about timing, about tactics, about the way the occupying forces should go about transforming Iraq, but they never broke on a question of principle. It was an extraordinary political event, which put Blair at the centre of a puzzle that his Cabinet colleagues in London found it difficult to solve.

He had influence, but did he have power? Such was his conviction that pre-emptive action could be justified in the contemporary world because of the threat of a confluence of rogue states and terrorist networks that he became a loyal partner to Bush. At moments when some of those close to him expected—or wanted—him to draw back, he resisted. Instead, he seemed to have a degree of ideological common cause with Washington neo-conservatives who were seen by the European political establishment as dangerously ambitious to create a world ordered to suit America's interests and no one else's, if necessary by war. In doing so, Blair sacrificed the outsider's freedom of action in return for a degree of respectability and influence in Washington which, he argued, would moderate the wilder possibilities canvassed on the outer fringes of the Right.

The result was to give Bush a stabilizing helping hand in confronting his critics at home and the chorus of antagonism abroad which greeted him almost everywhere he went. Blair became an adjunct of his presidency, in a way that Bush couldn't reciprocate. Just before the invasion of Iraq, Bush suggested that the climactic summit should be held in London. Blair said no; it would cause too much trouble. So they met in the middle of the Atlantic, on the Azores. Blair's defiance of that domestic unpopularity, and his conviction that he was right, even when Saddam Hussein's weapons of mass destruction appeared to vanish into thin air, made him stand out as an original—a different kind of politician. To some members of his own government it was an unattractive badge of honour. They thought he was wrong about Bush, wrong about the war, and wrong in giving so much weight to his moral convictions in dealing with the woes of the world.

One minister said of him: "We keep waiting for his *Love Actually* moment, and it never comes." In that film, Hugh Grant plays a foppish prime minister who is in thrall to an automaton of a president, but who nonetheless manages a moment of release when he cries out "a friend who bullies is no longer a friend". They have waited in vain for Blair to cry out. He sees no reason to.

Talking on the record in Downing Street in May 2004 about Iraq, Bush and his own future, Tony Blair remained utterly convinced that the war would some day be seen as justified. There were demonstrations in the streets, his own party was in agony over his policy, the Opposition was starting to snap at his heels for the first time since he came to power, but Blair had settled into this role as conviction politician, the niche first claimed by Margaret Thatcher. Would history prove him right? "Yes . . ." In less than a hundred years? "I sincerely hope so. . . ." And he laughed.

Yet this was at a moment when his party seemed to be seriously wondering for the first time whether the Blair era was almost at an end, and if his difficult relationship with Gordon Brown was back in the deep freeze. That old friendship, electrified by rivalry and strained by years of struggle for supremacy in government, is the counterpoint to Blair's partnership with Bush, completing the picture of a prime minister who has learned to conduct his politics at an intimate, informal level. Partly because Brown's presence and power meant that it had to, his premiership has become a very personal affair.

His fascination with the United States was largely fuelled by a friendship with Bill Clinton, whose closest foreign ally he became before he managed the trick again with Bush. The relationship with Washington became more important to his premiership than that with any of his ministers, save Brown, and by the time British troops arrived in Baghdad his leadership was defined abroad by its role in Washington. Though the bread-and-butter questions of prosperity, law and order and the rest might decide the general election in 2005, Blair became a war leader who decided his reputation should rest, for better or for worse, on whether or not he had been been right to respond to 9/11 and Saddam Hussein's defiance by throwing in his lot with Bush.

Everyone who has watched Blair through his career knows that just as it is always dangerous to underestimate his resilience—he keeps getting up off the floor just when you think it might be time for him to crawl into the corner—he never loses his capacity to surprise. In Washington, at the height of his popularity there, he demonstrated that talent for mystifying even as he impressed. After his speech to both Houses of Congress in July 2003, which was one of his most lustrous performances, he was cheered to the echo by both parties. But they were still not quite sure what to make of him. At the end of it, Senator Christopher Dodd of Connecticut, that most unreconstructed of Democrat liberals, was applauding in the aisle beside Senator Pete Domenici of New Mexico, a Republican. He said to Domenici that it was inspiring to hear such a speech from a liberal. Domenici, who is a wily old bird, said: "If he's a liberal, I'm a commie." Blair is remarkable for not caring very much how that question is answered.

He is strikingly individualistic in his politics and although part of his personality is cautious, there is a streak of danger running through it. He thinks and often acts alone. He defends Bush to a Labour Party which thinks he represents everything it should fight. He believes, still, that he will be vindicated in helping Bush to depose Saddam by the future that will unfold in Iraq after the difficult election in January 2005. Blair has nurtured a relationship with Washington because of certainties which have made him a unique figure. Towards the end of his second term he was struggling against political forces at home which believed Britain had had enough of that uniqueness and should escape from his era. Like Bush, fighting a difficult campaign for-re-election and confronting divisions painfully exacerbated by war, Blair was marked by the decisions he took in the immediate aftermath of 9/11, and still moved by the passions which it aroused and he believed were still too little understood by those who opposed him.

They were an odd couple—the Republican president who felt uncomfortable with Europe, and the European whose best American friend had been a Democratic president. Nothing prepared them for the partnership they'd make; nothing prepared those around them for what it would mean. Blair had to accept a heavy price for the warmth of his alliance. On the evening when he was preparing the televised speech to the country explaining his decision to send troops to Iraq, he was in his small office with Alastair Campbell, still in those days his confidant and spiky alter ego, wondering how to begin. Campbell said: "How about, 'my fellow Americans . . .'" For once, Blair didn't laugh.

He perplexed many of his friends. His conviction that he was right, even when no one could find the famous weapons of mass destruction in pursuit of which he said he went to war, made him stand out as a different kind of politician, which is what he wanted. Many of his ministers thought he was wrong about Bush, wrong about the war, wrong in giving so much weight to his moral conviction in dealing with the woes of the world. But they also recognized that if it was a mistake, it was on a grand scale. Blair has always preferred the sweep of a broad canvas to working with detail.

That characteristic was important in shaping the decisions that led to war. As he ploughed through the UN negotiations, which he hoped would prevent war, and the security council began to splinter in acrimony, Blair became impatient and began to see the dispute with Iraq increasingly in the simple terms which had influenced him since 9/11. As he put it to Lord Butler's inquiry in 2004: "What changed for me with September the eleventh was that I thought then 'You have to change your mindset . . . you have to go out and get after the different aspects of the threat . . . you have to deal with this otherwise the threat will grow . . .'" Though he succeeded in persuading the Americans to spend more time at the UN than they wanted, since they never believed Saddam could be persuaded to reach an accommodation on inspections, Blair was always driven by a sense of inevitability that grew in his mind. By the time he was convinced that force was justified, he appeared to have persuaded himself there was no alternative. This was not a view held by everyone in his Cabinet, nor in the Foreign Office, nor in MI6, nor in the Ministry of Defence. But it was his. He said he was still a reluctant warrior, but a determined one.

The process that convinced him to join the invasion was one which was strongly affected by this certainty in his mind. But the unravelling of the story of intelligence from Iraq in the Hutton and Butler inquiries demonstrated how uncertain the hard evidence was, and how the political demands from Downing Street tended to overwhelm the apparatus that was meant to measure and sort out raw information in a cautious and deliberate way. The political pace became so fast that the machine began to overheat.

Blair himself recognized what had gone wrong long afterwards when he encouraged MI6 reforms to try to improve the machinery for assessing material from the field, but the spies felt it was piquant that he was implying all the mistakes had been made by them and not by Downing Street. They believed, and so did some people in the Foreign Office, that a certainty had taken hold in the Prime Minister's office which would not be denied, and that the flow of information took on the shape that was demanded of it. An American satellite picture that *might* show a chemical weapons truck suddenly became a matter of excitement, defectors who spoke of active weapons programmes were believed because they appeared to confirm what was already taking root in the government's mind, suspicions of the motives of some informants were cast aside if the information seemed to fit the picture that was building up.

A telling description of this process comes from Carne Ross, who was a senior diplomat in the British delegation to the United Nations during the pre-war negotiations. He subsequently resigned. After leaving the diplomatic service, he said this:

"If ministers want a particular story to emerge, it has a way of emerging: the facts are made to fit the policy. It takes a brave if not foolhardy civil servant to resist this tide.

"This is not to claim that there was some secret cubicle in Whitehall (or Washington) where evidence of Iraq's weapons was deliberately fabricated, but something more subtle. Evidence is selected from the available mass, contradictions are excised, and the selected data are repeated, rephrased, polished (spun, if you prefer) until it seems neat, coherent and convincing, to the extent that those presenting it may believe it fully themselves."

To those who laboured in Whitehall in the Iraq crisis, these words ring true. Blair had to acknowledge more than a year after the invasion that the case which his government had put to the people was, at best, an inadequate version of the truth. Weapons of mass destruction could not be found, the "imminent threat" was not quite what it had seemed to be, and therefore the best argument for war was perhaps going to have to be a version of the "regime change" policy which had been Bush's from the beginning. The consequence was that those who had been sceptical of the case for war in the first place were confirmed in their belief, and a number of Blair's friends who had gone to war with him felt betrayed. The Labour Party was shaken by the experience and Blair discovered that although as he managed to retain a commanding position in the opinion polls, giving him every chance of winning a third term, his personal standing was gravely damaged.

This was the price of his alliance with Bush, a partnership which he had turned from the necessary relationship with an American president into a much deeper commitment. It reflected his personality and his political style, but it changed him too.

Apart from the political consequences of the Iraq invasion, which caused him serious difficulty, he was revealed by the experience to be a particular kind of politician—driven by a morally informed set of convictions which tended to spring from his feelings rather from cool analysis. He trusted his instincts. It also encouraged Blair to see himself as a lone figure struggling against a hostile tide, a tendency to which he was susceptible. The result was that in running his own government he was even more interested in strengthening the Downing Street machine—watching an executive president at work had fed a frustration which had always been there.

Above all, the experience that led him to Iraq and tied him to the United States made him an even more determined character. The firestorm of unpopularity which followed the invasion, the strains with Jacques Chirac and others which came along with it, and the wearying revelations of the Whitehall bungles which accompanied the preparations for war all affected Blair's outlook towards a third term. From a brief period of gloom and dispirited introspection in 2004, in which his family loomed large, he emerged apparently invigorated, determined to press on with public-service reform and a policy programme that he knew would challenge a substantial section of his party and, especially, Gordon Brown. His posture in the run-up to the general election which he planned for May 2005 was the product of the experience in which Bush, the most unpopular American president in Europe in living memory, had been his unlikely partner. The Blair ready to fight for a third term was the Blair who had been fired in the heat of that alliance.

The Iraq policy had weakened him at home, but the assertion that he made to his closest colleagues was that the experience had strengthened him. With Brown waiting for the succession to Downing Street that was meant as a warning. Blair wasn't finished yet.

It was a claim that would take time to be tested. If he won a third term, it might be with a majority that would corral him in a way that he hadn't known before. Brown might break publicly in way that he had (just) managed to resist so far. And Labour MPs might not prove as enthusiastic about market solutions in the public services as Blair liked to believe. There was also the question of Bush, now in his second term.

On one issue Blair was optimistic and on another he was worried. Before the American election, Blair told friends that he had a promise from Bush of a Middle East peace initiative which the Prime Minister thought might start to repair some of the damage done by Bush's inactivity during his first term. Condoleezza Rice's appointment as Secretary of State (welcomed in the Foreign Office and Downing Street, not least because she was David Manning's best friend in the administration) was followed by a visit to Israel-Palestine on her first trip overseas. Blair had reason to believe that Bush would at least try to put the pressure on the Israeli government that was needed (and could only come from Washington) and offer enough in friendship and money to the post-Arafat Palestinian leadership to produce an interim peace. But he was concerned about Iran.

The argument about Iran's nuclear programmes was complicated, but Britain, France and Germany remained convinced that diplomatic pressure could settle the up and down dispute with the

West which had been going on for quarter of a century. Washington was less sure. In the first State of the Union message of the second term, Bush took the trouble to tell Iranians who wanted reform that the United States stood with them. The unspoken thought was that they would stand together against a regime that was still part of the "axis of evil" with Iraq and North Korea that he had identified in 2002. His policy towards Teheran, where Jack Straw, the foreign secretary, had invested a great deal of diplomatic capital over many years was causing great disturbance in the Foreign Office.

Blair himself, characteristically optimistic, appeared convinced that Bush would not wish to embark on another military adventure, not least because of the snares he had encountered in Iraq, and because of the cost. But to some of those around him he seemed less alarmed that he might be. In one conversation, he surprised a questioner by revealing only a hazy knowledge of the hostage crisis in 1979–80 which had traumatized the United States and which was the issue on which the transition from Jimmy Carter to Ronald Reagan had turned. He had little knowledge of the background against which the debate about Iran was conducted in the United States. It was an insight into the real Blair.

Such lacunae are not unusual with him. Though he absorbs a brief quickly, and enjoys filling his brain with detail just before he needs it, he is not someone whose head swarms with information, especially if it is from the past. He learns when he has to, but he has a near-conscious desire to think afresh and to avoid getting bogged down in history. This, his critics say, is because he doesn't know any. Although that is not true there is some truth in it. Blair likes to write on a blank sheet of paper. One of the reasons for his easy relationship with Bush was that Bush was someone who worked in the same way (though he has much less interest—by some accounts, almost none—in the arguments about ideas which Blair enjoys when he gets into gear).

So even as European foreign ministries agonized about Iran, Blair remained confident that a crisis of Iraq proportions could be avoided. Ministers, concerned that he might be swept along by an

American policy which they found acceptable, were convinced, eventually, that he would indeed say no to military action if any were proposed.

It was a measure of the extent to which his relationship with Bush dominated the foreign-policy discussions that there was such worry that he might *not* say no. So profound was his commitment to the Iraq policy, even when he was infuriated by some of the American bungling in Baghdad after the invasion, that the loyalty involved seemed to overshadow everything else.

That may have been an illusion, but it was an understandable one. Bush was making an important effort at the start of his second term to repair relations with Europe—the visit to Brussels to see European Union and NATO leaders was a deliberate signal of intent from Washington—but there was still intense disquiet about his presidency, and even the promise of better cooperation between the State Department and the White House with Rice's "family" ties did not expunge it. Blair, whether he liked it or not, would remain the European leader who'd made common cause with the outsider.

There was still, however, something of a mystery about exactly what he would take from it. He certainly believed he had developed a strength in his international dealings, and he was convinced (to the consternation of his opponents in his own party) that he had honed a set of convictions that would carry him through. But what it would mean for the Labour Party was less clear.

He did get some advice after the American election, though from an unlikely quarter. The trade minister Douglas Alexander, a close associate of Gordon Brown, was an observer at the American conventions in the summer of 2004 and kept in close touch with the Kerry campaign. After Bush's victory in November, he wrote in the *Guardian* about the lessons for Labour, and argued that the "triangulation" strategy which Blair had taken from Clinton was dead. This was a way of solving a policy impasse by drawing lines from two irreconcilable positions—on Right and Left, for example—until they met, at the point of a triangle. And there you'd find some common ground where everyone might be happy. It won Clinton his re-election in 1996 and became a piece of Blairite strategy.

Now, said Alexander, the Republicans had shown that you could do it differently. They had built a political movement so strong that it shifted public sentiment. "The Right in America has understood that the purpose of politics is not simply to inhabit the centre ground. The point is to shift it, consciously and irrevocably, towards your vision of a good society. Their victory suggests that building strength in office demands not simply following public opinion but the fashioning of a new 'common sense'."

This was a direct challenge to the thinking of some of those around Blair, and perhaps to the Prime Minister himself. Labour must stand for something that would move people in the way the Republicans had with their socially conservative philosophy. In other words, Labour had to think ahead.

So from Blair's American ally came a challenge that went beyond Iraq and Iran. If the Prime Minister had indeed been strengthened by the experience, as he claimed he had, would he use that strength to learn the domestic lesson from Bush: if you want to keep winning, you have to move minds.

As Blair approached his election campaign his American experience, therefore, was central to his whole political outlook. It obviously consumed his attention day-to-day in Iraq, in the continuing "war on terror" but it also fed into Labour's own state of mind after two terms in office. Blair's difficulty was that he might find that learning the lesson of Bush's victory—the shift in the public mind—might prove the final break with Brown, because they were increasingly developing separate ideas about where Labour's natural territory should lie and how it should be defined.

That struggle, so long-standing and such a dominant part of modern Labour history, was bound like everything else into Blair's posture and policy after 9/11, his American epiphany. It was the experience that made him what he had become at the end of his eighth year in office, and one that, for better or worse, he seemed to be making the political story of his life.

# THE
# ACCIDENTAL
# AMERICAN

# CHAPTER 1

# UNLIKELY ALLIES

Sitting at Andrews Air Force Base in a snowstorm, a White House visit just over, Tony Blair was doing what he often does best—appearing relaxed and driven by urgency at the same time. He drank tea and spoke of George W. Bush, Saddam Hussein, Iraq, and war. I asked him what he would say to critics at home who saw him being led meekly to the battlefield by an American president. It was worse than that, he said: "If George Bush wasn't raising these questions, I'd be raising them myself."

Here was a British prime minister presenting himself as full of grit as any Texan, positioning his government deliberately along-side an administration preparing for war and insisting that if anyone was going to retreat from the coming fight, it wouldn't be him. Not a tremor of doubt was allowed to disturb the picture. If it came to it, he'd be even more eager than Bush to take on Iraq.

No scene catches the authentic Blair more clearly. He was determined, convinced that his instincts were right, and rather enjoying the sensation of being a leader going against the grain. Fifteen months later, with a war behind him and his popularity at its lowest level since coming to power, he hadn't changed his mind. If the Americans had been nervous about invading Iraq to disarm Saddam Hussein, would he have been trying to convince them?

"Well, you would need to do it with America. I would have been pressing them to take action. In the end, they are the only country with the overwhelming firepower to do this, but I would certainly have been pressing them to take action—hopefully to resolve it peacefully, but if not, ultimately as the last resort, to make sure that we took a stand on this issue of weapons of mass destruction, and the place to do it was Iraq because of the history of it."

His words on the last day of January 2003 had been no pose. Blair was about to catch a plane that would take him to a political crisis at home, where his own party was splintering around him and bigger demonstrations than the ones in the heady days of Vietnam were about to fill the streets. He was less popular there than he was in the United States.

His relaxed demeanor in Washington might therefore have been mainly a symptom of that popularity, the kind of physical ease that a politician finds coming with the balm of adulation. It was not. He had just had an unpleasant experience in the White House. After the two men engaged in warm and reassuring conversations in Bush's private quarters, they had come downstairs to the East Room for a press conference that seemed surprisingly awkward and somehow lacked the rhythm that such events are choreographed to produce. There was a sobering reason.

Before they left the first floor of the family quarters, Blair believed he had persuaded Bush to sound enthusiastic in public about the United Nations resolution that Britain now wanted to write in order to give a sounder basis to the war that they were both convinced would come in a month or two. Blair needed it to hold his Cabinet together and to keep his Party from exploding in rage. Bush seemed to be willing to oblige him.

But when they reconvened with their advisers before walking into the East Room for their press conference, the plan changed.

Ari Fleischer, the White House press secretary, asked Bush what he was going to say. The President looked at his pencilled long-hand notes and said he'd support Blair in asking for a second UN resolution, which would allow the Security Council to authorize military action if Saddam continued to defy the UN. Resolution 1441, which had passed in November and warned of "serious consequences," wasn't enough if there was going to be a war. Blair needed something more. Fleischer frowned. A statement of that sort from Bush would be an unwelcome head-line in the evening newscasts, perhaps suggesting that the Presi-dent was bending to the UN. He wanted no mention of a second resolution.

Condoleezza Rice, Bush's national security adviser, said she had spoken publicly in the past about the administration having no problem with another resolution if it could be negotiated with-out wasting time. Why not say it again? With Karl Rove, Bush's Svengali, nodding in agreement, Fleischer said that a presidential statement would make it a big story. Rice musing about a second resolution was one thing; Bush throwing his weight behind Blair to get one was quite another. Blair's officials looked at the Prime Minister. Would he insist that Bush say something in his support?

He didn't. It was a turning point. One of those present in the British delegation said afterwards: "All he had to say was— 'George, I need this.' He didn't. It was an important moment."

The importance was in setting the tone for the final six weeks before war. Long nights of diplomatic wrangling in the UN lay ahead, but American resistance to a resolution that would give weapons inspectors more time in Iraq meant that Blair had little chance of getting what he wanted. Those countries that wanted to avoid war didn't want to provide him with a trigger. They wanted to play for time. The Americans feared delay: troops were in place and an invasion had to come in March if they were to avoid the horror of fighting in the summer heat. Blair was caught in the middle. But as he had demonstrated in the White House on that January day, he had made his choice.

The press conference was awkward. With Blair looking nervous beside him, Bush dodged the question of a second resolution. In answer to the very first question, he turned instead to the timetable for war. The crisis would come to a head "in weeks, not months." Blair repeated the phrase. Everyone knew what it meant. War by Easter, whatever the UN Security Council might say. There was no hint that the United States would do anything to try to put together a new resolution, though that commitment was largely what Blair had come to Washington to secure. His motorcade left within the hour, speeding out to Andrews because the weather was closing in so fast that there was a danger his plane might be grounded for the night.

The Blair who spoke that night of his determination to pursue the confrontation with Saddam, therefore, was a political leader experiencing all at once the most delicious and painful consequences of his trade. At home, a rebellion was souring his party and threatening to shake his government into pieces. In Washington, he was luxuriating in the trust and friendship of a president but understanding that even when a "special relationship" became personal, it was circumscribed by the demands of domestic American politics, over which he could never hold sway. The result was the onset of a sensation familiar even to politicians who find themselves surfing through the highest waves of popularity and enjoying the passing thrills of defying gravity. Blair was alone.

It is a strange word to use of a man whose alliance with Bush had all Europe and much of the world watching him with fascination, and with various kinds of fear. Blair's prominence did not make him loved, but it made him irresistible. He was the politician who was somehow making a different kind of pattern in the sky, whose spectacular vapour trails lingered to torment those who came behind. And in the United States, he was the leader who seemed most fitted to the age of celebrity in which he'd come to prominence. His popularity ratings were high and in an era of twenty-four-hour news, his was the face that was identified and celebrated as America's friendliest in the hostile world outside. These were remarkable achievements and advantages. And yet, through it all, Blair had about him a solitary quality.

The reason for his apparent calm as he prepared for the flight from Andrews was that this was nothing new. He was quite used to isolation, and part of him even welcomed it. His political character had been shaped and is sustained by an urge to break away, which has caused him to make his biggest mistakes but has also put an individual mark on him. Moreover, in unravelling his fascination for Americans, and their fascination for him, this quality of distance is important.

It is one of the mechanisms he employed in making his alliance with Bush, and with Bill Clinton before him, and it also provides the clue to the strange pull he has exerted on many Americans, even among those who disagree profoundly with his support for Bush in the war in Iraq. In their mystification, they seem as fascinated as everyone else by the way this leader from the offshore island whose imperial days are long gone has been able to rise above the throng of leaders who make their hopeful way to the South Lawn to hear the band play and feel the happy clunk of the Oval Office door closing behind them.

Blair was the youngest prime minister since the eighteenth century, and the most inexperienced. That he came to power at a time when the United States was going to face its most dramatic and disturbing challenge for at least a generation was a matter of chance, and the events that threw him into such intimacy with two presidents were largely accidental.

His response, however, turned these chance events of politics into the definition of a new era. Blair was the leader who articulated and embodied the obsessions of a new century. He reacted against the ideologies, Right and Left, of his predecessors and consciously moulded himself as a leader for the age of globalization. His decision to call his own party New Labour, to the disdain of many of its loyal members and supporters, was no cheap gesture. He meant it. In the same way, he adopted a moral tone in speaking of the uncertainties of a post–Cold War world, again to the sound of grumbling from some of those around him. From the time of his election in 1997, though he did not have an intellectual approach to politics, he saw himself as the embodiment of change. The partnership between him and the President became the prism through which, for better or worse, the arguments about peace and war, about the clashes of cultures and religions, were to be filtered. The unanswered questions of the 1990s were no longer academic, but now pressing matters of politics that couldn't be pushed aside. The coming together of two characters in Washington and London determined how that process would begin. It was a surprise, because they seemed unlikely bedfellows—Blair leading a party that carried Britain's socialist tradition along with it and Bush from a political class and culture to whom leftism of even the mildest sort was shocking and mystifying. Yet for reasons that were in part personal and in part the consequence of melodramatic and unpredictable events, they found themselves thrown together.

Bush was a president lampooned for his international inexperience and gauche diplomacy; Blair a boyish prime minister whom the world was willing to court and indulge. In their alliance, they were both able to change. Bush could point to the support of an ally who represented that old European strain in world affairs that his administration had seemed to find difficult to comprehend, thereby implying that he might yet lay claim to a foreign policy that was more than a gunslinger's threat. Blair could try to surmount all the complicated jealousies and disputes that bedeviled Britain's relationship with the rest of Europe, and play out his dream of being the post–World War II prime minister who, more than any other, preserved the Atlantic alliance.

Their critics, in vast numbers in both countries, argued that both objectives were empty and dangerous at the same time. Bush found himself drawn into international accommodations that the neoconservatives in and around his administration found alarming and even sinister. At the same time, Democrats accused him of using the cover of a leader like the popular Blair to pursue a warmongering policy that would otherwise have been easier to expose on Capitol Hill and across the country.

Blair, on the other side of the looking glass, was caricatured as a poodle who had leapt into his master's lap and who was willing to make common cause with those same, suspicious right-wing thinkers in Washington who seemed to his own Labour Party to be the very antithesis of government from the Left. And for good measure he was accused of a betrayal of those American liberals who had feted him in the Clinton years and now sat puzzled as they watched him flit from Crawford to Camp David to the White House and back again, a pair of cowboy boots in his baggage. In summer 2004, Howard Dean, who tried and failed to win the Democratic nomination, told me in London: "We Democrats don't quite know what to make of Mr. Blair. We find ourselves closer to the view of the British people than to the Prime Minister."

Senator John Kerry, the party nominee, was required to be more diplomatic. But the view in his camp was the same as Dean's. Blair was a bit of a mystery.

The phenomenon of Blair was notable enough in Clinton's time. He was Washington's favorite guest and managed to etch a sharper profile in the American consciousness than had ever been drawn by John Major, whose visits to the United States had registered only as tiny blips on the radar screen and whose relationship with Clinton had never escaped the coolness that had trapped it from the beginning. By the time of Bush's arrival in Washington, Blair was established as a leader who was an important moral ally: he wouldn't flinch from supporting a president in trouble, as Clinton had seen.

Abroad, there was freshness about Blair that contrasted with the weariness that was beginning to weigh him down at home. He was finding himself mired in boggy ground and had long since lost the advantage of being new, different and fascinating in the way that all leaders are when they first arrive on the scene.

By the end of his first term, in summer 2001, Blair was already grateful for the happy lift that he felt in Washington. At home, he'd be assailed by voters wondering why the promised health service reforms hadn't eliminated the waiting time for a heart operation, or why the trains still didn't run on time, or whether he'd yet made up his mind whether it was a good time for Britain to join the single European currency (and, if so, when). In

America, there was none of this. He was the visiting friend in whom everyone seemed interested. Whether it was Ted Kennedy praising him for bringing relative peace to Northern Ireland or Bob Dole thanking him for pressing on in the Balkan war to get rid of Slobodan Milosevic, he was welcomed. All this played a part in Blair's character as a leader. He enjoyed the stage America gave him, and because he is an actor by instinct and a performer who savours occasions and moments of drama, he reciprocated.

The American affair that was kindled by Clinton and that flowered throughout his presidency continued to grow after the arrival of George W. Bush, to Blair's surprise and relief, and on September 11, 2001, turned into a thing of passionate intensity. He was closer to the President than any other foreign leader and spoke to him more often than quite a few senior members of the administration in Washington. The price was a certain detachment from all but his closest political colleagues on the other side of the Atlantic. And across the English Channel, on the European continent, where Blair had spent his first term in office trying to manage a reconciliation with presidents, chancellors, and prime ministers who saw Britain as a standoffish and reluctant partner in their enterprise of political integration, this new friend of the United States experienced a tangible chill. In France, for example, it was thought that you had to choose between being a European or an Atlanticist. You couldn't be both.

To compensate for those difficulties, Blair had his conversations with the Oval Office. They were long, frequent, and generally friendly. But he discovered that even a relationship like the one with Bush, which had been consummated in the days after 9/11 and which matured when they went to war in Afghanistan in search of Osama bin Laden, could not rebalance the scales. After all, he was not an American politician. Doting editorials, even in the *New York Times*, were read by almost no one who could vote for him; flattering findings in opinion polls in the United States might occasionally be reported in Britain with some awe, but for everyone who was impressed, there was someone else who would complain about the intimacy with Bush, a president who, from his earliest days in office, seemed to grate with the European political class and set their teeth on edge. Although Blair was drawn westward across the Atlantic in search of power and influence as well as by instinct, the consequence was that he seemed detached from the political culture on which he had to feed to survive.

Many of Blair's colleagues have spent long nighttime hours trying to explain the process that brought him so close to two American presidents from different political traditions. They understand the importance for any British prime minister of having a working relationship with the American president, who- ever it is, but they wonder whether the depth of Blair's relation- ship can be explained entirely by the trauma of 9/11 and the military challenges and dilemmas that came in its wake. They know that something else is at work. As they have pondered what it is, it is quite natural that they have begun to see Blair as a prime minister standing on his own, with a defiant look on his face and the air of a man who is deliberately and soberly setting himself apart from them.

Blair's alliance with Bush has always seemed to some of his closest colleagues in the Labour Party a bizarre infatuation, as if he were celebrating his fiftieth birthday with a classic midlife crisis by plunging into an affair with a stranger. But to the Prime Minister himself, deep in the throes of the new partnership after 9/11, there was nothing at all surprising or odd about it. If his instincts led him to Crawford, Texas, so be it. As a politician driven by feeling rather than by ideology, Blair has always trusted those instincts, believing they've never let him down. And even if they did, Blair's friends know that he wouldn't change. This was the way he plied his trade; the only way he could do it.

In this relationship, which developed with such startling inten- sity and speed on both sides, Blair found a partner with just as strong an attraction to the politics of touch and feel. From the moment of their first awkward joke at Camp David, about using the same toothpaste, these two leaders found that they operated in the same way. It surprised them, but each of them felt a certain childlike glee. Bush found a European leader who would defend him even as his effigies were going up in flames in the streets of Paris or Berlin; Blair discovered a president who appeared willing to forget his earlier dalliance with Clinton and to welcome his support with an open door and a shoulder squeeze. Wildly different though their backgrounds were, and deep though the cultural gulfs between them were, they began not only to like each other but to need each other. Somewhere beneath the surface a shared nervous system began to develop, enabling Blair to make the startling observation (in private) toward the end of 2003 that he thought his government as a whole now had a better relationship with the Bush team than it had with its predecessor administration, despite Clinton's personal closeness. And all this at a moment when his Labour Party was in collective despair about Washington's foreign policy. Blair enjoyed it all the more.

If there is a special relationship between Britain and America—and British foreign policy has rested on the assumption that there is—then its incarnation was in World War II in the pact forged by Franklin Delano Roosevelt and Winston Churchill. On the eve of his third inauguration and eleven months before Pearl Harbor, FDR wrote to Churchill in his own hand (calling him "a certain naval person" in their private code) with a verse he remembered from Longfellow:

> Sail on, O Ship of State!
> Sail on, O Union, strong and great!
> Humanity with all its fears,
> With all the hopes of future years,
> Is hanging breathless on thy fate!

This fruity, sentimental verse moved Churchill, who shed tears frequently and could turn the trick to political purposes with equal ease. He was aware in an instant of the use to which FDR's words could be put. He quoted them in a radio broadcast that night, and the effect was to hasten the assistance from across the Atlantic for which Britain was then desperate and which would be decisive in winning the war. From that moment on, through the bonding of the Marshall Plan for rebuilding Europe after 1945 and the early days of the Cold War, the relationship became routinely described as "special," even when the word applied much more to the inherited history and culture of the countries than to any depth of understanding between their leaders of the day. John F. Kennedy and Harold Macmillan were able to claim a particular warmth in their thousand days as leaders together, but even in the dark month of the Cuban missile crisis the contacts were much more infrequent than they became a generation later, and intimacy was impossible on crackly, unreliable phone lines and through the slow passages of the diplomatic bag across the ocean.

Reagan-Thatcher was the relationship always portrayed at the time as the apogee of the symbiotic link between the White House and Downing Street, but despite the heroic status that the Iron Lady was given in the United States, their political and cultural comfort together did not produce a daily closeness. Margaret Thatcher was certainly able to prevail on Reagan for important help in the Falklands War in 1982, and without her persuasiveness he would probably have been prevented by conservatives from giving Britain any help, for example in persuading Chile to allow discreet military activities on its territory.

Thatcher was a valuable ally of the United States in strongly encouraging the stationing of cruise missiles in Britain in the early 1980s (though the noisy political opposition at the time was ultimately feeble and never threatened her position as prime minister). But in the second half of his presidency, Reagan was often a trial to her.

At a summit with Mikhail Gorbachev in Reykjavik in 1986, she thought that he was about to be suckered into a deal that would dismantle the West's nuclear arsenal without adequate reciprocation, and she was right. From then on, she spoke of him to colleagues with affection but with an awareness of his failings. She felt genuine humiliation, for example, at the American invasion of the tiny Caribbean island of Grenada without notice— she even had to apologize for Reagan's act to the Queen, who was still head of state of the island, in a hangover from the days of Empire. Towards the end of the Reagan years, the relationship was one that depended on an emotional tie, and shared attitudes to communism and the free market, rather than on the joint working out of policy.

Blair's relationship with Bush works the other way round. It is practical. Until about six weeks before Bush's election in 2000, Blair had expected that Al Gore would be in the White House, carrying on Clintonism and attending conferences with the Prime Minister about the "third way" ideas he had developed with the White House, which were meant to bridge the awkward political gulf between the social concerns of the liberal Left and the power of individualism as championed on the Right. How cosy it all seemed. Instead it was to be "compassionate conservatism" from the statehouse in Austin. It was late in the campaign before Blair accepted that he was going to have to learn some fast footwork. The story of how it was done, and how the cataclysm at Ground Zero translated that early work into something durable—even impregnable—is part of the tale of these two leaders. But there are other ingredients, too.

Although Bush's dynastic roots are so important to him and he had always known what it was like to have government cars at the door and the Secret Service encamped in the garden, he shares with Blair an innocence about politics that is almost deliberate. This is not to say that he has ever been an inadequate campaigner (on his final visit to Britain as President, Clinton warned Blair never to underestimate Bush and told him that he was much tougher and wilier than he appeared). Nor is it wise to underestimate his ability to get his way, which is the aspect of his performance that most surprised Blair in their first meetings. But Bush approaches politics differently than many who take to the trade, particularly as compared to his immediate predecessor in the White House.

Bush is neither interested in ideology for its own sake nor in the manoeuvrings that excite so many people in the trade, and indeed whose lure is the very reason they take to it in the first place. Put Clinton in the midst of a crisis, with roomfuls of aides and analysts and an armful of phones, and soon he is engaged in an LBJ-like frenzy of persuasion and argument, laced with the trickery that comes with that kind of obsession. Nothing could excite him like a difficult negotiation, whether with Israelis and Palestinians at Wye Valley or in the midst of Blair's marathon sessions with the political parties in Northern Ireland trying to reach a tentative political settlement, when the Prime Minister on several occasions had the President awakened in the middle of the night in order to place a helpful, persuasive call to one of the recalcitrant participants who might be swayed by a word from the White House.

No one could imagine Bush taking such visceral enjoyment in these things, even if he felt like throwing himself into such a negotiation with gusto, which seems improbable. It is one of the marks of his political style. Blair does not share it, being a politician who has always had a weakness for back-of-the-envelope deals late at night and a lawyer's love of the last-minute absorption in a complicated case when time is running out. But there is a striking similarity in the way they see themselves operating in the political world.

Bush's instinct to stand back from the fray, to conduct meetings by staying above the argument, is matched in Blair's awareness of his own lack of traditional schooling in politics. Though he rose through the parliamentary ranks on the Opposition side of the House of Commons and made his reputation in the way that any future party leader and putative prime minister must, he came to government with no experience at all of office. It meant that he had his first experience of the workings of government on the day that he became Prime Minister.

Blair's innocence about government was more of a surprise in London than it would be in Washington, where four of the last five presidents have made virtues of never having served for a day in either house of Congress before becoming chief executive in the White House. The assumption in the Parliamentary system is that leaders are blooded in opposition and in junior office before they reach the top. In Blair's era, largely because of the dominance of Thatcher, it didn't happen. Blair was a phenomenon and he has always treasured the feeling that he is somehow different from the others. It would be easy to argue that he greatly exaggerates that difference—he has often approached the problems on his desk in a way that all previous prime ministers would recognize—but it is important to understand that he *feels* himself to be another sort of character. In part that is because he is always conscious of his instincts; they are what he cherishes most.

In late 2002, Bush said the same thing of himself to Bob Woodward in Crawford, Texas. "I'm not a textbook player, I'm a gut player." Woodward reported that a dozen times in the course of their conversation at the ranch, the President spoke of his instincts or his instinctive reactions. Blair could say the same thing.

Their approaches to decision-making are surprisingly similar, despite surface differences. Though Blair is at home in a seminar, of the sort that Clinton used to convene in the White House for long evenings of discourse and which now occur in Downing Street, Bush is not. But each sees himself as the leader who is never drawn into the melee of argument to the point of being submerged. Blair makes a virtue of the *ex cathedra* statement and the one-man policy, dropped like a fizzing grenade on the Cabinet table. It has caused him almost more trouble than anything else apart from war, but he has built his own political personality on that trait. Any other way of behaving would feel like a betrayal.

The strange affair between the two was therefore not so strange after all. Though one of Blair's senior ministers could ask, soon after Bush's election: "Has the man ever had an intellectual argument in his life?" and though the Prime Minister's friends took some time to believe his insistence that the President had some formidable attributes (some of them refusing to believe it to this day), Blair always felt comfortable in Bush's company. They're both informal, tactile, and downbeat in style. They're postwar men on whom the 1960s left their mark (though Bush's experience of its wilder side was certainly the more extensive). They have a weakness for charismatics and the power of a simple belief. Even on the vast territory where they disagree, and where their attitudes will never be reconciled, they seem to have decided to treasure the *way* they form their politics. Some shared instincts keep them comfortable.

That comfort is a paradox. It seems impossible that an administration whose heart beats to a neoconservative drum and draws so much of its strength from the fundamentalist Right could have bedded down with a Labour government whose social notions and commitments on tax and spending are from a tradition so different that it seems alien to most Americans. And how could a prime minister reared in the shadow of Labour history find himself riding the range with the first American president in living memory to make a virtue of unilateral action abroad and a doctrine of preemptive strike? The contradictions seem so profound as to be impossible to unravel. But they are not illusions; they are shaping the world.

Blair became immersed in America by accident, because he came to power at a moment when by chance one president was of an age with him and shared his outlook on the world and then, with another president in office, 9/11 drew him even closer. His reaction to those accidents turned them into the pillars of his premiership. Though he often tried at difficult moments to convince his electorate (and even his sceptical party) that he was overwhelmingly concerned with his domestic agenda, and though he felt desperation about delivering on social promises at home that had proved overblown and almost impossible to fulfil, he couldn't escape the joint ventures he pursued with the United States. Not for a moment would he give ground to the band of critics who said he'd been wrong, or reckless, or even malign—a majority of those questioned in polls in early 2004 were taking one of those views—but he understood the degree to which any failure in the day-to-day business of government was magnified by reference to the world outside, where his policy could be painted as a story of chaos by his critics. Far from making it easier to govern at home, his successes in the United States made it more difficult.

As he turned westward across the Atlantic, he could hear the cheers. Turning back to home, he could sense puzzlement, hostility, and even hatred. And beyond, in the rest of Europe, he faced a cold stare.

In the summer of 2003, these crosscurrents came together for Blair in a most painful way. On July 17, he addressed both houses of Congress on Capitol Hill and received a spectacular welcome of the sort that would lift the spirits of the weariest old politician, let alone one who had just turned fifty but still seemed able to appeal with remarkable penetration to the American political class and the people beyond.

But within twenty-four hours, he heard news that threw his government into a turmoil that lasted for the rest of that year and wreaked such damage on its spirit and its standing that it seemed certain to last until the day Blair left office. As he flew west to China from Washington, a simple but terrible message was passed to his plane. The government weapons expert who had been accused in recent days of being one of the sources for BBC reports on the preparations for war in Iraq that had infuriated the government had been found dead in a field in Oxfordshire and was presumed to have killed himself.

The Prime Minister who had enjoyed the seventeen interruptions to his speech for cheering in the House of Representatives and had just received the Medal of Freedom from the President of the United States was tossed into a political crisis. His reputation, the standing of his closest aides and ministers, the very integrity of the intelligence apparatus around him would be tested over many months by the independent inquiry that he set up immediately after Dr. David Kelly's death, and at the bigger and perhaps less forgiving court of public opinion. By the time Blair returned from his Far East tour, he seemed to have aged.

Blair, the accidental American, was in danger of being ensnared by that which he regarded as perhaps his greatest achievement.

He believed he had rescued the transatlantic relationship from a fatal rupture after 9/11, when America might have gone it alone, and then, concerning the challenge to Saddam, he further argued with colleagues who told him that he was wrong to say that a new age of American unilateralism had been thwarted by his absorption in the politics of Washington and his relationship with Bush.

Blair countered that without him, the Bush doctrine would have been cruder, more dangerous and much more unpalatable to those who were now telling him that he should never have become involved as a partner. As ever with Blair, he did not mind adopting a tone of some moral superiority when he made these arguments, which he had to do again and again, to Cabinet colleagues, to his political "family" and to Europeans who lined up at his door to ask why it was that he had thrown in his lot with the "warmonger" Bush.

Now, with Kelly's death threatening to stir up a political maelstrom and a host of domestic political difficulties piling up on his desk, there would be a reckoning.

Characteristically, Blair did not believe in the midst of these travails that his involvement with Bush and his policies had been a mistake. He was untouched by doubt. Some colleagues would claim to have noticed a flicker or two about the way war was waged in Iraq, but on the principle he was immovable. And on Bush himself? Resolute, to the despair of some of those who were his nearest and dearest in politics.

The story of their mutual fascination is one of the forces trying to shape an unruly world, and it offers a picture of how character is shaped by the seismic moments in politics. This President and Prime Minister startled and infuriated many of their friends by the depth of their unlikely alliance, and each had to accept that after the benefits there would be costs, more painful for Blair than for Bush.

How Blair came to imprint his political personality on America and fascinate so many of its people is the contemporary story of a leader who has reinterpreted the past and turned it to his own purposes. For Americans, Blair is something of a guide to them-selves. The accidents of politics and war helped to make him what he is, and they reveal his weaknesses and his strengths, but the determination with which he turned chance into a crusade has become a compelling motif for an age of confusion and fear.

CHAPTER 2

# FROM WESTPHALIA
# TO THE WEST WING

Prime ministers, even presidents, are often wary of placing themselves too boldly in the middle of a vast historical canvas, though
the temptation is always there. It invites scepticism, and sometimes ridicule. So those big maps are rolled out only occasionally.
Yet Tony Blair has no hesitation in portraying himself as a leader
who is comfortable in surveying the contours of history. Between
his arrival as the *ingénu* in 10 Downing Street in 1997 and the
eruption of the "war on terror" early in his second term, he turned
into a prime minister consciously portraying himself as a figure
with a task that had to be measured against the story of centuries.

In March 2004, he made a strikingly revealing speech in his
Sedgefield constituency. There was no grand stage, no gathering
of the political and diplomatic great and good, and the setting was
simple. The truth was that he had been anxious to make the
speech for some time. It had been gnawing at him, and the
opportunity was created to let him get it out. There was no point
in waiting for a platform—a lecture or a suitable parliamentary
occasion—because this was an exercise in the relief of frustration.

Of all Blair's speeches, none explains better how his mind was working. There was no artifice. The fact that one of his prominent party critics called it "drivel" immediately on hearing of it was confirmation to Blair that he was saying the right thing. This was unvarnished, raw defiance in the face of the criticism that was sapping his government and sending tremors of alarm through those who would be running his re-election campaign within eighteen months or so. It was the real Blair.

For the observer tracing how Blair's foreign policy brought him so close to the White House and how presidentialism began to seep into his own exercise of power, the description he gave of himself in this speech is the best starting point of all.

Describing the evolution of his thinking in foreign affairs, he placed himself at the centre of the international argument with no hint of nervousness or false modesty. And he showed how deeply he felt the tides of history lapping around him. In the most arresting passage of the speech, he swept back three and a half centuries to find a reference point against which to measure his task and his intent.

"Before September 11th," he said, "I was already reaching for a different philosophy in international relations from a traditional one that has held sway since the Treaty of Westphalia in 1648."

Westphalia! A name redolent of ancient Germanic disputes and deals, a seventeenth-century diplomatic marketplace and melting pot. In his search for a still point in a turning world, this twenty-first-century prime minister had settled on a surprising one.

Few prime ministers in Britain in recent times have felt able to speak in an unembarrassed way with such sweep. Since Churchill, for whom English history was as familiar and important as the air he breathed, the tendency has been to keep a brake on the rhetoric. As Empire disappeared and economic miseries began to exert a painful grip in the 1960s, it seemed absurd to try to recreate the sense of a politics in which a second-rank power still lived its history. Margaret Thatcher reacted instinctively against that tendency but showed an uncharacteristic lack of confidence in dealing with history. She trod warily in that territory. And Blair began his premiership without any sign that things would change.

He is no historian, anyway, being impatient with over-intellectualization. How strange it was, then, for him to assert that in his time he would be trying to rewrite the whole story of modern Europe.

Yet in inviting his audience to glance back at the seventeenth century, he was doing no less than that. The Treaty of Westphalia, he reminded them, could be seen as the agreement that determined that one country's internal affairs were for it alone and that interference could only be justified if a country was threatening you or breaking a treaty or if there was an obligation of alliance.

Some of them may have known what he was talking about, their minds pricked by some distant memory from school days. But they would have been few.

The four years of negotiation that produced the 1648 settlement were certainly momentous in the history of Europe, and one of the most celebrated diplomatic circuses ever to pitch its tents. The Thirty Years' War had sapped the strength of all the European powers. The collection of little states that would become a united Germany two centuries later was engaged in a civil war between Catholics and Protestants, and around their borders France and the Austrian empire were pitched against each other, the Spanish and the Dutch were struggling for supremacy after years of imperial rivalry, and the monarchs of Sweden and Denmark were engaged. Eventually the diplomats and the peace brokers began to trek in their carriages to Westphalia, near what is now the western border of Germany, to shake the kaleidoscope. There they settled the future of Europe and defined the role of the nation-state.

In essence, the peace guaranteed the independence of sovereign countries. The religious wars of the previous century came to an end and the Holy Roman Empire disappeared. The power system of the previous century and a half gave way to a new settlement. It did not stop religious conflict inside states (notably in Britain), but it fixed the internal architecture of Europe.

And this, said Tony Blair in Sedgefield in March 2004, was the peace that had come to an end. Indeed, he went further. There was an obligation on leaders to make sure that it did come to an end. By any standards, he was speaking with breathtaking confidence and even with a touch of chutzpah. The prime minister did not even say that he had been persuaded to this view by others. He spoke in the first person. "Let me attempt an explanation of how my own thinking, as a political leader, has evolved during these past few years," he said. The events of 9/11 had been a personal revelation: "What seemed inchoate came together."

No leader outside the United States speaks with quite the fervour about the September attacks as Blair. He went on to explain what everyone who knows him had realized from the start, from that moment when he got the news from New York just before he gave a short impromptu address to union leaders gathered for the annual Trades Union Congress—that the political revelation was akin to some kind of spiritual conversion. "What galvanized me was that it was a declaration of war by religious fanatics who were prepared to wage war without limit. They killed 3,000. But if they could have killed 30,000 or 300,000 they would have rejoiced in it."

His rhetoric would not have seemed overblown to an American audience. But even among those Cabinet colleagues who agreed wholeheartedly with his policy in going to war in Iraq (by far the most divisive of his premiership) and his analysis of the threat from international terrorism, when Blair warmed to this theme there was always a nervous shuffling of the feet and a lowering of the eyes. Support for the United States in principle was fine, and so was a resolute defence against terrorism, but it is often possible to detect in Blair a moment when he changes gear. The language becomes fiercer and imbued with the feeling of a personal crusade. He speaks as he sometimes feels—on his own.

In his March 5 speech, he said, for example: "From September 11, I could see the threat plainly. Here were terrorists prepared to bring about Armageddon."

Again, it is as if the Prime Minister is explaining a credo to those who refuse to believe in his sincerity. There was much in the agonized debate over the Iraq war in Britain that can explain some of that feeling and his anxiety to demonstrate how genuine his convictions were, but there is also something else at work. In addition to the frustration of dealing with critics who simply don't see the world as he does, his words reveal a determination that his policy shouldn't be seen simply as a matter of practical politics—putting armies in the right place, strengthening homeland security, forming alliances with other governments to challenge rogue states—but also as an expression of belief.

That is why it has worried a number of his colleagues. Robin Cook, foreign secretary for the whole of Blair's first term, has become a mordant commentator on the Blair view of the world. Since he resigned from the Cabinet in spring 2003 when it became clear it would not be possible to get a new United Nations mandate specifically authorizing war in Iraq, Cook has specialized in finely targeted public criticism that is usually stripped of personal bitterness (involving a considerable feat of self-discipline) but is nonetheless acidic.

The invasion of Iraq, he said on the anniversary of the start of the war, was the worst British foreign policy blunder since Suez, that botched and duplicitous invasion of Egypt in 1956 that became a byword for political ineptitude. The reference was particularly pointed, because in that crisis it was the United States that believed it had to realign Britain's moral compass, having been deceived about British plans. In Iraq, Cook thought it should be the other way round. The very word *Suez* had the same electric effect on succeeding generations of British politicians as a mention of the Bay of Pigs still has on anyone who remembers Washington in the 1960s. Even for those for whom the details are shrouded in dense mist, it is a touchstone.

Blair is no longer surprised by this kind of criticism. Some members of Parliament in his own party have suggested, after all, that he should be arraigned before the International Criminal Court for crimes against humanity in the invasion of Iraq; his policy brought more protesters onto the streets of London just before that war than had been seen in modern times; he has been lampooned by cartoonists as either a twenty-first-century Dr.

Strangelove with a trembling hand hovering on the button or as the drooling lapdog of an unpopular American president. The revered liberal commentator Hugo Young wrote in his last column in the *Guardian* before his death in 2003 that Blair was a tragic figure who brought credibility back to the political art but who had nonetheless surrendered Britain's national sovereignty "in abject thrall to Bush and his gang."

Blair's typical response to this has been to become even bolder in revealing the feelings that have been disturbing him. From time to time he has said that he is anxious to remind people of his government's domestic priorities, but he never conceals his belief that his second term in office has been possessed by a bigger question. When a prime minister talks of Armageddon, a feeling of inchoate forces coming together in a moment of spectacular violence, and a personal revelation, then it is difficult to assert that the business of government is a matter of tax rates and employment policies, however important they may be in the maintenance of day-to-day life.

Blair found himself happy to argue that history had forced him to speak of bigger things. His speech to his constituency ended with a telling phrase. A new type of struggle now engaged the world, he said, and he understood that the different attitudes it demanded of political leaders would be controversial. "In the end, believe your political leaders or not, as you will. But do so, at least having understood their minds."

For months, Blair had been expressing his irritation with aides and ministerial colleagues that he had not been able to make this point clearly enough. He felt as if the arguments swinging back and forth on the justification for war and his attitude to the United States were missing one important point. His policies might be open to the usual disciplines of political debate in Parliament and the country, but people had to know something about his reaction to 9/11 and his attitude to Iraq: it involved a belief that was outside the normal range.

The March speech had Blair's hand all over it, though the Westphalia idea itself seems to have come from Robert Cooper, a former foreign policy adviser in Downing Street. Though most of his speeches go through the familiar official mincing-machine of a prime minister's office, and they sometimes emerge from cut-and-paste exercises involving contributions from all sorts of sources, he has developed a habit of writing his own. This is not always welcome to those around him, but it has become his way on the big occasion. For his address to both houses of Congress in July 2003, he himself was the principal speechwriter. It was the same story when he spoke to the annual conference of his own party in October of that year. He knew that it was going to be a dangerous political task, but he didn't ask for a draft from anyone else. The party was in revolt over Iraq, and his own popularity was sinking. A group of Labour MPs had become serial rebels in Parliament, trooping regularly through the voting lobbies to register an opposition to their government which was so deeply felt that it had almost become disgust. Yet by the time he got to his conference hotel in Bournemouth on the last weekend of September, he had done very little about his speech except to wonder how defiant he should be.

He was due to speak in the traditional leader's slot that Tuesday afternoon. By Monday night, very little had been written, though his red box of official papers was stuffed with suggestions from ministers and increasingly fretful aides about the things he mustn't forget to say. He stayed up until 4 A.M. in his suite, scribbling away. He started again after breakfast, with nervous aides wondering whether they would be able to get the thing translated into an Autocue script in time for him to read it (they didn't). He was due in the hall at just after 2 P.M. A little over half an hour earlier, he was still writing, in longhand, in his room.

As it turned out, this piece of brinkmanship worked. He confessed privately later that he had been astonished at the warm welcome he received. Not a single boo was heard, though he had expected a fine display of anger from the many in the audience who believed he had betrayed their party's principles. Instead, he managed to mount a justification of his foreign policy as an honest implementation of a deeply held view. Take it or leave it, he said in effect, but don't accuse me of hypocrisy or double standards. The fact that he pulled it off encouraged him in his belief that when he allowed speeches to flow from his convictions, they succeeded.

In that conference speech of October 2003, Blair was able to blend together his party's concerns about the most pressing social questions—schools, health investment, and the rest—with his beliefs about Britain's role in the world, all under the comforting banner of conviction. "I can only go one way. I have no reverse gear," he said.

This, of course, was not a statement that could be taken literally. Like any political leader, Blair is capable of pirouetting on the spot when he has to, and of quietly disposing of awkward pledges when hostile winds begin to blow. But the attitude is the key to his character. As with Margaret Thatcher, in whose ideological force field he served his early time as a young parliamentarian in the 1980s, the impression of resolution is everything, even when the political brain is working away at stratagems for fallback positions and escape routes. The assertion of "no reverse gear" was too close an echo of a famous phrase of Thatcher's to be a coincidence. Twenty years before Blair's speech, she told a party conference threatening rebellion against some of her policies that "the lady's not for turning." It was a lame pun on a minor Christopher Fry verse play about witchcraft (The Lady's Not for Burning), written in the 1940s, which had been inserted by her favorite speechwriter and which mystified her, even after it had been explained. Nonetheless, it worked on the platform, and became something of a catchphrase for her.

So with Blair. He could hardly claim that he never changed his mind, nor abandoned policies when they became too troublesome, because he was no less prone to habit than any other leader; but he wanted to indicate that there was something about his political mind that sometimes caused it to become fixed and immovable, and for good reason. By now, those in his party realized it. They would have to accept it or move against him. Blair even managed a joke (of his own making) about it. "The time to trust a politician is not when they're taking the easy option. Any politician can do the popular things. I know—I used to do a few of them."

With British troops having been in Iraq for six months, his party knew that although many MPs sitting behind Blair in the House of Commons had grave doubts about the policy, and some were publicly calling it an act of recklessness or worse, the Prime Minister had become so convinced about the thrust of his foreign policy that he would never change. "I ask just one thing: attack my decision but at least understand why I took it and why I would take the same decision again."

These speeches of Blair's are good starting points to trace the trail leading from Downing Street to the White House, and to explain his style of governing. He reveals himself in his own words, as a leader who found himself on an expedition of learning in office and discovered that his mind was settling on a set of convictions that, once settled, seemed immutable. Strikingly, he does not describe the outcome as the product of thought or calculation. He turns instead to deeper feelings. He said in his Bournemouth speech: "I've never led this party by calculation. Policy you calculate; leadership comes by instinct."

With these words, the real Blair swims into focus. The instinct he speaks about is the part of his political personality that has brought him success at home and abroad, but which has also ruptured his relationship with a substantial section of his own party, and its supporters across Britain. In early 2004, one opinion poll, for the *Observer* newspaper, suggested that something close to a majority of the electorate wanted him to step down. For a prime minister who had never suffered a genuinely threatening bout of unpopularity since his landslide election in 1997, it was as if the old rules of the game that had seemed suspended for the whole of his first term in office had come back to remind him that he could not continue indefinitely to expect to defy political gravity.

He has discovered that belief is a quality easier to sell abroad than at home. "He's in his Jesus mode again," more than one Cabinet colleague has said of him after a meeting in which Blair has adopted a preachy, insistent tone. As the Iraq saga began to develop, one of the most common accusations from opponents of war was that Blair had been drawn to the Bush White House by a religious conviction that he found was better understood in the United States than at home. This is only a fragment of the truth, and one that is quite misleading. But a wider definition of moral conviction does help to explain how it was that Blair turned the historic closeness of London and Washington into something different in his era, and powerful enough to span two administrations of different political complexions. It is also the key to the puzzle that troubled so many leading Democrats as the 2004 presidential campaign began. How could Bill Clinton's best friend turn into a supporter of the American foreign policy that Senator John Kerry calls "the most reactionary, isolationist and reckless of modern times"? By straddling two administrations that took different views about how America's foreign interests should be pursued, Blair has helped to point up the dilemma so many Democrats have faced in supporting a "war on terror" and the need for strength after 9/11 while finding the Iraq invasion and its consequences unacceptable.

His persona has been something of a mirror for Americans. His initial popularity after the attacks in New York and Washington can easily be attributed to his eloquence in expressing sadness and solidarity, and to the old ties that suddenly felt stronger for many people in the United States when they heard, for example, "The Star-Spangled Banner" being played by the band at the changing of the guard outside Buckingham Palace on September 12. But there is more to it than that. Blair can be seen to have had a special affinity for the debates that wracked America in the aftermath of only its second "day of infamy" in living memory. They stirred precisely the worries that had begun to trouble him in a deeply personal way about terrorism in the post–Cold War world, and something in his anxiety found an echo among Americans. He became drawn into the forces shaping policy on the other side of the Atlantic and the arguments that flowed from the "war on terror."

With two successive American presidents, he had the seeming

luxury of frequent and lengthy phone calls and apparent intimacies at moments of the greatest crisis. But it would bring him much criticism as well as praise. As he committed his troops to war in Iraq just over two years after 9/11, a number of American friends who had feted him in the 1990s watched aghast as he praised Bush. From the Clintons' innermost circle came this dismissive description of his behavior: "The trouble is that he's started believing his own bullshit." Blair's aides began to worry what would happen if Bush were to be beaten by Kerry. Having done one somersault, could the trick be performed again?

At home, his critics spoke of a different kind of trick—one perpetrated by Bush. Robin Cook and others in the Labour Party who opposed the recourse to war in Iraq without specific UN sanction believed that Blair had been used as political cover for a policy that couldn't have been sold to Americans without him, since the appearance of the United States alone against Saddam Hussein would have raised many more awkward questions than the ones that in the end faced Bush in the preparations for war. In this reading, Blair is a dupe. Not only does he associate Britain with a policy that is wrong—destructive in the Middle East and in Europe and of the very transatlantic alliance in whose name it is carried out—but he has refused to take the opportunity that his American popularity after 9/11 gave him. A "no" from the beloved Tony Blair, say these critics, might have prevented war. That is not a view that finds much favour in Downing Street, even among those officials who were most apprehensive about war, for they have a professionally cool view of the realities of a White House relationship and in particular the speed with which it can turn from passion to estrangement. Nonetheless, it is a charge that has damaged Blair: the negative that is impossible to disprove.

Even if he could not have prevented war by distancing himself, of course, many of his supporters would have liked to see him do it as a matter of conscience. Blair didn't do it precisely because his conscience leaned the other way. His refusal to take opportunities to detach himself from Washington's plans when the United Nations' efforts began to fail was not a practical judgement about running out of options; it was a statement of belief. That was why it was so painful to many on the British Left. Blair is no Forrest Gump who was deceived by Bush. His allegiance is more mysterious, but it sits quite happily with his unorthodox political background. His political childhood was odd. His friendships were unusual. His transition from the putative prime minister who seemed determined to be all things to all people to single-minded warrior was unpredictable. As his two White House friends realized, he possessed that invaluable political gift—mystery. He was not easy to explain, and the more fascinating for it. For better or worse, this was a leader who might shape events in unexpected ways.

Blair's journey has been in part a matter of personality and intellectual attitude, in part a series of accidents. In politics, the strict ideologues who believe that the landscape will change its form at their command usually end up bewildered by its refusal to do so, just as the sinewy masters of mechanical politics are often defeated by the complexity of their own plots and machinations. Blair was in neither category, but was a blank page on which events could make their own mark.

He is a politician who came to office without feeling the reassuring weight of a settled ideology on his back, nor with any experience of the exercise of power. He is the only Prime Minister of the modern era in Britain to have had to learn the business of government after being elected to lead one. All his predecessors since the 1920s had served as ministers in previous administrations (usually in senior Cabinet posts) and had the feeling of returning to corridors of power whose twists and turns they knew. Blair had never been inside the Prime Minister's study, had never sat in the Cabinet room looking out towards the trees in St. James's Park, had never opened one of the boxes covered in red leather that ferry official papers to and from the government departments around Whitehall and are a minister's emblem of power.

It was an advantage. He had been leader of the Labour Party for only three years when he was elected Prime Minister, and youthful vigour and intellectual brio were all. The Conservative

Party, which had wielded untrammeled power through the 1980s under Thatcher, now constituted a spent, wheezing government fast running out of breath. It was visibly exhausted and, after eighteen years in power, the party knew in its heart that the time had come to depart. Talking to John Major in Downing Street in his last week as Prime Minister was to see a man already drawing the shadows around him. The rooms seemed bare, and a telling quietness was settling on everything. He spoke of a last rallying of the supporters who had seen his party through so many battles, but he didn't believe it. Much later, he wrote in his autobiography: "The players were acting out their roles, but the outcome was predetermined. All that was at stake was the scale of the defeat."

His government had been crippled above all by one poisonous ideological argument that had several times threatened to destroy it completely. The issue was Europe, and it had turned his party inside out. How closely should Britain be allied with those European nations pressing for increased integration inside the community that had started in the 1950s as the Common Market and was now the European Union? Major himself had signed the Maastricht Treaty in 1991, which bound the countries, including Britain, much closer together, in trade and in law, and which he believed would put Britain where he argued she must be, "at the heart of Europe."

But those in his party's Right wing, egged on by the retired but not retiring figure of Thatcher herself, would have none of it. They turned against Major and made his parliamentary life a misery. Major found himself scraping majorities together in a weary and undignified scramble to hold on to power.

In 1996, he had been driven to the most desperate of measures, resignation as leader of his party. He wanted the subsequent leadership election to give his government a blood transfusion and a hope of survival. He was duly re-elected by Conservative MPs as their leader, but not much changed and he lived out his last nine months or so in power as a figure who looked doomed.

The atmosphere as the sun set on the Conservatives had profound consequences for Blair. Although his Labour Party was well positioned for victory simply because its opponents had been in government without a break since 1979 and were reaping the whirlwind sown in the inevitable troubles of such a long life in power, he was able to use Major's travails to make his election seem much more than a natural changing of the guard. He could claim that an old order was passing away and he represented the excitement of the new, and be believed.

Circumstances allowed him to define himself not so much by what he represented but by what he was not. He wasn't what was called "old Labour"—in thrall to state-funded solutions as the answer to nearly every problem—and he was a break with the Conservative orthodoxy that had prevailed in Britain for nearly two decades. Thus, Blairism could be created. A famous Labour slogan of the day was "Things Can Only Get Better," and Blair was able to encourage the thought and ride the tide.

He decided soon after he became Labour leader in 1994 that in order to prepare for power he had to break spectacularly, and with a touch of melodrama, from his party's past. When he entered Parliament for the first time in 1983, Labour was a quivering wreck in danger of sinking into oblivion. A fierce struggle between those who wanted to follow a resolute socialist path and those who preferred centre-leftism had almost broken the party's back. It had suffered massive defections in Parliament and the country, and in many constituencies its members were engaged in such bitter ideological battles that they often felt like bloody hand-to-hand combat.

The drawing up of the election manifesto in 1983 had been a victory for the Left, and it committed a Labour government to remove nuclear weapons from Britain, to a widespread programme of nationalization of key industries, and to a negotiated withdrawal from the European Common Market unless a series of near impossible conditions were met by other member states. It was described by one leading Labour figure as "the longest suicide note in history," and it duly produced a dismal result for the party, the lowest share of the vote since the 1920s. Blair was a new MP in the diminished ranks that assembled in the Commons to face the might of the Thatcher Conservatives, about to embark on the most radical phase of their years in office.

For Blair and his contemporary, Gordon Brown, who had been elected in a Scottish constituency on the same day and would become his close friend, it was a dispiriting and bleak time. Their party seemed to be disintegrating around them, and they wondered if they had entered politics at the worst of moments, condemning themselves to a lifetime in impotent opposition. It was in this period that Blair's attitude to politics distilled.

As a law student at Oxford in the mid-1970s, he had attracted little interest. He wasn't a student activist and didn't join Labour until he was sitting his bar exams in London. Even then he showed no sign of a special talent for the game, nor unusual ambition. His wife, Cherie Booth, was a more natural political animal and was determined to find a parliamentary seat she could win. It was not until 1982 that Blair decided to give it a try, running in the by-election to choose a successor to a Conservative MP who had died in a constituency in Buckinghamshire where he had no chance of winning but might be able to demonstrate to his party that he had a talent. Somewhat to his surprise, he enjoyed it.

Those of us who met him on the road in that short campaign remember an eager candidate, raw but enthusiastic and cheery in the face of inevitable defeat. It was nonetheless a surprise to find that the following year he had swooped into a safe Labour seat in Durham and had beaten a number of local pretenders to become the candidate. In May 1983, close to his thirtieth birthday, he was in.

The shock of life in the Commons was profound. His conversation in those days was about how long his party could survive. The Thatcher revolution was at its flood tide—supply-side economics, the privatization of state-owned assets and industries, open confrontation with the trade unions, and strong support for Ronald Reagan's foreign and defence policies. Blair understood that Labour had to match this challenge or die and began to learn his trade, with Brown as his companion-in-arms and indeed as his mentor, for Brown had been a student politician and then a party insider who breathed politics in his sleep. The pair became Labour's twin hopes for the next generation of leaders, and in the course of the 1980s, while Neil Kinnock fought the bruising political battles that would capture the party for the centre-left, they established their positions.

Year by year they rose in the parliamentary party, rising to prominence in the leadership group after the unsuccessful election campaign of 1987 and becoming the centre of attention among the party's younger stars by the time the politics of the country seemed to stop for a moment in November 1990. In the course of a couple of weeks, Margaret Thatcher was driven from power in one of the most extraordinary passages of postwar British politics.

Blair watched from the Opposition benches as a parliamentary whirlpool engulfed her. She had been pursuing an economic course that cost her the angry resignation of the Chancellor of the Exchequer Nigel Lawson (possibly the most brilliant adornment of any of her Cabinets), and then, by her increasing hostility to her European allies and their plans for greater integration, she forced the resignation of another close colleague, Geoffrey Howe. The pillars were crumbling around her, but she seemed impervious. Howe's resignation speech in the House of Commons in which he explained why he had left the government, however, was an attack by stiletto and proved fatal. Sitting on the front bench surrounded by ministers who could hardly believe what they were hearing, Thatcher listened to the mild-mannered Howe assail her for stubbornness and lack of vision, for disloyalty to colleagues and disservice to the national interest, and suggest that it was time for her to go. Within twenty-four hours, her former defence secretary, Michael Heseltine, had challenged her for the leadership and the following week, panic-stricken Conservative MPs found themselves split over her future, aware that her unpopularity in the country now threatened their own futures at the next election.

She had a narrow lead in the first ballot of the leadership election but failed to win an outright majority. The following night she interviewed her Cabinet one by one, realized that her authority was gone and that she might well be beaten in the subsequent ballot. She went back to Downing Street, poured a large whisky, and told Denis that it was over. The next morning she told her Cabinet that she would leave office as soon as the party could choose a new leader and drove from Downing Street to Buckingham Palace to inform the Queen that she was resigning.

The fall of Thatcher unleashed passions in her party that were to poison it for a decade and more. Although John Major, was able to scrape a narrow victory over Labour in 1992 and take office for a new term in his own right, the sky was darkening for him. With the collapse of one of his principal policies, it turned black. In one afternoon a few months after the election, Britain withdrew from the European exchange rate mechanism, which linked the currencies of member states, after a chaotic run on the pound, and the Conservatives' jealously protected claim of financial competence was ruined. They lost the reputation with which they had managed to beat Labour in 1992 (presenting the Opposition as a high-taxing and reckless-spending party) and simultaneously let loose the argument over Europe that pitched Thatcherites against Major and his friends and began to make the party resemble the chaotic outfit that had been Labour a few years before.

Thus, the view from Blair's seat on the Opposition front bench was of a government consumed by subterranean arguments— between pro- and anti-Europeans—that had never been properly settled and had been allowed to fester. It was a lesson in what happened to parties that did not modernize and confront their difficulties. It had happened to Labour in the past; now it was tearing the Conservatives apart. Already he and Gordon Brown were working on schemes that they believed would revive Labour and give it a new face, and the cracks appearing in the Major government convinced them that they should move fast. How long could the Conservatives last?

After the 1992 election, Labour was led by John Smith, who had been a comradely father figure to both Blair and Brown since their arrival in the Commons. Upon his death from a heart attack in 1994, an event that was a terrible shock to both of them, they were thrown into a contest for the party leadership that would inevitably leave one of the friends a profoundly disappointed man. After a confused and sometimes bitter series of exchanges, and negotiations that have been the subject of recrimination and wild speculation ever since, Brown stepped aside in an act effectively guaranteeing Blair the leadership. The unresolved arguments of those weeks, and the ambition that they left unfulfilled, would return to shape much of the later story, but in 1994 Blair was Labour's youngest leader and, according to the opinion polls, likely to become Prime Minister.

He had, at most, three years to prepare. The effect of his parliamentary experiences showed immediately. To everyone's surprise he turned up at his first party conference as leader, in Labour's favourite conference town of Blackpool, and told his party that he wanted it to rip up its constitution. He was going to remove the famous Clause 4 of that document, which was the talisman for the Left, linking it to its socialist roots with a commitment to an economy based on state rather than private ownership. Blair had long thought the pledge was meaningless in the modern world and wanted to get rid of it. But he was confronting the party's most cherished folk memory, the belief that one day it might implement a socialist platform.

To Blair's surprise, the desperation among his colleagues for an election victory after four successive defeats was so great that the leader was going to be able to surmount almost any hurdle. Within a few months Clause 4 was gone and Blair was talking of his party as New Labour, a thing transformed. It allowed him to write a party platform on a blank sheet of paper, because old commitments were no longer sacred. He wanted to demonstrate that social justice and fiscal responsibility could work together. That was the philosophy, no more and no less. There was grumbling in the old Labour clubs in the party heartland, and the parliamentary Left spoke of a betrayal of socialism, but the urge to unity in advance of the election was so great that Blair survived.

By the time Major's government entered its last year, Blair had established a reputation for boldness and a certain kind of "reso-lution." Having developed a grudging respect for Thatcher's deter-mination in office in the mid-1980s and her refusal to be blown off course, Blair reveled in the description. His own party's desper-ation to avoid internal arguments in pursuit of victory, Major's inability to heal the splits in his own party, and a sense among middle-of-the-road voters that Labour was now "safe" for those who would never have voted for a socialist agenda meant that Blair found himself buoyed up and more popular than a Labour leader had been for a generation.

Even Rupert Murdoch's *Times* abandoned the Conservatives, and the *Sun*, his tabloid weapon of mass destruction, which had been turned against Labour for a generation and was the sounding board for Thatcherism, now backed Blair. With the grudging and astonishing support of the *Daily Mail*, he was in a position that no previous Labour leader could have imagined.

And, of course, he won. The majority on May 3, 1997, was huge—179. No government of one party had enjoyed parliamen-tary dominance of this sort in the modern era. The Conservatives were routed, having even fewer seats than Labour had managed in its horror election year of 1983, and Blair could contemplate a first term in office in which he could put through Parliament almost any legislation he wanted, and given the size of his majority and the crisis now visited on the Conservatives, he could look forward with confidence to another election victory at the end of it. His majority was on a scale that would make it almost impossible for it to be shifted in one campaign.

Blair thus came to office inexperienced but blessed. His majority seemed to give him freedom of action, and he had established in his own mind what kind of politics he enjoyed. The decision to press on with the idea of New Labour, and the arcane but sensitive business of Clause 4, emboldened him to believe that what he had thought of Thatcher in office all those years ago was indeed true. He would be another conviction politician.

From the start, therefore, like any lucky politician he had a feeling that he was different. The strange circumstances of his election, granting such power to someone with no history in government, made him unique. And his conscious disposal of the traditional Labour thinking that he believed had been hobbling the party when he first joined it let him think of government as an adventure in which a certain wilfulness could be allowed.

The story has some complicated twists, because Blair has a strong streak of caution in his makeup, and the life of his government has often turned on the struggle between those different sides of his character. But from his first day in office, when he began to establish the style in which he would conduct his business, part of his political personality was the one that Bill Clinton quickly came to know and George Bush would encounter years later.

He was a long way from the Treaty of Westphalia. Indeed, it is a safe bet that in 1997 he had either never heard of it or had long since consigned it to a dark, schoolboy's corner of his mind. In his first few weeks in office, he did discover in his intelligence briefings that there were deeper worries about what would become known as rogue states and about international terrorism than he had realized in Opposition (when he had no access whatever to any intelligence material gathered abroad), but his ideas about what patterns might emerge in the post–Cold War world were still crude. He had no formal experience in foreign affairs, and although he had taken the trouble to meet Clinton and was developing good relations with European leaders, he was a Prime Minister who was going to have to learn on the job. An open mind but a commitment to conviction politics: a recipe, his critics would say later, for disaster. For him it offered the excitement of a ride into the unknown.

But politics is not a matter of genetic determinism. As always, there was the unexpected, the chance event, the quirkiness of some leader in trouble or on a high, the working out of personal relationships that proved more complicated and painful than could have been imagined. No one examining the prospects for Blair's leadership in 1997 could have charted the events and foreseen the personal encounters that would turn him into a man whom some

Americans apparently wished could aspire someday to run for president himself. They were the accidents of his time, but they shaped his leadership as much as his own instincts and upbringing in politics.

When he came to office he did not think he would fight five wars in six years. He almost certainly did not know the name of the governor of Texas. He knew surprisingly little about the United States and had seen little of the country. The intricacies of American politics were a mystery that was only slowly unravelling for him. He believed that after the agonies of the Conservatives' failure to settle their attitude toward the new Europe, his principal task in foreign affairs would be to lay to rest Britain's long argument with itself about rapprochement with the old rivals across the English Channel. Like all prime ministers, he would want to win favours in the White House and preserve the relationship that was the traditional guarantor of security. But if he ever thought he would find himself risking his leadership because of it, he would have dismissed the idea as a passing fantasy and turned over in bed.

Yet in the end, Blair's premiership will be defined by what has happened as a result of this one relationship. Much of the next election will be fought largely about what has happened in schools and hospitals, about crime figures and jobs, and about taxes. Elections always are. But hovering over proceedings will be the story of the war on terror and Iraq, and its shadow will be long. Blair made a personal choice that was his own. Another prime minister might have taken a different road. He will be made to answer for his decision.

That decision not only changed his premiership but achieved something rare for any modern prime minister. For good or ill, Blair came to play a role in George W. Bush's America that helped to shape events in time of war.

A prime minister and a president who were both still learning the exercise of national power found themselves drawn together in an extraordinarily potent alliance that produced both delight and consternation in vast quantities. It was an unpredictable coming together of two men whose backgrounds in politics might have been expected to keep them apart and whose supporting tribes paid homage to quite different philosophies. Like a pair of adolescents in an illicit affair, they enjoyed the danger and the notoriety it might bring.

# CHAPTER 3

# THE ACCIDENT

Bush and Blair were thrown together by war, and little else. Without the September 11 attacks, and the war in Afghanistan that followed, their relationship would have had none of the tingling intimacy that came to characterize it within nine months of Bush's inauguration. No transatlantic relationship in their life-times had turned on such a moment, and it was that instant realization by Blair on a dark afternoon in Brighton that set the pattern for the next three years and, for him, necessitated a commitment that could not be reversed, even when it led him into a forest of political perils that seemed likely to swallow him up. And for Bush, there was suddenly a guarantee of support from abroad that he would make one of the pillars of his policy in war.

Blair is a creature of instinct, and his nature is to be moved unexpectedly. It is not too much to say that the counterpoint to his irritation at long briefings and detailed policy wrangles is his enjoyment of the moment that breaks the pattern. While Air Force One was taking off in Florida, where Bush had been addressing schoolchildren, and beginning its strange zigzag path across the country on its way back to Washington, Blair like Bush was already convinced that the rest of his time in office would be lived out under the shadows of the 9/11 disasters.

He came to this conclusion quickly and alone. As it happened, his foreign policy adviser, David Manning, wasn't within reach. He was in the United States. On the morning that everything changed, he was flying from Washington to New York. His was one of the last planes to land at Kennedy Airport before the cataclysm. From JFK he watched the clouds envelop lower Manhattan and made efforts to get back to Washington that would have been comic in other circumstances—persuading a reluctant cab driver to take him and a British honeymoon couple on a long meander through Brooklyn and Queens in search of a hotel where they could rest up. They finally found refuge in a place that rented rooms by the hour, for purposes they could easily guess. The phones were down, so Manning couldn't speak to the Prime Minister, who was now back in London convening emergency meetings of his Cabinet and security officials.

Blair, however, knew enough of Bush to understand that a military response was inevitable, and the prospect consumed much of his thinking before he spoke to the President almost exactly twenty-four hours after the first plane hit the World Trade Center. The President's precise words were: "I want to get moving." In speaking to Blair, Bush again used the word *war*, as he had with his aides on Air Force One before he arrived back in Washington. It would be some time before Blair would use that word in public. Yet even at this embryonic stage of the military campaigns that would dominate both their lives for years to come, Blair was beginning to sketch out in his mind the stance that would become his defence against criticism when the orders were given. It was that of the candid friend with the cautious temperament.

Throughout his career, Blair has embodied a paradoxical mixture of political attitudes. His years of opposition in the 1980s had convinced him that Margaret Thatcher's style of "conviction politics" was indeed the key to performance in office; by the time he was preparing to become Prime Minister, he was sure that only the kind of single-minded determination that she had made her trademark would make a government work. Yet he retained the caution that had always been part of his personality.

In the normal course of events, Blair is often slow to make up his mind. Coming to power in 1997, he led his government in some radical policies—on constitutional change, for example—but as a decision-maker, he often saw himself as the tortoise rather than the hare. In government, that attitude does not always have the fable's happy ending. It irritated members of his Cabinet, who thought him indecisive, and it stored up problems for his second term when a number of domestic issues came back to haunt him precisely because they had been allowed to fester in the early years. When he does jump, he makes a spectacular leap. But it often takes some time.

Therefore, after 9/11, the day when there was no time for thought and Blair's emotions were seized in a way that had not happened to him in government before, it was quite natural for him to want to slow things down. In his relations with Bush, he slipped almost without thinking into the role of the adviser at the shoulder who is preaching caution and playing for time. A couple of years later, when Blair's public image at home was that of the crusader with blazing eyes, this truth was often forgotten. But Blair's own justification for his policies in support of Bush—that he was a calming influence on some of the most warlike spirits in Washington—was a genuine belief, and an accurate account of the posture he adopted at the time. Whether it was wise—or right—to allow the closeness to flower into such a fusion of spirits was the question that would come to bedevil his premiership, but at the beginning it seemed to him an expression of his natural instincts: with convictions settled in the firestorm of 9/11, and bolstered by a deep emotion, he then wanted to proceed with caution.

In this attitude, and in Blair's counsel to the President over the following eighteen months or so, up to the moment when troops crossed the border into Iraq, lies the explanation for the relationship that puzzled so many of his supporters and colleagues in government. He could hardly talk publicly about the need for a restraining hand on the Bush administration—it would have seemed brash and would hardly have helped his cause in Washington—but it was what he believed in private, and it was the argument he used when some members of his Cabinet began to stir in anger at the sight of the road opening up ahead of them.

From the start of the crisis, Blair believed that he might be able to exert a much greater influence in Washington than he might have expected. First, he wanted to. The Clinton years had convinced him of the huge advantages of having a friend in the White House. Second, he had already developed a friendship with Bush. He also knew that he could find the words to express what he felt: the actor in him had always given him that advantage. He was ready to make his pitch. But he was also moved deeply by the attacks, and it was his belief in their impact that led to the commitments from which he could not later disentangle himself, and which gave precious support to Bush when he decided to move against Iraq in defiance of the United Nations. At the time, it did not seem to Blair to be an approach that would result in such a polarization between the United States and its allies on the one hand and what appeared to be the rest of the world on the other. Indeed, he argued that the only way to prevent the United States from a dangerous disappearance into isolationism was to maintain Britain's closeness to Bush.

In the beginning, there was nothing strange or unpopular about his attitude. There was public revulsion in Britain at the September attacks, and as it became clear in the early days that the most lurid predictions of American assaults in the Middle East were exaggerated, Blair was able to luxuriate in a widespread feeling that the cowboy Bush might be more measured than his critics across Europe had reckoned. For a brief season this was a political gift to Blair. In the first comments he made on September 11, he had seemed to many Americans to catch more eloquently than any other foreign leader the quality of their shock, and the embassy in London was giving him rave reviews in cables home for statements like this: "We therefore in Britain stand shoulder to shoulder with our American friends in this hour of tragedy, and we like them will not rest until this evil is driven from our world."

Significantly, Blair's language was already taking on an apocalyptic tone. Although in his discussions away from the public gaze, he was wondering how Bush would react and discussing the practicalities of trying to manage a response if the administration in Washington were to act unwisely and in haste, in his public posture he slipped easily into rhetoric that was his own and that demonstrated his natural lack of embarrassment at speaking of good and evil.

By the morning of September 12, having spoken to the French and Russian presidents and the German chancellor, Blair was the recipient of Bush's first call to a foreign leader since the attacks, made at breakfast time in Washington. It was hardly a moment for balancing political advantage in the scales, but Blair was aware through the early days of the "war on terror" how important his words would be in determining his influence in Washington.

He could hardly feel gratitude for the opportunity, since his defence chiefs and security advisers were telling him in their meetings in the bunker below Whitehall that they faced an unknown and therefore especially disturbing threat. The skies over London were cleared of planes, just as across the United States. For months Blair had been trying to establish some warmth in his relationship with Washington, aware that he was swimming against the tide in Europe.

In Europe, the new Bush administration was being caricatured as a trigger-happy band well before September. Although the full weight of neoconservative thinking wasn't yet understood in most European capitals, enough was known of Dick Cheney and Donald Rumsfeld, in particular, to raise the hackles of the dominant political class, which leaned gently to the Left. Jacques Chirac in Paris was an exception to that rule in strict ideological terms, but as President he was dealing with a socialist majority in the National Assembly and was also proud of his Gaullist heritage, which gave him an innate suspicion of all things American and an acute wariness about Washington foreign policy, whoever was President. The lack of knowledge of Bush, whom diplomats in Washington were still trying to understand, exacerbated the uneasiness that was the prevailing mood in London, Paris, and Berlin.

One of the indirect consequences of this atmosphere was an important strategic decision by Blair. After his re-election campaign in the summer of 2001, won easily against a Conservative Party still riven by the agonies which had sapped the Major government of its will to live five years before, he changed foreign secretaries. Everyone was surprised. Brown did not know it was about to happen, nor did Jack Straw, who was making preparations for an expected move from the Home Office to the Environment Department, and nor did the victim, Cook. Blair has always denied that his removal came about principally because of the aversion he had developed to some members of the administration in Washington—Cheney, in particular—but it remains true that the Bush administration shed no tears on his behalf. Cook had found himself becoming increasingly agitated about the drift of thinking in Washington.

Part of this sprang from the British position on Israel, which held that a Palestinian state was desirable and inevitable and had to be created as quickly as possible. With the State Department, the Foreign Office in London could still talk in the language that it had used for years, which had been quite welcome in Washington during the Clinton years. But from elsewhere around the White House came a distinct chill. Cook and other ministers concluded that they had ideological enemies in such officials as I. Lewis Libby in the vice president's office (who, after all, had been involved in writing the Likud election manifesto and was especially close to Benjamin Netanyahu). Just as Blair was trying to kindle some warmth with the new president, knowing that he had to work quickly to expunge the Republicans' memories of his intimacy with Clinton, his foreign policy ministers and officials were having to contend with a relationship that sometimes dipped into the cold zone. Just as there were many Labour ministers who were gripped by a visceral dislike of the Republican Right, Cheney and his colleagues would express to their Conservative friends in London their amazement that in the twenty-first century, British voters could still be electing a party to power that clung, however precariously and unconvincingly, to a socialist heritage.

Blair was determined to counterbalance that suspicion by proving to be Washington's best friend. A number of his Cabinet colleagues were suspicious and unhappy about his emphasis on the American relationship but he was single-minded in his policy. Much of this was a matter of practicality, in acknowledging that in international affairs, power flows from Washington. For a couple of generations, the desirability of a good relationship with the White House has been so obvious in Downing Street that it has not been seriously questioned.

Only one postwar prime minister set a different course. After his election in 1970, Edward Heath turned his Conservative government toward Europe. So great was his passion for British membership in the Common Market, as the nascent European Union was called at the time, that he subsumed much of his foreign policy to that end in the belief that the future of a second-division power lay in the developing European bloc and not of the role of supporting player to the American superpower. He succeeded in signing a treaty of membership in 1973 and changing the pattern of Britain's international relationships, perhaps even starting the slow business of altering the country's traditional feeling for its own independence, but his reluctance to work on the transatlantic link meant that his dealings with Richard Nixon were frosty. Heath had no high regard for him, and in any case all his instincts about American foreign policy were tinged with a natural wariness, sometimes coming close to the gut dislike that tended to prevail in Paris. But with the exception of that European interlude, Downing Street has in modern times always been a supplicant in its dealings with American power.

Blair was especially conscious of this for two reasons: his political affair with Clinton, and his shock at Bush's election.

Any explanation of Blair's relationship with Bush must begin with Clinton. It was he who welcomed Blair to the world stage, and he who discovered within a couple of years that this whipper-snapper of a prime minister was urging him—a president of the United States!—to commit troops to the Balkans and engage in a deeper military campaign than his political antennae and his administration advisers judged wise. In the growth of their friendship, you can detect in Blair the development of the muscularity that he'd show to Bush, and much of the confidence that would seem to his critics later in his leadership to become arrogance.

They met first before either was in power, in the period when Clinton was beginning a patchy and mostly unsatisfactory relationship with John Major. Blair, with Gordon Brown, went to Washington immediately after the 1992 presidential election to try to learn something about how the Democrats had managed to unseat George H.W. Bush. Sidney Blumenthal, then a journalist, who would eventually metamorphose to become the White House aide charged with oiling the wheels of the relationship with Downing Street, arranged a dinner at his home for the Blairs and Hillary Clinton, and the following day the two men met for the first time.

Contact was maintained and the friendship grew. It was piquant that Major invited Blair for his first visit to 10 Downing Street (the only one before he became prime minister) to a reception for the visiting Clinton in 1994. By then, Blair was already adapting the first phase of Clinton's presidency as a template for his own thinking about power. He was privately determined to dispense with much more traditional Labour thinking than his party yet realized, and in trying to find a way to describe a political philosophy that was neither "old Labour" nor the right-wingery of the Thatcher years, he was naturally inclined to like what he saw in the White House. Clinton's famous "triangulation" of policy, finding a way of escaping from the competing attitudes of old and taking off in what seemed to be a new direction, with the added attraction of a philosophical diagram attached to it, was attractive to him.

Those in the Labour Party who were nervous about all this pointed out that such excursions into the unknown were particularly easy for Blair because he carried no ideological baggage with him and travelled light. This was quite true. To Blair, it was no cause for embarrassment. He felt the exhilaration of a politician without guilt: he had nothing to apologize for, nothing to explain. He was charting a course for himself.

This was the Blair who found Clinton a natural soulmate. They had both come to power by finding new language to try to undermine conservative philosophies that had held sway for years, and although both would be accused of quickly losing a radical edge in office, they were able, in those early days, to enjoy the sense that they were inventing a new kind of politics. Such feelings are almost always illusory, and Blair would realize toward the end of his first term how grindingly destructive were the familiar problems of modern democracies—the sluggishness of bureaucracy, the tension between the political imperative to act and the wisdom of long-term thinking, the impossibility of personal control over all the policy that flows from government. Nonetheless, those first years would seem later to be almost carefree compared with the morass of Iraq and the impenetrable difficulties of the "war on terror."

When he came to office five months after Clinton's second inauguration, the pair immediately fashioned a striking intimacy. It was helped by Blair's personality and working habits. He is unstuffy and informal, and from the moment he became Prime Minister, he also established a routine that was surprising and a little alarming to officials in government departments who had not encountered it before. He worked in a tiny office off the Cabinet Room in No. 10 and insisted on conducting many of his meetings without the presence of aides and officials, to their disquiet. His inner circle was small and there was not much more than a nod to the notion of collective decision-making, which Cabinet government in the parliamentary system is meant to embody. By the end of his first term, the principal complaint from restless ministers was that there was too much private policy-making in the prime minister's office.

Early on, they started to use the word that would hang in the air throughout his time in power, and give a sharp edge to his American friendships—*presidentialism*.

One of the three telephones on Blair's desk was marked simply "Washington." He used it a great deal. It was acknowledged in both capitals that they spent more time talking to each other than either did with any other world leader.

This had huge practical benefits for Blair. In trying to negotiate a peace in Northern Ireland, bringing the political representatives of the IRA to the table to draw up a political settlement instead of waging a terrorist war in the streets, Clinton was an indispensable ally. On several occasions, while Blair was stuck in day-and-night negotiations in Belfast between the parties and factions that were being asked to put aside generations of hatred, Clinton was willing to be roused from his bed to make a call to one side or the other, twisting an arm or offering support and the promise of a reward if the deal was done. Although the Good Friday Agreement in 1999 was a preliminary rather than a final peace, it was an important political achievement for Blair, and he probably could not have achieved it without Clinton.

The quality of their friendship was given a sparkling illustration when Blair made his longest official visit to Washington in February 1998. The White House announced proudly that there would be the biggest banquet since Nixon had entertained the Chinese with famous lavishness in 1972, and the best table settings were produced for Blair—the Eisenhower gold-base plates, Reagan china, and Kennedy Morgantown crystal. The vermeil and silver candelabra held gold-tapered candles that cast their flickering light on a typically Clintonesque ménage, the Washington political establishment rubbing shoulders with Hollywood and allowing Barbra Streisand to cuddle a rather wide-eyed Blair, Harrison Ford to enjoy his first visit to the White House, and Elton John and

Stevie Wonder to croon happily at their pianos for the cabaret after dinner.

A prime minister of less than a year's standing, Blair was understandably lifted by all this. Even so, he had to endure an excruciatingly awkward joint press conference in the East Room of the White House on his last day in Washington, at which the American press was able to question Clinton for the first time for many weeks about the latest twists and turns in the Monica Lewinsky affair, which was about to reach its torrid climax. His Washington ambassador, Sir Christopher Meyer, was fond of telling his staff that they must not use the hackneyed phrase "special relationship," beloved of prime ministers for decades, because it implied an inevitability and some smugness, but no one watching Clinton and Blair together could doubt that a special bond had been forged between them.

One of the consequences was to strengthen Blair's natural confidence. Cautious he might be, but when his mind was settled he was immovable. The year after his White House visit, he was emboldened enough to do what all his recent predecessors had often thought unwise (and probably pointless)—to try to encourage a reluctant American president to go to war.

The crisis in the Balkans in the mid-1990s sent a tremor through Europe. The collapse of Yugoslavia, a nation that had been artificially constructed after World War II, was the signal for historic hatreds to spew into the streets, and it forced the rest of Europe to observe the return of barbarism to a continent that believed it had moved beyond such crudities. Serbs and Croats, Orthodox Christians and Muslims, old-style Stalinist Communists and nationalist partisans sank into an orgy of violence. Blair was of the generation that had been spared military service and grew up with the expectation that war in Europe was a horrid memory that would never again transform itself into a reality. Apart from the strange few weeks of the Falklands War in 1982 his only knowledge of war was the struggle with the IRA in Northern Ireland, a depressingly domestic dispute.

By the time he came to office, having seen the violence between Croats and Serbs, and then between Communist-led Christians and Bosnian Muslims, culminating in the sacking of Sarajevo, he was seized by a passion. Clinton had a different view. When Slobodan Milosevic tried to fulfill his principal political ambition of bringing Kosovo back into a greater Serbia, and did so with brute force, it was an act with little resonance in the United States. The President knew perfectly well that few Americans could stick a pin into the Balkans on a map, let alone Kosovo itself. The intricacies of nationalist and religious divides in south-eastern Europe were a mystery. Sarajevo might be remembered just as the city where Archduke Ferdinand's assassination started the chain reaction that loaded the guns for World War I, but that was a long time ago and the place was a long way off.

But by halfway through his second year in office, Blair was determined that force must be used to resist what he saw as a mixture of despotism and anarchy. To him, Milosevic became a figure as sinister as Saddam Hussein himself, and when refugees began to pour out of Kosovo into Macedonia, clinging to tractors and carts and taking to mountain passes in the hope of escape, Blair found his gorge rising. The Left of his party was deeply uneasy about military action against Serbia, despite the near universal revulsion against Milosevic's policies in the previous few years, but Blair established a pattern that would later become familiar.

He quickly became the most hawkish of European leaders and, despite being a leader with less than two years of power under his belt, was convinced that a campaign of air strikes would not be an adequate response to the war being waged by Milosevic. By chance, NATO was celebrating its fiftieth birthday in Washington in April 1999, and it was the occasion of a difficult passage in the Clinton-Blair friendship. It would never quite seem the same again, losing some of the near innocent fun that once character-ized their encounters. Blair was pushing a little too hard for the President's comfort.

As General Wesley Clark, the former supreme Allied commander of NATO, points out in his memoirs, this was the war that Washington did not want. Clinton was hemmed in by domestic and family difficulties (Ms. Lewinsky then appearing a rather bigger threat to his standing in office than Mr. Milosevic), and the State Department and the Pentagon could not agree on a strategy. Into this mess stepped a surprisingly bullish Blair. There had already been one difficult telephone call in which the President of the United States felt it necessary to point out to the British Prime Minister the relative powers of their jobs, and their standing in the world. There had been shouting from a red-faced President whose capacity for losing his temper was well known in the White House and had aides scuttling for their hideaways when it happened. It did not stop Blair, though he was startled at the time by Clinton's vehemence.

In fact, this confrontation seems to have strengthened in Blair the feeling of growing up in office. He had an impregnable parliamentary majority at home and a fairly quiescent Cabinet that was unlikely to turn against him, even in war, and he made clear to everyone that he was enjoying office. The Balkan crisis certainly touched him emotionally—he shared Clinton's sense of shame that the West had turned away from Rwanda when genocide engulfed it—but confidence was now running strong. He pressed on.

In Washington, he was aggressive enough to lobby the President persistently in the fringes of the NATO meeting for a greater commitment in the Balkans than Clinton or many of his advisers wanted. Although the Secretary of State, Madeleine Albright, was hawkish throughout the crisis (her Middle European background giving her a sharp feeling for the convulsions in the region), it took more than a month for Clinton to send the signal that he would, if necessary, commit American ground troops to a campaign that had once been thought mistakenly to be winnable in the air.

When Blair's friend and courtier, Peter Mandelson, arrived back from a Democratic Leadership Council seminar in Florida in early June, he brought the news that the Prime Minister was anxious to hear. In a conversation before dinner, Clinton had told Mandelson that if he believed it necessary, he would indeed commit ground troops to battle. Ferocious Russian pressure was brought to bear at last, and the capitulation of Milosevic a day or two later allowed Clinton a justifiable claim of victory; in London, it persuaded Blair that he had been the decisive influence in Washington. Historians will argue about the truth of it, but Blair's conviction that his intervention tipped the scales was an important part of his development. He had won a war.

The victory was particularly sweet because of Clinton's early reluctance. Blair was able to argue that despite the scepticism of other European leaders and opposition in official Washington, he had changed Clinton's mind. He used the Washington visit to make a bold assertion about his own role in shaping the postwar world. Making a trip to Chicago for a few hours—Mayor Daley closed the freeways for his motorcade in the kind of salute that even then Blair was beginning to find familiar and to enjoy—he spoke to the Economic Club about global interdependence. He'd refer to this in his "end of Westphalia" speech almost exactly five years later, and he still sees it as an important statement of beliefs that were beginning to form a solid pattern in his mind.

Once again, Blair delivered a speech that was not a Foreign Office text that fitted in with its professionals' long-term thinking. Blair was already developing a stronger foreign policy machine in his own office and calling on a number of historians and defence analysts to feed his own thinking. The guts of the Chicago speech came from Professor Lawrence Freedman of King's College, London University. The British embassy, which would usually expect to provide drafts for speeches of this kind, was hardly involved.

Blair argued that the existence of Western states themselves was no longer threatened, as they had seemed to be in the Cold War. "Now our actions are guided by a more subtle blend of mutual self-interest and moral purpose in defending the values we cherish. In the end values and interests merge. If we can establish and spread the values of liberty, the rule of law, human rights and an open society then that is in our national interests too. The spread of our values makes us safer."

Having expressed himself in that way, touching on sentiments that are much more familiar to American political leaders than to Europeans, who are less likely to speak of foreign policy as a matter of moral purpose, Blair went on to talk about the circumstances in which intervention against a rogue state could be justified, though the "rogue" term hadn't yet entered his lexicon. He didn't want to jettison too easily the principle of non-interference—but he articulated his case by pointing out that in some cases, as with the killing in Kosovo, it was impossible for the world to stand by. National interest was involved when refugees were pouring across the border in a combustible part of Europe. Military action should only come when every effort at peace had failed, but when it did, there had to be a commitment to long-term involvement.

In this speech, the Blair of the Iraq war begins to take shape in the shadows. He mentions Milosevic and Saddam Hussein in the same breath, advocates a deeper moral component to foreign policy in the confusions of the post-Cold War world, and reveals his nagging belief that if globalization was changing the economic rules for the world, so were the threats of terrorism and genocide in unstable states now that they were no longer frozen in a pattern policed by two superpowers.

He ended with a classic Blairite assertion, a biblical reference that came naturally to him: "Just as with the parable of the individuals and the talents, so those nations which have the power have the responsibility." The world could not afford isolationism.

The rookie Prime Minister—who was having his first quarrels with an American President and was about to fly back to Washington to try to persuade him to make a military decision about which Clinton was extremely sceptical—was sticking his head over the parapet. Watching him in Chicago that day, however, was to see him at the peak of his confidence. The weariness and the wounds of later years weren't yet taking their toll, and he seemed like a leader—secure at home, still an object of fascination in Europe and feted in Washington—who believed he could think aloud and be listened to.

He had resisted uneasiness in his party, outright hostility from his fellow European leaders, and wariness in Washington to press the case for NATO's first serious engagement in its fifty-year history. Although Clinton did not accept for a moment this description of affairs, it is a fact that a White House official told a senior British correspondent in Washington during NATO's April summit: "The leader of this NATO coalition isn't Bill Clinton, it's Tony Blair."

The uneasy Left of Blair's Labour Party was correct to identify 1999 as the period in which he enjoyed a delicious flexing of the muscles and found for the first time that the intense diplomacy of these crises was intellectually and emotionally rewarding. He had no doubt at all that his attitude about pressing for the NATO campaign was morally justified and politically astute. When the time came four years later to face the prospect of war against Saddam Hussein, the Milosevic experience was still in the fore-front of his mind. By 2003, the Serbian leader was standing trial at the International Criminal Court in The Hague, seemingly complete in his humiliation. For Blair, that victory was the underpinning that helped to convince him that despite deep public unease in Britain and bitter hostility in much of the rest of Europe, he was in the right about Iraq.

The odd alliance with Bush, so surprising to so many of the friends of the two men, has its roots in Blair's experiences with Clinton. Without him, Bush would not have had such a friend in Blair.

Yet when Bush began his run for the presidency, the profound hope in Downing Street was that he would not win. All of us who spoke to Blair's circle during the autumn of 2000 can remember the long faces as the word came back from the campaign about Al Gore's miserable progress. By early October, there was genuine disturbance in Downing Street about what lay ahead. It had even been suggested, so one of his staff said, that Christmas might be spent with the Gores. At the end, Gore's last rallying week before he sank in the Florida imbroglio gave the Blairites the hope that the old gang might yet sail into a second term, but in truth they knew it was over.

From the Washington embassy, Christopher Meyer had been sending messages for months warning the Foreign Office and Downing Street to take Bush more seriously than had been the habit. He had twice gone to the governor's mansion in Texas to prepare the way and had identified Condoleezza Rice (not Cheney or Rumsfeld, let it be noted) as potentially the most friendly point of contact should the Republicans move into the White House. Rice was a happy choice for Blair, since she became the natural conduit to the National Security Office for Downing Street after 9/11, and she and David Manning became accustomed to speaking daily. By the time he was translated from the foreign policy adviser's office in Downing Street to the Washington embassy three months after the invasion of Iraq, Manning was almost part of the extended family that connected Rice to the President's most intimate circle.

The Rice-Manning connection had established the groundwork for Blair's relationship with Bush, but he still needed luck. It came in the malign form of the September attacks. A tentative friendship was galvanized by a shaft of electricity that transformed the political atmosphere and forced leaders to live their lives in an utterly changed world. Some of Blair's friends think that one of the most regrettable outcomes of September 11 was the bond he forged with Bush. Political colleagues who had always had reservations about him, like Robin Cook, are open about the consequences of the alliance, believing that the strength of the personal relationship made it impossible for Blair to have contemplated seriously disengaging from the American policy to effect regime change in Iraq, with or without the support of the United Nations. Therefore, they conclude, his closeness to Bush was a betrayal of the national interest.

In all that lay ahead, and in the rush of events after 9/11, Blair showed not a flicker of doubt. According to his advisers, he was certainly concerned with preventing an American over-reaction and did not believe it was time to threaten Saddam with the attack that some around Bush thought was justified. Though even then Blair thought there was a case for the threat, he wanted time. In March 2004, when the former White House security coordinator, Richard A. Clarke, told the Kean Commission investigating the events of 9/11 that Donald Rumsfeld had spoken of war against Iraq on the very day of the September attacks, it came as no surprise in Downing Street, where the sulphurous quality of some of the Middle East rhetoric in Washington had been making people queasy for some time. But in his attitude to Bush, Blair had no doubt.

There were two primary reasons that moved him to such certainty. The first was that in their opening meeting at Camp David in February of that year, they found their conversations easier than they had expected. The diplomatic foreplay had gone well. Second, Blair was personally convulsed by the events of 9/11 and felt drawn into the resulting agony in a way that some other leaders would have resisted as a matter of discipline.

When they arranged that first meeting for February 2001, the month after Bush's inauguration, a vast amount of preparation was done. Blair was nervous. Although the relationship with Clinton had been punctured by periods of irritation on both sides after the Kosovo affair, the President had paid a warm farewell visit in December to Chequers, and they parted as friends. Advice poured in from the Washington embassy about Bush's style and attitude, and Blair spent an unusual amount of time in preparation. But Bush seemed concerned, too. His officials made meticulous preparations for the visit: there was much worrying, for example, about how informal they could be at their first encounter.

As it turned out, Blair was the one who perhaps betrayed the fragility of the atmosphere, asking first how they should address each other. He wanted to avoid "Mr. President." They immediately opted for first names. Blair came home relieved. His early judgement was the one he has repeated often since, and never changed:

Bush is quicker in conversation than you expect, more decisive than you've been led to believe, but he isn't interested in talking in terms of ideas, only practicalities. Bush's first public reaction at Camp David described the comfort of their conversation. "You know where you are with him." That was what Bush wanted.

These encounters are awkward affairs, first dates played out for the cameras with all the half-conscious grappling for a comfortable body language that is the fate of the nervous suitor. The accounts spread afterwards by the anxious aides are often exaggerated and tailored to embellish an image they have already created, and it is frankly difficult to know what the atmosphere was inside the room or on the golf cart trundling through the trees at Camp David. It was clear in Downing Street, however, that Blair came home and expelled a long sigh of relief.

So he was comfortable with Bush. Even as the President began to be lampooned across Europe, mocked for his malapropisms and painted by cartoonists as a clueless cowboy, and the Labour Party rumbled ominously about the neoconservative rhetoric of some in the administration, Blair thought he had a relationship that would prosper.

The 9/11 attacks forced the pace. In the next few days afterwards, Blair seemed to be everywhere. The first leader to talk to Bush, he was in Berlin and Paris within the week, talking to other Europeans and General Pervez Musharraf in Pakistan. Outside church on that first Sunday, for the first time he consciously echoed Bush in talking of "war." He'd go to Washington on September 20.

That morning before leaving for the United States, he had breakfast in Paris with President Jacques Chirac, who had by chance been able to see Bush the previous day during a long-planned visit to the United States (after which Chirac pointedly refused to use the word "war" in expressing his condolences to the American people and promising support). At such moments of crisis, diplomats are careful in what they say—but in Paris and London there is a long-established race to pre-eminence between the leaders (a practice long before Blair and even Chirac came along). There was therefore some irritation in London that Chirac had been received first, albeit by chance. Blair's visit, they hoped, would establish that it was Britain's voice that was more important. Such are the ways of the diplomats.

As he flew west, there was already disquiet in London about the atmosphere in the White House. On September 12, Bush had described the attacks as "an act of war." When he said "we will be patient, we will be focused," you could almost feel the relief in Downing Street and the Foreign Office. But it evaporated with his closing words: "This will be a monumental struggle between good and evil."

Blair shared some of the nervousness. Knowing the obsession in some corners of Washington about Iraq, he feared an early push to war there. He knew that for some in the administration it was a hangover from the "unfinished business" of Desert Storm, the Gulf War of 1991, when Bush's father had not pushed all the way to Baghdad to depose Saddam (not least because under the UN resolutions that authorized that invasion it would have been illegal). Blair had been told by his intelligence advisers within a few hours of the attacks that they were convinced beyond doubt that the hand of al-Qaeda was responsible; he was given no evidence to suggest any credible link with Iraq. He therefore decided that his policy must be to try to influence Bush as best he could to attack targets directly associated with the terrorists.

But the difference between Blair and some of those advising him was that he found the "good and evil" rhetoric less scary than they did.

In Chicago two years before, he had spoken of a just war in Kosovo based on values rather than territorial ambition. Bismarck, the nineteenth-century architect of the European balance of power, had been wrong when he said the Balkans weren't worth the bones of a single Pomeranian grenadier. Tear-stained refugees and the heart-rending tales of cruelty, Blair had said then, proved that an evil dictator must not be allowed to rampage unchecked or "we will have to spill infinitely more blood and treasure to stop him later."

No British prime minister had been so willing to use the word *evil* since the defeat of the Nazis sixty years earlier. When Ronald Reagan spoke of the Soviet Union as an evil empire, even Margaret Thatcher was careful not to give the phrase much of a public echo, though she agreed with him wholeheartedly. She was the most ideological of postwar prime ministers, insisting that some things were right and some things wrong (and, of course, that she could always identify accurately the difference between the two), and during the two-month Falklands War she had spoken of General Galtieri's junta with the fervor of a single-minded warrior. But even the rhetoric of the Iron Lady herself rationed the use of *evil*. Blair, leading a party that was dedicated in large part to unravelling the domestic legacy of Thatcherism and fashioning a new internationalism, might be thought an unlikely figure to outdo her in this respect. But this is his essence.

His religious convictions are probably deeper than those of any British leader since Gladstone was in power in the Victorian twilight, and they make it easy for him to talk in moral absolutes. There is a good deal of misunderstanding about the nature of his Christianity. For example, he feels no kinship whatever with the fundamentalist Right in the United States and is embarrassed when it is assumed that as a devout man, he cherishes their political influence. But he is comfortable with the language of judgement. He is also attracted by the politics of the simple assertion. The more his government became bogged down in the inevitable mistakes and failures of power—hospital reforms that seem sluggish, a reform of the school exam system that goes wrong, a government minister who is revealed embarrassingly to be not up to the job—the more he relished the opportunity to speak of his own foreign policy in black-and-white terms.

Since he came to office, Blair had been spending a great deal of time in the tortuous negotiations that are a consequence of European Union membership (all deals, compromises, and uneasy consensus) and now understood how labyrinthine a political negotiation could be after brokering the Northern Ireland peace talks that swallowed up so much energy in his first term. He thus found some release in the world beyond, where he believed he had the opportunity to write on a blank page. The problems were even more intractable, but they presented an opportunity for the kind of moral politics that he was beginning to enjoy. He could talk about right and wrong.

He was not naive enough to believe that the world's problems were easier than the ones he dealt with at home, but part of Blair enjoys the feeling of going against the grain so much that in the trail of speeches and interviews through his first years in power, it is easy to detect a leader who is trying to construct a language of his own for describing the world. Maybe this is because he came to office with less detailed knowledge of foreign affairs than almost any of his predecessors, and found himself able to think freely: that is certainly how he sometimes explains it. Perhaps it springs from something deeper, a natural affection for the world stage as a performing space and an enjoyment of the telling phrase and satisfyingly turned cadence. For a prime minister already reaching for a vocabulary like this, the last quarter of 2001 was an inspiration as well as a traumatic period in politics. In the two months after 9/11, he had more than fifty meetings with foreign leaders, in Washington, across Europe, and in the Middle East, as well as at home. If he was not talking by phone with President Khatami of Iran ("You *talk* to these guys?" Bush said to him in Washington), he was talking to Chirac about his Washington visit, or to the nervous Russians, or to President Musharraf of Pakistan (who, usefully for Blair, had trained at Sandhurst). He was in a perpetual whirl, and at every turn seemed buoyed up by the experience. The effect on him was profound, and it influenced the way his life with Bush would develop in the succeeding years.

When he arrived in Washington on September 20 after a few hours in New York to inspect the rubble at Ground Zero, Blair had the meeting with Bush that is now seen as the most important of their early conversations. For twenty minutes they were alone in the Blue Room at the White House, and when Blair came out he seemed to his Washington ambassador and his Downing Street aides to be in a notably determined mood. Something had been settled. His principal aim, to tell Bush that he would support an attack on the Taliban and al-Qaeda in Afghanistan, but not (for the moment) on Iraq, had been achieved. Bush had already decided that Iraq must wait, a decision settled at Camp David four days earlier. In return, Blair was ready to commit himself to stand with Bush, despite the acute nervousness already disturbing his government at home. Just before he left, the International Development Secretary, Clare Short, had broken ranks to say that the bombardment of Afghan civilians would be "unbearable."

But Blair was now on board. An hour later, he got a standing ovation on Capitol Hill in the course of the President's address to both houses simply for being there. "Thank you, friend," said Bush.

When he flew to Brussels through the night to brief European leaders on his conversations in Washington, he was able to take some satisfaction in his efforts to restrict Bush's response to 9/11 to an American move in Afghanistan. He had indeed brought some influence to bear, but it was almost certainly not decisive. In the weekend after 9/11, Colin Powell and the State Department had prevailed in an argument with the hawks about America's response, arguing that an international coalition could not be assembled to take on Iraq. Even Cheney, whose itch to get at Saddam was known to everyone in the administration, accepted the view of the Joint Chiefs that military sense dictated an Afghan strategy and, for the moment, nothing else. They left Camp David with a policy settled, albeit with an unresolved long-term argument about where the "war on terror" should take them, and when.

However limited Blair's direct influence on White House policy in these early days had been, his ranking as perhaps the closest of the "friends" who were rallying to Bush was profoundly significant for him. So great was the impact of 9/11 on his feelings and on his thinking that within a few weeks he was routinely talking in a language that he had not used before, and he seemed confidently to be taking on a mantle that he was quite willing to describe as having been provided by destiny.

By the time he became the first Western leader to visit Afghanistan after the defeat of the Taliban, in the dead of a 2002 January night on his way back from India and Pakistan, Blair had spent four months in constant movement from continent to continent, capital to capital, and was relishing the role that had developed from that White House meeting in September as the bridge builder for Bush with countries that were less reconciled to the military consequences of 9/11 than he was himself. Although he often presented himself in private as largely a restraining influence on Washington hawks, in public he appeared as an utterly confident supporter of Bush, apparently untroubled by the criticism raining down on the President from much of Europe, from his own Labour supporters, and (though still mostly *sotto voce*) from around his own Cabinet table.

The apogee of this transformation in Blair came in his speech to his annual party conference in early October, an occasion that often results in a ragbag speech designed to appeal to every constituent interest in the hall, usually topped off with a melodramatic flourish to enliven the delegates who must soon troop home to resume the weary business of politics in the streets. In 2001, Blair crafted the speech himself and ditched most of the usual lists of pledges and boasts that are expected. Instead, he performed a kind of act of rhetorical levitation that marked a personal high point in his premiership, and which, for those who were already tiring of his style and growing suspicious of his foreign policy objectives, appeared less of an ascent than a descent into dangerous simplicity.

The speech explains much of what moved Blair after 9/11 and how it was that he came to stay by Bush's side when the arguments over Iraq became fractious and bitter. It remains the most telling statement of his feelings in that period and was the platform on which he constructed the alliance with the United States, which he refused to reconsider even when his commitment to United Nations authorization for an Iraq invasion proved impossible to achieve.

No other words by Blair catch more dramatically the transformation he felt in 2001, described in terms that made it seem almost like a religious epiphany. "Out of the shadow of this evil should emerge lasting good," he said. History had reached a turning point. There could be no negotiation with the Taliban, only surrender on their part. Anyone giving succour to terrorism was "every bit as guilty" as those who had attacked New York and Washington. Once again using the failure to intervene in Rwanda as the exemplar of weakness in the international community, he appeared to promise a war (though he used the word only twice) on every injustice at home and abroad—from child poverty in Western cities to climate change to the plight of the whole continent of Africa, which was "a scar on the conscience of the world."

This speech, remarkable in being covered fully in early evening newscasts in the United States as well as on twenty-four-hour news channels, was dizzying. Reminded of the English poet most easily moved by imperial conquest and the glory of war, Matthew Parris wrote in *The Times:* "His ambitions left Kipling looking wimpish."

The words that rang most clearly from the speech were *duty, courage, danger, fear*—and, of course, *victory* and *defeat.* Rousing though the tone was, Blair delivered it as much as a sober warning as a call to arms. No one could doubt the anxiety that seemed entwined with his determination. During it, there were periods of unusual silence in the conference hall in Brighton, as if his words themselves were having a shocking effect. Afterwards, the reactions began to take the form that would shape the debate about war over the next three years, in Britain and America. With his eloquence—unquestioned even by his critics—Blair was sharpening the questions that would divide most Western nationals in the years ahead and force him into the decisions that would help determine not only his own future as Prime Minister, but the direction of American policy, too. On that Tuesday afternoon in Brighton, his choice was clear.

On the Left of his party there was still some reluctance to speak of a war-mongering Prime Minister, so raw was the post-9/11 atmosphere. Only a handful of dissidents were starting to make their unease public. But in private, the divide was opening up fast. Some liberal commentators were convinced, and apparently carried away (Polly Toynbee writing in the *Guardian* that it was "the speech of a lifetime" in which his commitment to justice and equality had been explained as never before). Inside his own government, the stirrings of dissent could be felt; and in the Foreign Office, a place where such an ambitious and rhetorically lush text would never make it to the Autocue, a distinct drawing-in of breath. Africa, the Middle East, climate change, world poverty, victory in the Balkans as a model for victory in Afghanistan, a foreign policy driven by values of freedom rather than national self-interest and the practicalities of power politics—and all in one afternoon. Too much for even the most starry-eyed diplomat-evangelist.

But there was nothing fake about this speech. Blair wrote most of it himself, and it had the ring of his private conversation translated to the stage. He was indeed moved by connections that he now saw between the injustices of the world and the threat of terrorism, between the impoverishment of nations and the denial of democracy. As a credo, it was powerful enough to sharpen dramatically the edge of his profile, on both sides of the Atlantic. In Washington, where he was already emerging as the likeliest to stay loyal when the going got rough, his words seemed the nearest echo of the sentiments of mainstream Americans (perhaps delivered with easier eloquence than could be managed in the White House or its environs). At home, they placed Blair where he most liked to be—on his own. Like it or loathe it, this was a speech that only he could have given.

Was this the moment when the road to Baghdad opened up and became the only path for him? The kaleidoscope, he said in Brighton, had been shaken and the world had to make sense of the flux. His reading of the pieces would now place him firmly in the camp of an American president more unpopular elsewhere in the world than any since Johnson at the height of Vietnam; and

Bush was presiding, by his own acknowledgment, over an America still divided down the middle as it had been at the moment of his election. Never in his lifetime had a prime minister taken such a risky course in making a principal alliance. Nor had any been able to claim such a role in shaping a policy that, in the world of one superpower, would attempt to change the rules that they had all lived by after World War II.

During these three months or so after the September attacks, Blair made the commitments, emotionally and politically, that would determine the rest of his premiership. They were also decisions that had consequences far beyond the borders of Britain, in bolstering American policy when it was engendering opposition and hatred in many parts of the world. The story goes from Ground Zero to that conference hall in Brighton, to a dozen and more capitals round the world, to the windy corridors of the United Nations in New York, and on to the streets of Baghdad. His choice—for choice it was—was important.

It did not come from intellectual torment or ideological analysis, nor solely from the pressures that bear down on any supplicant prime minister who deals with the powers that flow from the Oval Office. Blair's convictions were simpler than that, as his friends and enemies both acknowledge. Although he embroiled himself in the negotiations and compromises that are the day-to-day life of any leader, he was driven by unmistakable and surprisingly resilient instincts. They led him to war, and to a strange kind of international celebrity that encompassed political isolation.

By chance, it was he who had the freedom of action when the twin towers were struck. By accident, Bush found an ally whose instincts were surprisingly close to his own. By an unpredictable combination of circumstances, they found themselves in a position to argue that they were writing the blueprint for the history of the twenty-first century.

Blair was an enthusiast for the enterprise, believing that he had no choice but to make it the engine of his leadership. In doing so, he helped to invent the most potent alliance of the post–Cold War world. Not only was it powerful, the object of some envy and much hatred, but it was fascinating for its peculiarity. Nothing revealed more about these men than the strangeness of their coming together.

CHAPTER 4

# THE AXIS
# OF FRIENDSHIP

Blair is sitting in the garden of 10 Downing Street in the early summer sunshine. The news from Iraq is bad. Saddam Hussein has been gone for more than a year and is in a prison cell in Qatar, but there are daily eruptions of violence against coalition troops. Every day Blair is asked why he still believes it was right to go to war; whether it was ideology, or religion, or an unlikely political affair with the American Right that drove him on. He says something surprising: "I never quite understand what people mean by this neocon thing."

While he speaks, the Labour Party is pulsating with talk of a leadership crisis. The deputy prime minister, John Prescott, has acknowledged in public what everyone knows in private—that when they meet, his ministers are beginning to think beyond the Blair era and ponder what might follow. They are not planning a coup, but they think his premiership is in the autumn of its days. They certainly have a view on "the neocon thing." In the Labour Party, Blair's alliance with Bush is more unpopular than ever and, quietly, the party is extending its feelers to Senator John Kerry's campaign to assure him that whatever the Prime Minister may think, they are still natural Democrats, and they hope he wins. They are wrestling with an insoluble ideological problem. How can a Labour leader lie down so happily with an administration whose right-wing pulse beats strong and which Kerry says is running a foreign policy that has shattered the historic alliances it claims to be protecting? Many in his party are beside themselves with puzzlement and anger. Yet Blair brushes aside the ideological problems as if they don't exist.

Asked if he had read the founding text of the neoconservatives who have been the warriors of the administration and were the cheerleaders for the invasion that he joined, "The Project for the New American Century," Blair replies: "I can't say I have . . . What's in it?" There follows a short and only slightly embarrassed chuckle. He is a prime minister accused by his own party of having made an ideological pact with devilish right-wingers, whom Labour MPs think are bent on the creation of a new American empire, and for whom in their eyes Blair's friend Bush is a pawn. Yet he is hazy about the thinking that has convulsed his own party. He is only interested in his own.

Typically, Blair affects a certain degree of surprise that his own analysis has found him some odd bedfellows, and it is just as typical that he isn't bothered by it. Referring to those who adhere to the founding principles of the neoconservative project—an unembarrassed belief in the primacy of American values, a commitment to pre-emptive action in supporting them abroad, a dislike of all the ideas that huddle under the umbrella of "internationalism"—Blair says: "I come at this from a completely different perspective—a progressive perspective that says there should not be a doctrine of nonintervention in every set of circumstances. Why should the Left never support that?

"Why should we say that we should never intervene in a situation where people are brutally repressive. I mean, I can't understand why we should be saying that. I can understand a right-wing conservative saying that.

"Now I think after 9/11 from the other perspective there are people on the Right who have said—and I think this is where the progressive and the right-wing cases come together—not 'we've got to go out and impose American values.' What I think people are saying, and this is certainly my belief, is that the greater the spread of freedom and democracy, the greater the possibility of security. Why? Because it is states that are repressed, that are dictatorial, that give their people no freedom, that don't allow them to exercise democratic rights that in my experience and judgment are the states that end up threatening others."

Blair did not reach this view by turning to the high-priests of neoconservatism—the journalist and conservative polemicist Bill Kristol, Rumsfeld's deputy Paul Wolfowitz, nor even the ever-present Richard Perle, who had been demonized in the Labour Party twenty years before by Denis Healey as "the prince of darkness" for his promotion of the Star Wars project when he served in the Reagan administration—but arrived there by his own propulsion. In his Chicago speech in 1999, he had shown himself to be well on the way. By the time Bush was elected he was anxious to move further, apparently unaware of the parallel path being taken by some whose views on matters other than the war on terror—particularly about how Israel and the Palestinians should settle their affairs, or what role there should be for the United Nations—were quite different from his own, and whose rhetoric he would find unsettling. But they were facing the same way.

To Blair, there was no contradiction in thinking about pre-emptive action as legitimate in a disordered world and simul-taneously holding to ideas of internationalism associated with liberal democratic thinking and traditionally excoriated on the American Right. Condoleezza Rice said during the 2000 presiden-tial campaign, in criticizing the Clinton approach to foreign affairs, that the outgoing administration believed "that the support of many states—or even better, of institutions like the United Nations—is essential to the legitimate exercise of power." Blair would describe that internationalist view as his own, but he found himself in the early months of the Bush administration comfort-ably discussing the state of the world in terms that sat quite happily beside those of Rice, and even some of those to her right in the administration who were already breathing fire.

His political personality was split. When talking to his own party, as in his conference speech soon after 9/11, he naturally reached for the language of international cooperation and consensus. It was Labour's tradition, and he was comfortable with it. But he was also becoming convinced that a disordered world—the process he associated with terrorism—demanded new thinking. He was just as attracted to the idea of pre-emptive action as he was to the strengthening of international institutions, whether NATO, the European Union, or the United Nations. It was inevitable that the two instincts would collide, because an America acting alone would inevitably find itself in conflict with the organizations that wanted to strengthen collective decision-making as a counterbalance to the influence of one superpower. He staked much of his foreign policy on his ability to resolve contradictions that his own Foreign Office, most of his Cabinet, and his party thought were irreconcilable.

Above all, he tried to be the fulcrum of a balance between Europe and the United States. It was not a stark choice between one or the other, because like all his recent predecessors, he thought that the national interest lay in maximizing influence in both directions, and he convinced himself that he could be the one European leader who could be Washington's friend without sacrificing influence in capitals nearer home.

The idea that the Prime Minister was suckered into playing the submissive partner is too simple. No British prime minister could play a dominating role in Washington, of course, because the flow of power is one-way. He (or even she) is bound to be subordinate, but influence is subtle and can transform both leaders, almost without their noticing. Blair's relationship with Bush changed him as a prime minister. It was a change that dismayed his party (perplexing some of his most important Cabinet colleagues) and brought him great unpopularity; yet it was one that undoubtedly brought him the satisfaction of feeling he had found his mission.

At the height of his Iraq troubles, with piles of pictures sitting on his desk showing the horrors from Abu Ghraib prison and the sound of antiwar demonstrators in the street outside calling "Not in my name," Blair was still convinced that his alliance had been right. He took that view not simply because he thought his policy in the Middle East was justified. To his surprise, in dealing with a politician from a background so different it might have been on another planet, a man whose values were so profoundly American as to appear distant and almost quaint, he discovered a strange kind of freedom.

The friendship they started to enjoy was one that Blair conducted on his own. It engendered little sympathy in those around him, except inasmuch as American policy was the elephant sitting on the Cabinet table that could never be ignored, and he used it as an intellectual and political release. There were no rules about what he must think, no political traditions to be followed like textbooks, no wearisome committees to be negotiated in getting a policy through the Cabinet and into the bureaucratic machine. It was direct and assertive, and the kind of politics Blair liked.

A prime minister and a president can make agreements that stick. They are unlikely to be unscrambled by the officials back in the office. Indeed, Blair's attraction to the relationship with Washington was increased by his enjoyment of doing business in this way. The regular summits of European leaders—which now punctuate all their calendars with two-day sessions of argument and deal making—are cumbersome by nature. One-on-one policy-making is a happier business. It also suited Blair's style. In London, he had broken much of the pattern in the Prime Minister's office. Because of the relationship with Gordon Brown, that was essential to the good working of government, and because of its fingertip sensitivity, he did a great deal of business with Brown in private in his den. Civil servants were alarmed—no note taking!—and after a year or so, they began to insert themselves into the conversations. But many consultations remained private. Well into his second term, Blair's diary had large spaces that were simply marked "GB" for his session with the Chancellor, and it was at those times that much of the most important business of government was done, or attempted.

With Bush, he realized after their first meeting that he had a friendship that could be developed. From the beginning it did not seem to occur to him that he might face any profound difficulties, anything more than disputes over detail or passing arguments—a trade dispute over steel tariffs, for example. He was naturally sensitive to the accusation that he was a weak partner but always made clear that he trusted Bush never to put him in too humiliating a position. He told Michael Cockerell of the BBC in summer 2002 for a documentary on the transatlantic relationship: "In the end, Britain is a sovereign nation. Britain decides its own policy and although I back America I would never back America if I thought they were doing something wrong. I wouldn't support it." Significantly, he then added: "But I've never found that, and I don't expect to find it in the future."

That is a remarkable statement, revealing the depth of Blair's belief in the thrust of American policy. No other important European leader would have given such a blanket statement of faith. From the start, Blair was willing to give Bush the benefit of the doubt. In doing that he deliberately edged away from his party— something that didn't disturb him at all—and consciously staked much of his premiership on the judgement he had made about Bush. The consequences of that decision would not become clear until long after 9/11, but even at their first meeting, Blair knew that he was making an important decision in his own mind. He made it for a particular reason.

His mind was turning to Afghanistan and the Taliban. The doctrine laid out in Chicago in 1999 justified intervention in other countries' affairs on humanitarian grounds when all diplomatic options had been exhausted. With what he believed the success of the Kosovo campaign behind him, he was already contemplating Afghanistan. Around the time of his first meeting with Bush in February 2001, he asked the Foreign Office (to its surprise) for a report on the state of the country—the strength of the Taliban regime, the extent of its violations of human rights, the scale of the heroin traffic that originated in Afghan poppy fields and led to the streets of British cities, and the threat from al-Qaeda, a network that was then little known to the public at large but was looming large in his mind. In his first conversation with Bush, he pondered the possibility of action being necessary in Afghanistan under the "Blair doctrine" stated in the Chicago speech.

Thus, six months before 9/11, five months before the now notorious President's daily briefing in the White House identifying Osama bin Laden as being "determined to strike in the U.S.," Blair was pressing an alarm bell. He did not know then that inside the administration there was a struggle going on over the importance or otherwise of al-Qaeda. Richard A. Clarke, head of counterterrorism in the White House, was frustrated at his inability to get to Bush to give him a detailed briefing on the threat he believed would come from Osama bin Laden. When he did brief officials in April, two months after Blair visited Bush in Crawford, he was surprised that Paul Wolfowitz, the deputy defense secretary, was unimpressed by bin Laden and interested principally in Iraq. As Wolfowitz put it to them: "Well, I just don't understand why we are beginning by talking about this one man bin Laden." Clarke said al-Qaeda posed an immediate and serious threat. It was clear that although the State Department agreed with him, the Pentagon did not. In the first months of the administration, the Pentagon took an antagonistic position on the question of terrorism and retained it through the Iraq war and its aftermath three years later.

Blair was part of this argument. In London, he had turned himself into a one-man early warning system and was demanding assessments in Whitehall about the dangers that might flow from Afghanistan. This was not a public exercise, but in the foreign policy machine operating in Downing Street—to the weary frustration of the Foreign Office, which was getting used to the leakage of power to the prime minister's office—Kabul was a name on everyone's lips. The result was that Blair became an important element in the education of Bush about the "war on terror." The Bush tutorial did not begin formally until after 9/11, but in Blair's mind, the combatants were lining up long before the planes took off.

In a conversation with Bush in the spring, Blair even raised the prospect with Bush that they would find themselves at war in Afghanistan. Convinced by his Balkan experiences that military intervention could work, he was turning his mind to bin Laden's base. There was no public acknowledgement of this in Britain, although the head of the diplomatic service, Sir John Kerr, did tell the Foreign Affairs Committee of the House of Commons in March that Afghanistan was one of the principal worries in his office.

The basis of the relationship between Prime Minister and President was therefore established in the months before the crisis: Bush trusted Blair in part because he had been saying for months that the risk came from Afghanistan. Blair's natural instinct toward "presidentialism" meant that he preferred personal diplomacy and direct dealings with Bush. From the start, they talked a good deal. It was often rambling stuff, however. Afterward, transcripts were circulated in the White House and Downing Street. It was quite common for a phone call to go from the British embassy to Condi Rice's office, or the other way round, asking: "What do we think they mean here?" According to someone with access to all the transcripts: "They are not rich in detail." That catches the flavor of their dealings from the beginning. The conversations were informal, open, and surprisingly trusting. To Blair, that was an advantage. To Cook, his foreign secretary at the time, it was a harbinger of trouble ahead. The Prime Minister was apparently treating the President with the same intimate familiarity he was accustomed to showing Gordon Brown, though without the rows and sulks. It meant that he would protect the privacy of the relationship in the belief that it was the way to enhance its power. Blair's style was dictating the way the relationship between the two countries was going to develop, and from the beginning there were many in the foreign policy establishment who didn't like it. They had worried about it in the Clinton years, but with a president being urged by his colleagues to pursue a much more aggressive and controversial American policy abroad, they smelled danger.

Blair sensed something else. He was able to appear to Bush as a positive force. He was not arguing a defensive case—warning against aggression, playing down threats, promoting the cautious view. He was sounding the alarm. When 9/11 came he was seen as one of the prophets who had predicted the doom, and therefore one who could be counted on to understand its consequences.

Without understanding it fully, Blair had become an important adjunct to the administration in its first months. When the lapses in intelligence and analysis before 9/11 began to be uncovered by the Kean Commission three years later, it became clear how powerful these early discussions must have been. With Bush wallowing in a degree of ignorance, he was susceptible to the power of persuasion by his new friend across the ocean.

In return, Blair was given a welcome that he had believed impossible after Gore's defeat. Where it would lead he could not know, but he told his colleagues in this period that he had secured a place at the top table that would ensure that the British view was heeded in Washington.

Robin Cook suspected from the first that it was a delusion and that the Prime Minister would be drawn into an alliance from which it would be impossible to escape when the sky turned dark. But for Blair it was the evidence that he, personally, could be the bridge between Europe and the United States. He would secure the transatlantic relationship, increase Britain's influence in the European Union, and guarantee favoured status for the British view in the White House. So the argument went. It was optimistic, as is typical with Blair. Across the street in the Foreign Office, there was much more concern. Even then, the Bush foreign policy was a worrying phenomenon because it was so hazy. But by the summer of 2001 it was clear that whatever it turned out to be, Blair would support it.

The period after 9/11 did everything to convince Blair that he had been right. Because of his conviction that the attacks could be the precursors of an international catastrophe, he used his special position with Bush—and his public standing in the United States as almost an honorary American—to be the leading figure abroad promoting the Afghan campaign that began in October and an assiduous advocate across the Middle East of the thinking that had united him with Bush. By this stage, he had cast away the language that most leaders use to lower the temperature at moments of crisis and was revelling in the centrality of his role. The reason was clear. If asked why he had an apocalyptic vision of Armageddon, he says: "Well, I believe that there is a serious risk of that and I believe the risk is not a risk that you can run. In other words, I am not saying for a certainty it will happen, but I am saying that the risk is sufficiently serious that the balance of risk tilts you towards acting and not waiting till it happens." Few political leaders would answer a question including the word *Armageddon* without first trying to take the sting out of the language.

By the time he decided to go to war in Iraq, he had already come to believe that here was a risk greater than any that had been taken seriously by any other prime minister since World War II. None had believed a Soviet strike was likely. It was the principal preoccupation of defence policy, but it was theoretical rather than real. Blair was now seized by an alarm that he'd never experienced. He spoke of *apocalypse, Armageddon, meltdown*. Even making allowance for Blair's thespian tendencies, these are strong words. In the context of the Middle East, they conjure up an historic nightmare. Blair used them quite deliberately.

His concern about Afghanistan meant that when victory in Afghanistan was claimed at around the turn of 2001, Blair was happy to be there first. On a freezing January night four months after 9/11, he landed at an airfield outside Kabul. He was on the ground for no more than an hour or two, but it was exhilarating for him. He was the first leader of the victorious coalition to claim victory on Afghan soil. Never mind that bin Laden, the object of the American assault, was in a cave or on a distant mountaintop. This was liberation.

The circumstances were appropriately odd. As he walked from

his plane across an airfield still pitted with mines, a welcoming posse of Afghan warlords huddled in a shed to greet him, some of them with daggers in their belts. They seemed an unlikely government-in-waiting. A few of them, Blair knew, had histories as bloody as any of the Taliban leaders who had been driven from power. But their turbans and knives, and the iron handshakes they exchanged with Blair in an awkward greeting, were the symbols of victory. It was for this that Blair had spent the previous weeks shuttling through the Middle East, coaxing the Pakistanis into surreptitious help along the border, arguing that the American desire for revenge could be turned into something more positive: the removal of an obnoxious regime, which seemed to encapsulate the grim menace of bin Laden himself.

By the end of 2001, Blair's relief that the United States was engaged in an Afghan campaign and not an assault on Baghdad had become something more. As so often, he found virtue in political necessity. The war in Afghanistan was the "right" response to 9/11, as he had agreed with Bush in September, and now it became for him the emblem of a Western response that went beyond revenge. Arriving at that darkened airfield from Delhi, where he'd been talking about the threat of a nuclear exchange between India and Pakistan over Kashmir, Afghanistan became the first victory in the war Bush had announced on September 12. Two years later they would still be fighting there; bin Laden would still be a will-o'-the-wisp somewhere in the mountains; political institutions would be shaky; generals would still be asking for more troops to pacify rebel areas. But it was a victory at the time. On the plane taking him on to the Gulf state of Oman and then home, Blair was ready to argue that just as the war in Kosovo had righted a wrong in the removal of Milosevic, so the disappearance of the Taliban was more than a natural consequence of an American response to the al-Qaeda attack: it was a morally just outcome.

His general foreboding as the new year began was therefore touched by some exhilaration. It was not shared by all of his Cabinet.

Although a military response to 9/11 was known to be inevitable from those first days and although there was relief that Bush had targeted Afghanistan alone, Blair's government was already suffering tremors. In the months after he told his party conference, "Let us re-order the world around us," some of his senior ministers were becoming queasy at the prospect. That unease turned to rampant alarm at the end of January, with Bush's State of the Union speech.

In the history of Blair's support for Bush, the speech was a turning point. There was distaste in London at the language, and nervousness about the consequences. Blair might have begun at this moment to suggest that the British approach was different. He didn't. In the course of the following nine months, he became a partner in the policy it represented and unwilling to put any distance between him and the President.

Bush's phrase "an axis of evil" may not have been meant to sound as alarming as it did. He may well have been avoiding too much emphasis on Iraq alone. The inclusion of North Korea and Iran could be seen as softening the anti-Iraq rhetoric, and that was certainly the rationalization of the State Department. In Europe, however, the effect was quite different. In the Labour Party, Bush now appeared to be talking of a wider war. It was precisely the kind of language that set teeth on edge. Even if no one believed that missiles would be pointed at Pyongyang in anger, nor that Iran would be a target, the path stretching before Blair appeared to be strewn with dangers and horrors. Even a prime minister capable of summoning up apocalyptic rhetoric in responding to 9/11 could hardly use the word *evil* to describe a regime in Teheran with which Britain was conducting an intense effort at détente. But Blair did not gulp. He told his colleagues that he well understood the pressure that had caused Bush to speak on Capitol Hill as he did. Around the Cabinet table, however, the pessimism was beginning to disturb his government.

Those ministers, like Cook, who were stirring uneasily, would have been even more disturbed had they known what Blair was told around the time of the State of the Union speech. He learned from his Washington embassy the fact that would change his premiership: that a timetable had been set for the invasion of Iraq. By the time Bush rose to speak on January 29, it was known at 3100 Massachusetts Avenue that planning had begun. When the information was passed to Blair as a fact, there was a schedule attached. Sir Christopher Meyer, the ambassador, was able to add another fact, which would become an alarming one. The plan was to avoid letting the confrontation with Saddam drag into the autumn of 2003, but to attack in the spring. The summer was excluded. Blair now knew that the White House had set what would almost certainly become an inexorable course toward Baghdad. He did not consider for a moment distancing himself from that aim. Knowing Bush as he now did, he believed he could exercise influence on the way the push to war was measured. But he knew, too, that it was all but unstoppable.

In the Pentagon, the remorseless logistics of war began to be assembled. Although there was nervousness there, along with a mistrust of Rumsfeld's willingness to commit enough troops to do the job, the wheels had begun to turn. In London, the same process began, but with even less enthusiasm. In the Ministry of Defence, and across the River Thames at the headquarters of MI6, the view was that war could—and should—be avoided. There was no enthusiasm whatever for war with Saddam.

But Blair himself was going through a profound change. He argues that he never faced the prospect of war with enthusiasm; but in the course of 2002, he moved from a position of nervousness and even scepticism to a more resigned state. It calmed him, and disturbed his colleagues. After the State of the Union speech, a number of them noted that their astonishment at the "axis of evil" was not shared by the Prime Minister. He would not have used it himself, and thought it crude and unhelpful, but he saw no reason to use it to distance himself from Bush.

The Cabinet discussed Iraq for the first time at length in early March. Robin Cook, who sat almost directly across the table from Blair, noted in his diary: "For the first time I can recall in five years, Tony was out on a limb." In his account of that meeting,

Blair is arguing that Britain has no alternative but to remain the candid friend in the hope of bringing influence to bear on the White House. When Cook himself raises the Israel-Palestine crisis and his fears that any hope of peace will slip away with an Iraq war, Blair insists that only by staying close to Bush can he influence American policy for the better; when Cook worries about relations with Europe, Blair says that the German chancellor, Gerhard Schroeder, and the French prime minister, Lionel Jospin, have both told him that they understand that Britain cannot oppose the Americans. His version of the choice is that there is none: Britain will support Bush.

His colleagues could hardly disagree. A prime minister inherits the assumption that since power flows from the Oval Office (especially in the direction of the Middle East), there is no rival to the President as his obvious object of affection. Blair never questioned the inevitability of American primacy. He had seen it work with Clinton; he had to make it work with Bush.

But the complaint that began to be heard from his ministers in private was different. They did not doubt the strength of the ties that bound Downing Street to the White House, underpinned and perhaps dominated by the defence and intelligence relationship that acted like a marriage contract, and they understood that it would have been all but impossible for Blair to stay out, for example, of the coalition that invaded Afghanistan (even if he had thought it a good idea). Practical politics did not allow it. Their concern was about a deeper attitude that they began to see developing in Blair. One of his advisers later put it like this: "There were six or seven moments in the Iraq story when he could have drawn back. The first time was probably early in 2002. He could have, and he didn't. It was clear then where we were heading."

The period between the State of the Union speech at the end of January 2002 and Blair's visit to the Bush ranch in Crawford, Texas, in early April is the decisive period in Blair's conversion to war. In part of his mind, he seemed to struggle against it; in another compartment, he had accepted its inevitability. As always with Blair, this conflict was expressed in rhetoric of a personal kind. When he spoke at the George H.W. Bush Presidential Library at the end of his Texas visit, no one required decoding equipment to work out that the ideas first put together in his conference speech six months before had now taken root and were flourishing. "I advocate an enlightened self-interest that puts fighting for our values right at the heart of the policies necessary to protect our nations," he said. His use of "fighting" was not accidental, the context making it clear that he saw the struggle as one that was only partly intellectual. It would involve physical conflict, too.

Recalling his Chicago speech in 1999, he said that people had accused him of being guilty of "Panglossian idealism," believing in the best of all possible things in the best of all possible worlds. Not at all, said Blair. His idea of "a doctrine of international community" was practical enough to be the justification for war in the Balkans. There was no effort to conceal how his mind was moving.

"Osama bin Laden's philosophy is not just a security threat to us. It is an assault on our hearts and minds. It represents extremism, cruelty, intolerance of different cultures and lifestyles. It can't be fought just with guns. It must be fought by moderate Islam against extreme Islam, by the virtues of religious and political tolerance triumphing over bigotry."

During this speech, James Baker III, former secretary of state and Bush family retainer, whose poker player's face seldom cracks into anything but a cheerless smile, found it impossible to conceal his excitement. He had seldom heard a finer speech, he said. The Republican establishment gathered at Blair's feet heard an analysis of the world that played to their deepest feelings. His commitment came at a price, said Blair. "It means that when America is fighting for those values, then, however tough we fight with her. No grandstanding, no offering implausible but impractical advice from the touchline. No wishing away the hard not the easy choices on terrorism and WMD, or making peace in the Middle East, but working together side by side."

No one listening to this could doubt how far Blair had come. He might not have written a blank cheque for war, but the pen was loaded and in his hand. Intellectually, he was providing the continuo accompaniment to the rougher and perhaps cruder statements by Bush, who was still hoping to smoke bin Laden out of his hole and bring him in dead or alive. Blair offered a patina of sophistication but promised that when the posse disappeared into the hills in a cloud of dust, he would be riding along.

The question for his Cabinet colleagues at home was whether in his private conversations with Bush, he had attached any conditions to this enthusiasm for the struggle ahead, which he seemed to envisage as a generation-long battle of minds, with wars attached. He had; but far from being the protection from war that most of his Cabinet sought, they became the stuff of the struggle that would divide his government and eventually leave him almost alone. As one of his closest colleagues in his dealings with the White House put it after the war, "They were the conditions that never became conditions, and that was really the trouble."

At the beginning, the conditions had seemed clear enough—in line with past British practice under governments of different parties, and with the necessary political attribute of being able to provide Blair with cover in his own party if it should come to war in Iraq. There were two components. The United Nations must be involved in any invasion in the Middle East, and there must be progress in bringing Israelis and Palestinians back into negotiations on a final settlement. With those guarantees, Blair could hope that he could carry his party with him, as well as public opinion. Even at this early stage, polls suggested that UN involvement was important if the public was to be convinced that it was sensible to join an American convoy en route to Baghdad. A penumbra of suspicion already surrounded Bush in the public mind, and Blair's convictions about his judgement and clear-sightedness were not widely shared. When he met sceptical Labour MPs in small groups at Downing Street, which he was doing regularly to try to maintain some familiarity with a party that was becoming estranged, he would startle them with the portrait of a man who, in Blair's description, they hardly recognized: "Straightforward, able to get to the point quickly, decisive, cleverer than you think," he would say. They would leave unconvinced.

Blair was not dissembling. By this stage he had convinced himself of a relationship with Bush that had caught up with, and perhaps even surpassed, his Clinton affair. Blair, however, was now sure that he understood the administration and, therefore, could make his influence tell. This was the calculation that was put to the test in Crawford in April 2002, in a visit that became Blair's turning point. Although he still believed that war could be avoided, his absorption in the logic of Bush's argument with Saddam was now such that he could not escape its coils. Robin Cook and Clare Short, the other Cabinet minister who was showing the most obvious public signs of hostility to Blair, were wrong to conclude that he had committed himself irrevocably to the American cause in those conversations at Crawford. He had not. There was still some agony to come. But he did make one decision that was to prove just as important.

He made no argument against the targeting of Saddam, nor against the belief that bringing down his regime would benefit the Middle East. Nothing said at Crawford led Bush to believe that Blair wouldn't stay the course. On the contrary, the President had every reason to believe that Blair would argue his case to the rest of the world. Blair did nothing to dissuade him. His purpose in Texas was to erect some hurdles for Bush to cross before war could begin, not to argue that it would be hard to justify; to that extent, he abandoned the argument of principle against attacking Iraq. Asked why, one of his Cabinet colleagues said simply, "Because he believed in it."

Blair had crossed the Rubicon. With his advisers, he'd worked out a strategy to try to persuade the Americans to go back to the UN, but he put it to Bush in terms suggesting that he believed it would strengthen the assault on Iraq. While some of his colleagues at home believed that a long negotiation at the UN would make war much less likely—and perhaps impossible, because of the opposition that would inevitably emerge—Blair used no such argument with Bush. Aware of the hostility to the UN and all its efforts by those around Bush, led by Cheney, Blair was making the case that it would strengthen the Americans' hand. He could hardly argue that it was the best way of preventing war, since he now knew that the planning was underway and that a decision in principle had been taken, so he adopted a defensive manoeuvre.

Similarly with the Middle East, Blair persuaded himself that Bush could be eased into a rerun of the last Clinton negotiation under Ehud Barak's premiership in Israel, which had produced a plan setting out a path that might lead to the creation of two states. It was turned down by the Palestinians, because Yasser Arafat could not have persuaded his people of its benefits. The Foreign Office were not surprised at the outcome: the contorted geography of the plan was never going to seem to the Palestinians like an embryonic state. But Blair wanted to try again. He knew that Arafat was weakening fast—Blair despaired at the corruption swirling around the ageing leader and knew that his powers of persuasion with his people were rapidly waning—but he wanted progress. British policy in the Middle East had for a generation rested on the end of the Israeli occupation of the West Bank and Gaza and the emergence of a Palestinian state, and Blair believed that Bush could be persuaded toward what, in European terms, would be a progressive policy.

So he asked Bush to send Colin Powell to Israel. Bush's announcement was notably downbeat and betrayed the rampant lack of enthusiasm for the new venture in all sectors except parts of the State Department. For Blair, however, it was progress.

He therefore went to Crawford in April believing that he could demonstrate to his wary colleagues at home that he was making progress. Did they believe the Americans would ignore the UN? Did they think that Washington had abandoned the Palestinians? He believed he could prove they were wrong and demonstrate as a result that his closeness to Bush had benefits. He was a man of influence.

But nothing that happened in Crawford altered the timetable

that was already on a chart on Rumsfeld's wall; nothing weakened the conviction that "regime change" in Iraq was the right policy, whether weapons of mass destruction threatened the West or not; nothing signalled the start of a wholehearted American involvement in a resumption of the efforts that had begun nearly a decade earlier in Oslo to negotiate a two-state solution in Israel-Palestine on the basis of important concessions on both sides. Instead, Bush was convinced that Blair would be with him all the way and Blair became even more persuaded that the fundamental thinking on Iraq was something with which he could not disagree. He was not yet convinced that war was inevitable, nor did he think that he was being asked to give an iron commitment to support for it, but he came home from Texas with the knowledge, perhaps lurking just under the surface of his political consciousness, that there was no way back.

His statement to the House of Commons betrayed the discomfort. He wanted to repeat the statements he had made in the United States about the importance of confronting Saddam, yet he wanted to reassure his audience at home that such influence as he had was being used to prevent the kind of eager rush to war of which Bush was suspected. The fact that Bush was more cautious than many of his critics assumed scarcely mattered: Blair was faced with a wall of suspicion. He had to find a way around it.

His words did not reassure his Cabinet: "There is no doubt that the region would be a better place without Saddam Hussein." That was hardly a controversial view, but it was hardly the point. His own Foreign Office had spent twenty years wondering how best to deal with his awkward presence and had concluded after the first Gulf War that containment was the answer. They never believed that the Middle East would benefit from another invasion. When Blair did look ahead, his words betrayed his belief that the Americans were set on war: "The method of achieving that [the removal of Saddam] is, as I said, open to consultation and deliberation."

Consultation and deliberation. Compromise and time. They were the twin pillars of his policy. But from April onward, though

Blair's efforts to get the sanction of the UN Security Council for an invasion were real and though he invested great energy in them to the end, those pillars always seemed to wobble. After coming back from Texas, Blair was aware that his efforts to engage the UN might fail. When questions were raised in Cabinet about the necessity of formal resolutions authorizing war, he refused to commit himself to a policy that would depend on the UN. And in the Middle East, the Foreign Office was reporting that it could see no sign of wholehearted American engagement in the process laid out in the road map—there were gestures, made mostly by Powell, but no substance. Compared with Clinton's obsessive engagement, Bush's involvement was distant, never suggesting a robust commitment.

Yet it was upon this that Blair depended. He was moving by now toward an engagement with the United States that was bound to cause him immense trouble at home. Unless he could persuade Bush to genuflect to the UN and offer him the *quid pro quo* of progress in Israel, he realized that he would face Cabinet resignations and that he might be drawn into a war that would be deeply damaging.

The extraordinary truth of the spring of 2002, however, is that he took little notice of these perils. The Crawford meeting is remarkable in that both leaders used the encounter to demonstrate their closeness but it actually revealed something quite different: the extent to which each did not understand the other's problem.

At the very time when the new "special relationship" was being hailed in London and Washington, Bush and Blair were confronting the differences between them, without realizing what was happening. Their conversations that April convinced them both that they would see the "war on terror" through the next few years as staunch allies, whether war was required in Iraq or not. But each revealed in the way he dealt with the other an ignorance of the political weaknesses on the other side of the Atlantic. They were not coming closer; they were trapped in an illusion.

Blair did not understand the depth of the neoconservative

obsession with Saddam, and Bush did not appreciate the difficulties Blair was already beginning to have to face in Britain. Each was deluded into believing, by the straightforwardness of their personal dealings, that such problems as existed would be solved by the strength of this joint leadership. They were wrong. Each would be damaged by the optimism that attended those Crawford talks.

Bush greatly underestimated Blair's potential political weakness. This was due in part to his hazy understanding of the parliamentary system, and more generally the politics of Europe, which he spoke of as if they were the machinations of strange life forms on a distant planet. It was not until nearly a year later, at the height of the failed effort to get a second UN resolution authorizing war, that Bush began to be troubled about his friend's capacity to survive.

In 2002, he found it impossible to believe that when Blair spoke with such simplicity about his commitment to stand alongside the United States in good times and bad, he was not speaking for his whole government. When Blair spoke of his Cabinet, Bush thought he was talking about a group of executives like his own, hand-picked to implement the orders of a chief executive in the White House. But no word is more confusing than "Cabinet" in comparing the two systems.

Blair's Cabinet consisted of parliamentarians, all but a handful elected to the Commons. Their jobs were in the Prime Minister's gift, but every minister relies on parliamentary support (and most of them use it from time to time in the daily struggles with Number 10 which are the stuff of life in government). Conversely, a minister who loses his party's support in the Commons is finished. A weak and miserable stand at the dispatch box has often marked the end of a parliamentary career. Despite the tendency of prime ministers to centralize power, and Blair's creation of a virtual Prime Minister's department in Downing Street to act as an executive core in Whitehall, the tradition by which the Prime Minister is only *primus inter pares* in the Cabinet has refused to die, though it has often seemed to be about to breathe its last. It has remained true that prime ministers who lose the support of their Cabinets sacrifice the authority they require to command their majority in the Commons.

American mystification at this process, akin to the way the mysteries of cricket appear to baseball players, was obvious in the resignation of Margaret Thatcher in 1990. Her supporters in the United States simply could not understand how such a thing could happen. In part, their lack of understanding flowed from ignorance over the policy that alienated her own party—the disastrous "poll tax" that sank her—but there was a more profound incomprehension. How could it be that a prime minister with a majority of more than 100 in the House of Commons, who had not been defeated on any major policy question in Parliament, packed up her tent and left? Vague talk about "authority" seems an inadequate explanation, but it is the truth.

No vote in Parliament, no vote in Cabinet, just the understanding that she could no longer exercise power.

In 2002, Blair was far from that position. The Conservatives had never been ahead in the polls since he was elected in 1997—an unprecedented and bizarre state of politics—and although he had been in power for six years, with the seven-year-itch not far away, he had no reason to be particularly nervous. But any prime minister understands that the approach of war sharpens the atmosphere and disturbs the flow of politics. Even before the irrevocable decisions were made, Blair understood that his party might turn against him.

Naturally, he tended to talk to Bush about this in jocular terms. In a partnership where one is much stronger than the other, commanding the superpower with its armies and its irresistible influence, the junior is not likely to draw too much attention to his potential weakness. Blair enjoyed the fact that at the start of their relationship, he knew many more world leaders than Bush. He was gently patronizing in his advice about how to deal with Vladimir Putin and spoke about some Arab leaders as if he were taking Bush through a speed-learning course in geopolitics. It was much later before he discussed frankly the depth of his political problems. And, according to some of those around Bush, the White House had little idea of the pressures that would begin to bear down on him as war came closer.

Sir Christopher Meyer, in the embassy, had spoken to Condi Rice of the dangers that lay ahead, and Jack Straw was in a position to be frank with Colin Powell about what an unruly beast the Labour Party might still turn out to be, but Bush himself appeared to believe simply that Blair was the kind of ally he dreamed of. Blair's political weight would allow the United States to use the word *coalition* when it came to Iraq, even if the United Nations were not involved. With due respect to Mauritius, or Poland, or even Spain, there could be no respectable coalition without a major power, and Britain's place as one of the permanent five members of the Security Council was evidence of that standing. Even without its historic engagement in the Middle East, its role as one of the three principal countries of the European Union and its global influence, which far outstretched its economic or military power, would be guarantee enough that this was no unilateralist adventure by the United States.

Bush was not only aware of State Department pressure to internationalize his Middle East policy but was receiving lectures from elsewhere. From Jim Baker and Brent Scowcroft, in particular, who were the most notable remnants of his father's administration, he was given unmistakable advice that if a war were to be launched against Saddam, it had to be an international effort. Anything else would expose the United States to new perils, which it would be well to avoid.

So Blair mattered. But he did not matter enough for Bush to avoid some of the language that would cause Blair huge embarrassment and political difficulty as they progressed along the path to war. Bush had some understanding of the unpopularity that was beginning to trouble his friend, but it was in another country, and besides, he had his own problems to concern him in Washington. Blair was solid; that was what counted.

He had little understanding of how quickly Blair might be isolated in Britain and in Europe if the policy went wrong. This would hardly affect Bush's own political position, which could not really be affected one way or another by the standing of any British prime minister, but his lack of feel for Blair's position was a symptom of a wider failure to grasp America's potential weakness around the world, which would eventually begin to haunt him. Had he understood earlier how idiosyncratic and politically dangerous Blair's policy was, he might have avoided some of the statements and decisions that greatly complicated his foreign policy as his first term approached its end in the welter of a threatening campaign brought against him by John Kerry.

On Blair's side the misunderstanding was deeper, with consequences for him that proved more damaging than any other in his time as Prime Minister. From the beginning, he failed to comprehend the vigour of the neoconservative argument that was closing in on the Oval Office.

It had grave political implications for him. By the time troops had been in Iraq for more than a year and the prisoner abuse scandal broke, Blair was identified by his voters as being in league with the Washington hawks. In fact, he'd been trying to outmanoeuvre them for eighteen months, but his identification with the administration was so strong and was such an emblem of his foreign policy that he could not escape. Had he understood earlier those with whom he was dealing in Washington, some friends believe he might have taken the first steps to distance himself before it was too late. This may be special pleading. Blair's own conviction drove him into Bush's arms, and he appeared to consider the embrace a welcome and reassuring one. It may be that he would never have considered behaving differently, but in asking why Blair appeared so uncritical in the early days, it is important to realize how patchy his comprehension of the administration was at the start.

He knew, of course, that Powell represented an approach to the world with which he felt at home. The State Department sailed on, tacking a little to the right compared with the Clinton days, but still recognizably the same ship of state that successive British governments had learned to understand. It was not going to veer away. From the moment Straw was made foreign secretary in the summer of 2001, he began to work on a relationship with Powell that became as close as the one that bound Robin Cook to Madeleine Albright in the Clinton era. That alliance had produced rather less than it seemed to promise, but it was warm and intimate. So was Straw's with Powell, particularly when the Blair government began to panic at the likelihood of a war without UN sanction. Beyond that, Blair knew principally of Rice.

There was a reason. Despite his success with Clinton and his absorption in Washington's ways during his presidency, Blair was not a student of America. As a young man, he had spent his spare time in Europe. Not for him the trek on Route 66 on a Greyhound bus, once the favored summer expedition of British students. He worked in a bar in Paris instead. His experience outside Washington is very limited. And his circle of friends is restricted. Two of them have been presidents.

In reading the politics of the Bush administration, Blair was therefore handicapped. The roots of neoconservatism were unknown to him. He would look blank at any mention of Senator Henry "Scoop" Jackson, around whom so many neocons then had clustered and developed their ideas. And the ideology of American conservatism, so different from its British counterpart, was something that he understood only vaguely. Even at the level of practical politics, Blair's touch in American politics is not sure. As late as October 2003, he was surprised when someone pointed out to him that the first primary of election year, in New Hampshire, would be coming up in January. "As soon as that", he said. He is not naturally attuned to the ups and downs of the electoral cycle, nor to the ideas that make up the weft and weave of the Washington debate.

As a result, he underestimated the depth of the ideology with which he began to fall in step. After 9/11, when he started to speak of inchoate fears and forces that came together on that morning, he was unconsciously echoing the neoconservative mantra. His attraction to the idea of enlightened intervention, his sense that old theories of "spheres of influence" in the world were passing away, his alarm at the likely alliance of rogue states and shadowy terrorist networks all paralleled the train of thought being encouraged by the neocons. Blair's worldview was quite different from theirs in other respects—he was instinctively committed to the United Nations, he wanted to increase the power of the European Union as a bloc, he had grave doubts about any American Middle East policy tied too closely to the urgings of an Israeli government (particularly if it was dominated by Likud), and he used the language of collectivism when speaking of endemic world problems like poverty and AIDS in Africa.

The neocons were exotic, but they did not trouble Blair because he knew little of them. Nowhere in Whitehall was there an attitude towards Iraq like the one adopted by the Cheney-Rumsfeld-Wolfowitz group in the administration. For example, Richard Clarke revealed that Wolfowitz's scepticism about the importance of bin Laden stemmed from his stubborn belief that the 1993 attack on the World Trade Center had a "state sponsor"—almost certainly Iraq—though that theory had long since been discounted by most analysts who had examined it. "Just because the FBI and the CIA have failed to find the linkages doesn't mean they don't exist," he told Clarke. In other words, the belief in the reach of Saddam's tentacles did not require evidence: enough was known of his rhetoric and his intentions to make it certain that he was involved.

The Pentagon even dispatched a former director of the CIA, James Woolsey, on a mysterious mission to Britain in late 2001 in search of evidence to prove Iraq's complicity in the 1993 attack. He found none, but he did cause plenty of embarrassment. The U.S. embassy in London had difficulty explaining the nature of his visit to the Foreign Office. They laid it at the Pentagon's door. By then, enough was known about the character of the administration for it to be suspected that this was a rogue mission. It certainly was. The chief constable in Swansea, eventually phoned the embassy in Grosvenor Square to say that he had been contacted by a local college about a visitor who was seeking information on students and said he was a former head of the CIA. The embassy, squirming as it did so, confirmed that indeed he was. Woolsey's hopes of finding a clue in university records that would link students to al-Qaeda and Iraq exploded. The main significance in London was to remind the government that there was some unorthodox thinking inside the Bush administration.

Wolfowitz's view represented a strain of thinking familiar in Washington but foreign to Blair. No one in his government adopted the approach to foreign policy that was being pressed on Bush and a reluctant State Department from that quarter. Told that John Bolton, the one senior official at State who subscribed to the neoconservative agenda, had proposed in the 1990s the virtual abolition of the UN, Blair was astonished. Yet never did he find it odd that his own convictions were bringing him into the ambit of neoconservative thought.

The mystification was two-way, of course. Blair was a Labour Prime Minister leading a government that spoke in language many neoconservatives found deeply unappealing. Blair's party conference speech in 1999, for example, was devoted almost entirely to the argument that Labour's duty was to reverse the consequences of a century that had been dominated by conservative thinking and to usher in "a progressive century" on liberal principles. Although the neoconservatives' argument supporting a new American nationalism in foreign policy and an aggressive interventionism was accompanied by social attitudes that had a liberal tinge, Blair himself seemed to have very little in common with them. He led a party that represented everything neoconservative thinking excoriated and that had always had a thread of anti-Americanism running through it. All their Conservative friends in Britain told tales of a government that was shifty, politically correct in its attitudes, obsessed with the presentation of its policies rather than with their substance, and in its European policy determined to strengthen the ties that meant more and more of British domestic policy was being filtered through the EU bureaucracy in Brussels. In short, it was old-fashioned internationalism epitomized.

Yet in the course of 2002, Bush and Blair cemented their alliance. Blair's refusal to recoil at the "axis of evil" was a signal. Their Crawford meeting in April established the basis on which Blair might be prepared to go to war in Iraq. By Camp David in September, he was convinced.

In these few months, Blair made his commitment. He was convinced that the challenge he had warned Bush about before 9/11 was now presenting itself. His personal relationship with Bush was strong, and it belied their differences in background and belief. They might argue about climate change, the subject on which Blair believes Bush is most wrongheaded, or about a trade dispute like the fight with the EU that caused Bush to slap high tariffs on steel, but they agreed so strongly about the consequences of 9/11 that everything else seemed secondary.

Blair had become a kind of accidental American. He was drawn into the thinking that was taking Bush to war, and he decided that his support for Washington was the only guarantee that the transatlantic relationship sustaining NATO would survive. He made himself the anvil on which he thought it could be re-moulded for an age of terrorism and uncertainty.

His decision was as much of a break as it was an attempt to preserve an historic friendship. In committing himself irrevocably to Bush, he was challenging the majority view of his government and his party, and posing a question for the new Europe to which he had also made promises. Was it possible to be a good European and an American, too?

By forging his own axis of friendship with Bush, Blair claimed that it was. Robert Kagan, in his *Paradise and Power*, a text treasured by neoconservatives, argued that Europe and the United States are drifting apart, with the Europeans imagining themselves in "a post-historical paradise of peace and relative prosperity," while the United States continues to try to exercise power in an archaic world of threats and challenges. "Americans are from Mars and Europeans are from Venus," said Kagan. In that universe, Blair is the traveller who tries to make the journey that others think impossible.

Although he believed he was making an historic commitment that transcended the here and now, Blair had to accept that it would be during war in Iraq that it would be decided whether it was wise or foolish.

# CHAPTER 5

# THE COWBOY

What might George W. Bush like to see during his state visit to Britain? In the months of planning for such occasions, which throw diplomats and royal courtiers together in an orgy of protocol and politics, such questions present opportunities and risks. When the Queen's vast archives were scoured for special treats when he visited in November 2003, they devised a neat solution. Out of the vaults came some souvenirs from the Victorian era. They found the memorabilia from an outing Queen Victoria had particularly enjoyed in her Golden Jubilee year of 1887—to Buffalo Bill's Wild West Show.

Victoria saw Annie Oakley, Buffalo Bill himself, fearsome "Indians" threatening to scalp anyone they met (and being beaten back, always), and bucking broncos, elk, and buffalo, all cavorting in the performance that entranced Europe for a decade. What better to remind the President of home?

If there was a mischievous edge to the suggestion that this was the culture with which he might feel most kinship, it was not meant to be very sharp. But it seemed entirely appropriate that in the course of a visit heavy with the traditional trappings of formal greetings, toasts, and exchanges of gifts, his hosts should acknowledge that this president had a strangely exotic air.

To the thousands of demonstrators who were roaming London trying to find a way through almost as many police and troops deployed to keep him secure, any exoticism was of the most unwelcome and unattractive kind. Effigies of him were everywhere, shops were emptied of rubber Bush masks and little books of Bushisms, and the speech to Parliament that might have been expected on such a visit was not arranged because of the number of Labour MPs who might stage a theatrical walkout. For weeks beforehand, his arrival was only spoken of in the context of security—how Scotland Yard and the Secret Service were having a hard time getting along together, how a request for air traffic routes over London to be diverted for the course of the visit was turned down, how the President would move around the capital and then north to Tony Blair's constituency in a bubble that would seal him from the world.

But no president since Woodrow Wilson had been invited to sleep in Buckingham Palace, the curious detail that, in the arcane world of formal dealings between leaders, makes the difference between a state visit and a piece of presidential or political tourism. The problems were not going to be allowed to prevent a special gesture being made. These details are decided by governments and not monarchs—the Queen issues the invitation, but on the prime minister's say-so and without any real independence of action—and none of Blair's recent predecessors had gone so far as to grant the full accolade. When the visit was agreed on in principle the previous year, Blair did so in the knowledge that Bush would be treading on difficult ground, in a country where he was regarded with more suspicion than warmth. Although Buffalo Bill's appearance was meant as a piece of friendly amusement before dinner, much as a president might show a prime minister in Washington some piece of charred carpet from the burning of the White House by the British in 1812, it did catch something of the outlandishness of Bush in the eyes of his hosts.

As with so many little gestures between public figures, it said as much about those who arranged it as it did about the recipient.

Among those who decided to dig out the story of Victoria's trip to the Earls Court arena, there was probably little knowledge of the way this show had made the West seem less wild, even as it was pretending to terrify its audiences with acts of bravery as man, beast, and Red Indian engaged in their primitive struggle. One of Buffalo Bill Cody's odd legacies was the turning of "cow boy" from something of a class-ridden insult in two words, describing someone who was as rough as could be and unlikely ever to be able to greet a lady or handle a knife and fork, into one word that was attached with some affection to one of the foot soldiers of the frontier. He sanitized them. The romance in the word was rather different in Europe, though Tony Blair grew up on the imported diet of American Westerns that filled the screens in the 1950s and early 1960s. Few Britons understood how the power of the drive westward still refreshed American culture, and it was hard for them to understand that for many people west of the Mississippi, it was not only a term of endearment but maybe a kind of compliment, too.

But perhaps it was a nicely turned joke by some cheeky Foreign Office functionary who did know this but also understood that in contemporary vocabulary, "cowboy" retains some of its earlier meaning. Householders remind themselves after a bad experience with a plumber or a roofer that cowboys are the people you can't trust.

The style of the visit, of course, was meant to convey the opposite message. The state banquet at the palace spoke of warmth and respect, with every detail perfectly arranged. The formal exchange of toasts between Queen and President even had a touch of familiarity about them. Bush was particularly valued by her for one gesture that she considered thoughtful. He'd placed as his ambassador in London William Farish III, a family friend and financial adviser who was a stranger to politics and diplomacy but a familiar character in the world of racing, where the Queen was at home. She'd visited his Kentucky stud farm in the past, and when they met they were certainly both happier talking about the prospects for the Breeders' Cup or the Derby than about troop deployments in Iraq. He was probably the only American ambassador anywhere in the world, with the possible exception of a couple of the Gulf states, who was able to talk to his host head of state about a particular bloodstock problem or the nightmare of a cracked fetlock and not be cut off with a glassy stare. At the palace, such dinner-table conversation is prized.

Bush therefore felt comfortable with this welcome. He was kept away from demonstrators and the awkward squad in politics, and persuaded that he was indeed a valued friend, whatever the newspapers were saying. It was all slightly fake, of course. Bush and Blair had discussed how awkward the visit was going to be. Blair's Cabinet ministers had worried for weeks about a disastrous piece of PR; the polls were telling them that Bush's unpopularity was rising with every month that went by. The President decided to joke about it; he'd been told it was the best thing to do. In his speech at the Banqueting House in Whitehall, he said it was good to visit a country where freedom of speech was exercised, something he said he knew was being demonstrated in the streets around him. The room in which he spoke, under a ceiling painted by Rubens, was a suitable venue for one who was stirring up wrath in the streets. Outside one of the windows behind the platform on which Bush stood was the site where Charles I had been led to the scaffold to have his head chopped off in 1649. On this occasion, the defender of the status quo was secure. But the relationship he celebrated in a speech carefully crafted to try to reassure his audience that he was an internationalist in outlook was not as healthy as the state visit had been designed to suggest.

"The truth is that for the first time for as long as anyone can remember we have a president who doesn't really like Europe," said a State Department official who has watched Bush from close quarters and was involved in planning the visit. It is a surprising but telling description.

You might expect the younger Bush to have instincts well attuned to European ways. His father's political career was honed in a way that fitted the East Coast establishment milieu in which he was raised, obligatory trips to Paris and London being regarded as part of growing up. Even when George H.W. Bush was a Houston congressman, no one thought of him as anything other than a son of Senator Prescott Bush and of Yale, on whom a cowboy hat would always be a slightly absurd adornment. As CIA director he adored the clubbish network of dewy-eyed spies and analysts who carried tales from the corners of the earth, and he saw NATO and its ministers and soldiers as the defenders of the world he had fought for in World War II.

In Europe, the elder Bush was known to be an obsessive internationalist. During Desert Storm he personally conducted much of the diplomacy that brought a coalition into being for the fight with Saddam, got the imprimatur of the United Nations for the enterprise, and kept it going when some of its Arab members agonized about the consequences of the arrival of tens of thousands of American troops on their doorsteps. An American diplomat in the Paris embassy at the time recalled that the President himself would be on the phone at odd hours of the day and night asking them to get the Élysée Palace on the line. His son's calls in that direction twelve years later would be few and far between. It would not have occurred to Bush Sr. to defy the UN mandate for the war by pressing on to Baghdad for a show-down with Saddam. He was a president who liked a world with rules.

That was one of the reasons Margaret Thatcher had been exasperated with him in autumn 1990 and was quite happy when it was reported in the British press that she had gone to see him in Aspen, Colorado, to tell him to "stop wobbling" after Saddam's invasion of Kuwait. She was reported, accurately, to want him to stiffen his sinews and flew off to see him, waving the metaphorical handbag that was her political coat-of-arms, well aware that he had never shared her admiration for the pleasing simplicities of pure Reaganism. Although she didn't know it then, one of her last international acts would be to remind a president of the United States that he must not go "soft" in the Middle East when the negotiators and diplomats asked for more time and warned of the dangerous legacies of war. How she would have preferred it if she had been dealing with the 43rd president, with whom Tony Blair found that his role was reversed. Instead of stiffening the sinews, he found himself trying to persuade the President to take a long, slow breath.

That difference is matched in the way George W. Bush has played his cards in Europe, where he is not his father's son. In addition to having an attitude that is markedly different, he has consciously built a political image in which he appears as the reverse—the photographic negative—of the picture familiar to Europeans from the early 1990s. Whether seeming more at home clearing brush on his ranch than on the golf course, or being told, "You did good, Bushie," by the First Lady at Buckingham Palace after his toast at the banquet, or telling the world that he wanted to smoke Osama bin Laden out of his hole, this president has appeared to be something quite different, both in style and in the way he looks at the world outside America's borders.

After Vladimir Putin became president of Russia, Bush said to Blair, "Once KGB, always KGB," and Blair still claims some credit for having persuaded him that Putin, though he did indeed bear the authoritarian stamp of his old service, was a politician who wanted to do business with the world.

And as for Europe—"old Europe" as Donald Rumsfeld called it in a famous aside that caused the administration more difficulty in Britain, France, and Germany—Bush saw it as a continent turning in on itself and harbouring anti-American instincts that probably had their origin in Paris but were disturbingly evident in almost any capital he could name, as if they spread like a poisonous gas. It was no accident that the administration reserved its warmest words for the countries of Eastern Europe that had survived life in the Soviet bloc and were now electing presidents and parliaments and opening their markets. To Washington, the European Union seemed at its worst when it ran on a Paris-Berlin axis and at its best when it was opening its eastern borders to let in the new democracies, as on May 1, 2004, when its membership increased to twenty-five with the entry of such countries as the Czech Republic and Hungary, which were once pillars of the Warsaw Pact, and Estonia, Latvia, and Lithuania, which had been largely quiescent outposts of the Soviet Union for most of Bush's life.

The President whose inheritance was a kind of privileged internationalism seemed to be in reaction against it. More than Nixon, Carter, Reagan, or Clinton—all with backgrounds from which they had to make a hazardous personal journey to the rest of the world—he came to office with a suspicion of the influences that would try to change the America he and his party wanted to champion. Far from celebrating his background and the dynastic ambitions of his family, he seemed to be rowing in the opposite direction.

He was right, of course, in identifying the hostility abroad. From outside, the drift of thinking in the Republican Party during the Clinton years seemed alarming to many European political leaders, including Blair. Even in European Conservative parties, whose natural ally the Republicans were, the rise of the American conservatism of the 1990s was regarded with a degree of puzzlement and, sometimes, shock.

Whereas Blair and his liberal-left colleagues were anxious to learn the lessons of the Clinton campaigns and adopted his pollsters and advisers (like Stan Greenburg, Dick Morris, George Stephanopolous, and Sidney Blumenthal), the Conservatives had a much more up-and-down relationship with the Republicans. Many friendships had been formed in government in the Reagan-Bush years—Dick Cheney, for example, kept in close touch with ministers he had worked with in the Margaret Thatcher–John Major era—but American conservatism was taking some turns that the centre-right in Europe saw as having little relevance to their own campaigns. Newt Gingrich's Contract with America in 1994 was regarded in European terms as eccentric—"potty" was a favorite word among moderate Tories—and the startling rise of the religious Right and, in particular, its identification with Israel had little resonance across the Atlantic. For a Conservative, this was not much help in trying to work out how to fight back against a resurgent Labour Party. They could make common cause in a complaint about high taxes, but even in that shared area of concern, the Conservatives were committed to a much higher level of taxation for public spending purposes than fiscal conservatives in the United States would regard as acceptable.

The ideological divide on the Right, which made it difficult for Conservatives to import much American rhetoric, was symptomatic of a deeper political change. Blair took power less than a decade after the crumbling of the Berlin Wall and the collapse of communism. He was faced with redefining the Western alliance at a time when the emergence of the United States as a single superpower meant it was seen in a harsher light.

It should not have been a surprise. In Britain, anti-Americanism and its young cousin, American agnosticism, have a long history. In every modern era, fascination with the bold and the radical from the New World has been matched by suspicion and dislike. A popular culture that colonizes much of the world so effortlessly cannot expect to escape without dissent, and even in Britain, with a shared language and ties of family that have kept the countries close, the tide of resentment has risen regularly and has turned from time to time into hostility.

For the political generation now in power in Britain, that suspicion was planted in the Vietnam era. When Europe was convulsed in 1968 by the student uprisings that began in Paris, the United States stood like a kind of angry Big Brother behind the various establishments that were being attacked. The paving stones thrown at riot police outside the Sorbonne were aimed just as deliberately at Lyndon Johnson and the Vietnam warriors. It was the first great intercontinental issue for the postwar generation, for which the foundation of the Campaign for Nuclear Disarmament and the British protests at the arrival of the Polaris submarines in the early 1960s were a preliminary. The tweed-jacketed, pipe-smoking protesters of that time—dominated by left-wing intellectuals, radical churchmen, and a small ragbag of dogged Soviet sympathizers—were supplanted by a much broader radical movement that found the Johnson administration easy to dislike.

They might march in support of the Czechoslovakian dissidents who watched Soviet tanks arrive in Prague in 1968, but they did not translate that dislike of Russian imperialism into an identification with all that was American. They wore Levis and listened to American music, but they excoriated its president as the symbol of an old world that they wanted to pass away. In the early 1980s, Reagan provoked another outburst of feeling with the decision to deploy Tomahawk and Pershing missiles in Europe. With Margaret Thatcher's unwavering support, the missiles arrived at Greenham Common and produced mass demonstrations across Britain. It was all forgotten by the end of the decade, when the Warsaw Pact had folded up like a child's paper fighter plane, and Mikhail Gorbachev was touring the world as the amiable symbol of a vanished creed. But when Blair became a member of Parliament in 1983, there was still a remnant of pro-Soviet thinking in the party, though it was tiny and often comic in its crudity, and there was a good deal of anti-Americanism.

David Blunkett, who as home secretary in Blair's second term became his most pugnacious and hawkish minister, exemplifies the way things were. Blunkett became a hard-line dispenser of law-and-order, loathed by the Left for his attitude to civil liberties, but had once been a leading left-winger himself. When he was leader of Sheffield Council in 1983 he gave a BBC interview in which he discussed the tradition of raising the American flag above the town hall. "Independence Day. It would be nice if we were independent of the United States, wouldn't it?" he said. Even some of Blair's closest colleagues once held very different views.

The party leader in 1983 was Michael Foot, who came from a political tradition that was deeply antagonistic to American policy as it had developed throughout the Cold War, not because the Soviet Union was "better" but because the United States was thought to represent a new imperialism unhealthy by nature.

Foot himself had not visited the United States since the early 1950s, a fact used by his opponents (some of them in his own party) to suggest that he was hardly fitted to be a prime minister in the modern era. Although he is a kindly, bookish man just as interested in discussing a Swift essay or a Shelley poem as in talking about defence policy, he gave voice to a worldview based on the premise that the United States was the greatest threat to peace. Although Foot was an electoral liability for Labour, and widely seen as the remnant of an era that was passing away, he touched feelings of resentment about American power that were strong.

This history is important, even though the 1983 election is a distant memory and Michael Foot resigned quickly afterward in humiliation, for it is the undercurrent that still disturbs the glib talk of a "special relationship." More than 8 million people voted for the Labour manifesto in 1983 (just under one-third of those who took part in the election), and though a good number did so through gritted teeth, its writing was an important reflection of a strain in British politics that can easily be stirred up. Many of those who serve in Blair's Cabinet marched with the Campaign for Nuclear Disarmament when the cruise missile crisis caused it to spring back to life after two decades of slumber. Blair himself was a CND member: it was almost obligatory as a Labour candidate to be able to flash the badge at your party meetings. He never imbibed or spouted the anti-American rhetoric that accompanied that campaign, but his party and many of its supporters were moved by it. Reagan, in his day, was caricatured as the same kind of stumbling figure as Bush, and when his TV ads for the 1984 reelection campaign—"Morning Again in America"—were shown in Britain they caused widespread amusement, because they were viewed as examples of the corny hokum to which British election campaigns hadn't yet succumbed.

Bush, therefore, has a history that weighs him down when he crosses the Atlantic. The U.S. publisher of this book, Peter Osnos, recalled a dinner in London when he was finishing his term as the *Washington Post*'s correspondent there in the mid-1980s. Neil Kinnock was the new Labour leader, a supporter of Foot's who had embarked on a programme of policy reform to avoid another debacle like the 1983 election. All the talk was of modernization. Yet in an awkward exchange of views after dinner, Osnos remembered Kinnock talking of a visit to Moscow, from which he'd just returned, in terms that suggested there was a great deal of hope in the Soviet Union and much to be admired. They had been talking, too, about Reagan, and the implication was that a visit to Washington would be less congenial. Now, Kinnock was no knee-jerk anti-American, and in his long apprenticeship on the political left never flirted for a moment with the dwindling band of dinosaurs in the pro-Soviet faction, but Osnos was struck deeply by the passionate suspicion of American policy that clearly moved a man who was going to fight the next British general election as Labour's candidate for prime minister.

No British journalist would find such a conversation odd, because those feelings course routinely just beneath the surface of politics. Just after 9/11, the American ambassador in London, Philip Lader, was reduced to tears during a recording of *Question Time* when confronted with the accusation that American policy had itself brought on the attacks. The implication was that New York and Washington had got what America deserved. That was not the prevailing view, but public unease about the policies of the superpower (especially in the Middle East) was deep enough to produce painful eruptions.

In British journalism, such accomplished polemicists as John Pilger have long made the case for a British policy independent of the United States as a matter of morality. No government has come close to breaking the link, for economic and defence reasons that every prime minister has found compelling, but all have been aware of the danger of an American president seeming to treat the British as residents of that fabled and much-feared patch of territory, the fifty-first state. Prime ministers have all understood that the relationship is more fragile in the public mind than the regular exchanges of affection between White House and Downing Street might imply.

As a lesson in the dangers inherent in the relationship, Blair could look back to the last Prime Minister to lead the Labour Party out of the wilderness, in 1964. Labour had been out of power since 1950, and Harold Wilson was a forty-something leader who had some of Kennedy's vigour, that favourite word of the age, in a way that Blair was thought to have thirty years later. Although it seems strange to think of it now in Britain, where he is remembered overwhelmingly as a political manipulator rather than a great reforming leader, Wilson had to ride the tide of the 1960s when the world was changing around him. He had to play a tricky hand with LBJ, whose policies in Vietnam had turned the Labour Party firmly against him. Wilson had arm's-length dealings with the President, positively glacial compared to the intimacies of Thatcher and Blair, and realized that as the war began to spiral into disaster, he must keep Britain out. Anything else would have consumed the Labour Party in agony and probably ended his premiership.

It stands as the great example of how British prime ministers find themselves in severe difficulty when Americans engage in military action that strains the Western alliance by failing to excite popular support. The rhetoric of a partnership formed on the D-Day beaches in 1944, said to be indissoluble, proves surprisingly thin at times.

Wilson's Vietnam crisis was quite different from Blair's. For Britain, there was no war. The risible suggestion of his informal security adviser and confidant, George Wigg, that it would be a useful symbol of support for the United States if the band of the Grenadier Guards was seen marching through the streets of Saigon, was treated with gentle contempt.

He understood well that on the mainstream Left, Johnson's war was anathema, and his experience is an illustration of the pressures that close in on any British prime minister who finds that on an issue of war and peace, the Americans are on the other side. The nuclear relationship, sealed when Harold Macmillan agreed in 1962 to accept Kennedy's missiles, was one that Wilson wanted to keep. That commitment, with the guaranteed pooling of intelligence that went along with it, was above all what made the relationship "special." There was no escaping it.

Caught in those coils, Wilson's Vietnam experience was miserable. He tried to keep a relationship with LBJ by offering some words of support and advice. It wasn't enough. He recorded in his memoirs that Johnson was interested in military support and not much else, telling him in 1966: "I won't tell you how to run Malaysia and you don't tell us how to run Vietnam. If you want to help us some in Vietnam, send us some men and send us some folks to deal with those guerrillas." It was impossible for Wilson to oblige, yet he was trying to protect the currency in an atmosphere of darkening economic gloom and could hardly offend the financial superpower to the point where Britain wasn't seen as deserving ally that couldn't be allowed to become too weak.

Wilson's shoulder-grabbing, persuasive style was a faint Yorkshire echo of Johnson's own serpentine skills, honed in his Capitol Hill years. A man of formidable intellectual sharpness, Wilson was a street politician, too, and he enjoyed the dramatic gesture in politics. He decided to capitalize on his knowledge of the Russians to try to act as peacemaker, but far from revealing the Prime Minister as a valuable broker with Washington and Moscow, the effort left him humiliated and angry, looking like a leader who should have known better than to try.

His chosen strategy hinged on the visit to Britain of the Russian prime minister, Alexei Kosygin, in February 1967. Wilson wanted to use the chance timing, which fell during the traditional Tet truce at the Vietnamese New Year, to harness Soviet influence in North Vietnam and his own relationship with LBJ to turn the truce into an extended cease-fire and, eventually, peace. He duly presented a plan to Kosygin that involved an American bombing pause and a subsequent scale-down of military activity on both sides.

Johnson, however, was pursuing his own plan. Without telling Wilson, he sent a message to the North Vietnamese leader, Ho Chi Minh, which proposed an end to American bombing *after* the North Vietnamese stopped incursions over the border into South Vietnam. Johnson wanted a reply in twelve hours. An embarrassed Wilson now had to get a message to Kosygin, who was even then heading for King's Cross Station and the night train to Scotland. In those far-off days, he would be incommunicado as he rattled north and the deadline would almost have passed by the time he pulled into Glasgow. Thus, one of Wilson's private secretaries arrived at the station moments before the departure of the train to press into Kosygin's hand the new plan from Washington that changed everything.

There was no deal, no Wilson coup, no end to the war. While Wilson was pacing around Chequers waiting for the hot-line phone to ring, and assuring Kosygin that he was the one go-between who could extract the superpowers from the Vietnam quagmire, Johnson was suspicious that the British were softening his terms for an end to the bombing and did nothing. Walt Rostow, Johnson's principal foreign affairs adviser, gave a succinct answer to the complaint of the former CIA director who had acted as special envoy to the Prime Minister: "Well, we don't give a goddam about you, and we don't give a goddam about Wilson."

The story is more than an insight into Wilson's personal difficulty with a president who was now sinking into the great mistake that would drive him from office. It reveals how the weight of the American relationship takes a heavy toll on any British prime minister.

After his failure, which by all accounts drove him to a fury in his humiliation, Wilson found himself not so much having lost an opportunity as having been revealed as weak. He even had to admit that at the height of the affair, when the discrepancy between his offer to Kosygin and the President's demands to Ho Chi Minh was revealed, he did not speak directly to Johnson. Did not, or could not? As an exercise in superpower politics, it was a lesson in impotence, too.

That failure had a profound effect on Wilson's premiership. Although popular concern about Vietnam in Britain was confined largely to the political class on the Left and to students who were breathing the exhilarating fumes of rebellion from Paris, the Prime Minister's inability to distance himself from an increasingly discredited policy in Washington became a token of impotence.

Confidence in Labour plummeted, and Wilson was lampooned on the Left as the leader who had not had the guts to break with Johnson.

Long years later, his refusal to countenance the use of British troops, despite heavy American pressure, would be seen as an act of some bravery; at the time, his verbal gymnastics in trying to give moral support to the United States while keeping some distance from Johnson conjured up a picture of political discomfort that stuck in the public mind. For a leader whose weakness was the impression that wheeler-dealing was more important than principle, it was devastating. Those in his own party who were already muttering about the betrayal of socialist principles by a government wrestling with intractable social and economic problems were now given the chance to accuse him of looking like one of the beagles LBJ notoriously once picked up by their ears for photographers on his ranch. And in the world beyond the Labour Party, he looked like a man with a world leader's pretensions but not much more.

Despite avoiding military involvement, Wilson reaped a terrible whirlwind in Vietnam. As the crisis turned America into a pariah for many of the next generation of political activists, he was given a cruel lesson in the consequences of the relationship that was now built into any British premiership. When policy was mutually beneficial, nothing could be more satisfying than the intimacy it guaranteed; when priorities diverged suddenly, especially under military orders, nothing could be more painful.

Even three and a half decades later, Blair's friendship with Bush was marked by this history. He had been a schoolboy during Vietnam who had shown no interest in politics until it was all over, with the 1960s' language of protest already seeming a little dated. But the pressures that had damaged Wilson so badly in a Cold War crisis were remarkably similar in an era that had left the superpower rivalry behind and, on the surface, appeared to present the Prime Minister with entirely different problems. Blair discovered, somewhat to his surprise, that the innate suspicion about the irresistible power of the United States was easily turned into an awkward political force. The disappearance of the Soviet Union from the landscape had made the problem worse. There was no longer an easy choice at moments of crisis, but rather a permanent suspicion of the behaviour of the one remaining superpower, to which Britain was assumed to be tied by culture and treaty. Even while the neoconservatives in the United States began to turn the freedom of the post–Cold War age into the confident and aggressive principles of "The Project for the New American Century," embracing theories of pre-emptive strike and a new nationalism, Blair was beginning to understand that in a world where the traditional threats of global conflict had been removed, America's motives were likely to be subjected to far more sceptical scrutiny than in the period before the Cold War was "won."

That realization was sharpened by the fact that closer social and perhaps cultural ties did not make the politics of the relationship any easier. Anyone who thought that in the rubble of the Berlin Wall there would be the foundations of a Western alliance free of trouble, jealousy and rivalry would be disappointed. New tensions were inevitable of course, but Blair was the Prime Minister fated to have to deal with them when they became most painful. Unlike Wilson long before him, he developed a close friendship with two presidents, and unlike Wilson, he was able at first to get public support for involvement in a war led by the United States; but like his Labour predecessor he discovered how fickle and awkward the politics of the relationship always seemed to be.

The contemporary pressures that bore down on him were very different from those of the 1960s, but they were just as awkward to repel. Although transatlantic traffic had increased to the point where there was almost a London-New York shuttle and young-sters from Britain could expect to have visited the States at least once by the time they were in their mid-twenties, and though the cultural flow to and fro across the ocean seemed richer than ever, Blair's Britain evinced a certain discomfort with modern America. It was more than just the kind of hatred of the Starbucks culture put into words by Michael Moore (who could fill the London

Palladium ten times over every night for one of his one-man anti-Bush shows), and it demonstrated that increased closeness in the age of globalization might be an illusion.

Why should it be assumed that a common language and the shared world outlook of the Cold War will sustain perpetual closeness in the twenty-first century? In politics, for example, Blair has discovered how strange—even alien—American practices have come to appear to a country that has always been thought to be closer to its historic partners than any other in Europe.

Take religion, which has given Blair much more trouble than he thought likely when he came to power. His lack of embarrassment at being a practising Christian is striking in itself, because his party is generally suspicious of those who wear their spiritual convictions on their sleeves. Labour history has a proud religious element, particularly in nonconformism in England and Wales. It was famously said of Labour that it owed more to Methodism than Marx, developing a socialism that was not dogmatically ideological but more a reflection of the nonconformist spirit in which community responsibilities were connected with God-given obligations to others. But despite this legacy, religion in British politics has long been a tricky affair, best avoided by those with ambition. No prime minister in the second half of the twentieth century before Blair spoke comfortably about belief, and political manners seemed to dictate that such things were for digestion in private, at home, and certainly not on a public platform.

Blair agrees broadly with that view, but because of his willingness to discuss his religious views and his certainty in them, he's often been portrayed as a peculiarly pious character. He is not. Very seldom has he looked more uncomfortable on television than when he was asked on the BBC in 2003 if he and Bush prayed together. No, he said, looking surprised at the question and very embarrassed. One Methodist minister did tell a senior Labour colleague of Blair's that he had been told by a pastor in Washington that Bush confirmed that they had prayed together. However, Blair draws a distinction between moments when the President asks for a moment's reflection, and full-scale praying. He wouldn't suggest it, and would find it odd. To Americans who have become used to public displays of religious devotion in politics, and in some quarters a naked competitiveness in getting nearer to God, this seems strange. British politicians find it even stranger to hear the routine invocations of the Almighty on public platforms in the United States. Standing with some British friends at a Bush rally in St. Louis in the 2000 campaign and hearing the then senator John Ashcroft lead 10,000 or so supporters in prayer for the votes to see him through (it failed, of course) was to understand how religion has carved a cultural gulf between the systems. There is no Bible Belt in Britain. Although evangelicals have a voice, it is not loud. No politician in high office need worry about having a particular religious view, or none at all. When Michael Howard became the first Jewish leader of the Conservative Party since Disraeli in 2003, his religion was hardly mentioned. Indeed, the only circumstance in which religion would be likely to become an important national issue would be if a leading figure appeared *too* devout.

Blair has tried to avoid falling into this trap. It got him into some trouble with the Catholic hierarchy. His wife, Cherie Booth, is Catholic and their children have been raised in the faith. Blair himself remains a member of the Church of England but attends Catholic services on Sundays. On abortion, he has made it clear that although he and his wife would not contemplate one, he believes it is a matter of choice for individuals and wouldn't presume to tell others what to do. The late Cardinal Thomas Winning of Glasgow, leader of the Catholic Church in Scotland, engaged in a long public argument with the Prime Minister about this view, which he thought disgraceful. The cardinal was an important figure to the Labour Party, because the bulk of his flock in the industrial west of Scotland were natural Labour voters, but Blair did not budge on the issue. They ended up almost not speaking to each other.

Yet in British politics, Blair is still seen as a peculiarly religious man. Most of his Cabinet would declare themselves Christian, more or less, but only a tiny minority would be seen in a church except for weddings and funerals. They are uncomfortable when Blair reaches for a piece of biblical language, which he does with ease, because it grates with the political style they know. The fundamentalist strain in Republican politics in the United States has therefore caused Blair great difficulty. In the run-up to war in Iraq, it was routinely said by opponents that Britain was being hijacked for a crusade—Bush's use of the word soon after 9/11 sent a shudder through Downing Street—which was being organized by born-again fundamentalists as an assault on Islam.

It was painful for Blair to be placed in this company, because he is rather proud of his interest in other religions, particularly Islam. He knows the Koran well and can quote from it. Chelsea Clinton, of all people, once told him that she carried a copy on her travels and he started to do the same. He cites this as evidence that he has an inquiring mind about religion, not a closed one. His views are certainly liberal.

When the Church of England was choosing a new Archbishop of Canterbury in 2003 it fell to him, because of the historic establishment of that church in the state, to forward a name to the Queen for approval (another monarchical formality in which her own view can play no part). The church's appointments body would put forward two names to Downing Street with the preferred one at the top. Blair was privately delighted to learn that it was that of Rowan Williams, archbishop of Wales, and was enthusiastic about his appointment. He had been his candidate all along. Williams is a liberal theologian excoriated by conservative elements in the church for alleged transgressions on questions of fundamental belief. He is unconventional, having said, for example, that he'd like to be a guest on The Simpsons (like Blair). He regards Bible-believing evangelicals as simply wrong, and Blair shares that view of those who are fond of literal adherence to scripture.

The language and style of the Bush administration is therefore alien to British political culture. If Blair is regarded suspiciously by many voters as a little too churchy at times and prone to dreamy piety in speeches, it is not surprising that a political system where

God is invoked regularly, and especially at times of war, appears unattractive to them.

Bush therefore struggles to span the divide. The natural comfort he feels with Blair, not least because of his professed faith, is not extended to other members of the Blair government. And the feeling is mutual: to all but one or two in the Labour government, the thought of an invitation to a prayer breakfast, of the sort that happens in rooms across Capitol Hill each morning, would be truly shocking: to them, politics is about everything *but* religion.

The American religious Right has no European equivalent. Nor is there a European cultural understanding of the warmth George W. Bush's language evokes from many Americans.

When Bush announced that he remembered the old posters in the West that said "Wanted—Dead or Alive" and applied it to Osama bin Laden, he wasn't making a surprising political point. It would have been surprising after 9/11 if any leader in his position had expressed different sentiments. But something about that phrase helped to fill out the image of Bush that had been building up for months in Britain. It was the picture of a man who reached for a childhood cliché rather than a subtle thought; the politician whose one-liners weren't evidence of an earthy humanity but of a lack of imagination.

This president played to his caricature with a devotion that made it seem real. From the moment the Florida muddle turned the end of the election in 2000 into the farce of the hanging chads and the missing ballots, the lawyers and the judges, Bush was fated to appear abroad as the lucky president. Whatever the truth that lay locked in the boxes and however ill-judged most of the Gore campaign had been through the autumn, Bush seemed something of an accident. Few people around Blair understood Bush's own skills as a campaigner and the grip he was able to exert on a broad swath of support. They believed that he had lost the popular vote, that Florida was a mess presided over by brother Jeb Bush in the governor's office, that the Supreme Court's involvement was thought by many constitutional scholars to have been wrong, and so on. Like a cartoon character who is beaten and crushed but springs back into shape like a piece of rubber, Bush seemed The President Who Shouldn't Be There But Is.

The consequence of this was more profound than the spread of Bush jokes or glee at some new episode of mis-speaking. Bush seemed to show that American political culture, often admired and appreciated in Europe, had become a little weird and even alien.

Clinton was always regarded as something of an oddity in Britain, though he came to be widely liked. In part this was Blair's doing, his largely happy relationship turning even the strangeness of the Lewinsky affair into a blemish on an otherwise regular guy, rather than a cause of disgust. The impeachment hearings and the agony of Democrats who believed they'd been lied to were matters for Americans: abroad, Clinton was able to surmount it all with a style that intrigued people. Partly because of his natural eloquence, Clinton was, in the end, an intimate.

Bush suffered by contrast. Although his Banqueting House speech during the November 2003 state visit was crafted as an answer to many of the questions asked of him—it was a defence of internationalism, even of collective action among nations—it was reported, and interpreted, as still falling short of a convincing reply to the criticism that swirled around him. In part this was because British troops were finding it hard going in Iraq, in a war still widely seen as America's revenge rather than an exercise in liberation. And it was also clear that in his first two years, Bush had failed to translate his caricature into something more familiar and reassuring.

He would always be the Unlikely President. How strange that a dynastic succession, as his parents saw it, should result in such discomfort. But it was not suggested even by his strongest supporters that he had succeeded in creating the warm glow that by the end of Reagan's first term had evidently pacified many natural Democrats, and Blair faced great difficulty in convincing his own colleagues that this was a president with whom it was sensible to have a closeness that went beyond the normal and inevitable partnership that any leaders of the two countries would have.

The more Blair spoke of the need to stand shoulder to shoulder with Bush and the historic importance of their mission in Iraq, the more he felt a political chill at home. The more he tried to persuade the public that Bush was brighter, more decisive, and more farsighted than the picture they had built up in their minds, the more the populace seemed to worry about the Prime Minister's judgement. At the start of 2004, polls were showing Blair as still enormously popular in the United States, at a moment when he was losing his lead to the Conservatives for the first time in nearly seven years in power. In British polls, Bush sagged and never seemed able to persuade those who were involved in "his" war on the other side of the ocean that he was the leader they might hope for on such a mission. British voters had no sympathy for Saddam, but neither would they support a war unless it was a United Nations enterprise.

As a result of the war, feelings of mistrust turned into a bitterness about the United States that was troubling to the U.S. embassy in London. Satirists who dismembered Bush on television were to be expected, but the depth of the unease in the streets was alarming. In popular culture, Washington-bashing was all the rage.

When John le Carré published his nineteenth novel at the end of 2003, it turned out to be an eloquent but bitterly personal denunciation of America's role in the world. *Absolute Friends*, in which an American operative perpetrates a violent act of betrayal against a friend and against Europe, was savagely reviewed in the United States, being seen by some as a paean of hatred. It had a mixed reception in Britain, too, but it stands as an illustration of the degree to which the political closeness of the two countries in the Bush era had underneath it a deep well of suspicion.

Le Carré has nine American grandchildren and enthuses about the great democratic traditions of the country and its genius in reinventing itself and managing change. But he also reflects an elderly Englishman's horror at a superpower he believes has gone out of control. In his home on the Cornish cliffs in the last month of 2003, looking out to the Atlantic where nothing but sea lies between him and America, he watched the seagulls wheeling up from the cliffs, gazed westward, and wondered if he would ever see the "real" America again.

"What we are seeing at the moment is a piece of theatre staged between fundamentalists on both sides. The fundamentalism of American thinking to my mind is just as great a threat to the world as the fundamentalism of Islamic thinking. The distinction is between tolerant people and intolerant people and that doesn't necessarily divide on national borders.

"A junta took possession of American democracy and instilled a sense of fear. It put the nation on a war footing, and curtailed civil liberties in a shameful way. Abrogation of treaties, the spread of arms—it just goes on and on and on. The distinction between corporate power and political power in this administration is totally blurred, and the sense of messianic purpose means that I think we are looking at a very dangerously poised America.

"I think in becoming a minstrel for the American cause, Blair in many ways encouraged it and legitimized the Americans' action in their own eyes. If he had turned the other way he might have helped to prevent them, but I don't think he ever wanted to prevent them."

It would be quite wrong to take this view as the settled conviction of the British people. It is far from that. But it would also be wrong to dismiss it as some kind of aberrant obsession from a writer who has spent his life dealing with the ambiguity of loyalty and the difficulty in the world of politics and espionage of separating right from wrong, a writer who is therefore obsessed by betrayal. Feelings of betrayal and of dislike directed at the United States in Britain have never been so strong in modern times, even at this moment when the two leaders have never been closer. The paradox is of Blair and Bush's making, and the task of unravelling it is one of Blair's daunting challenges in the years that are left to him.

Across the English Channel in continental Europe it is even worse. At the height of the UN negotiations on Iraq, when anti-French feeling reached a dizzying climax and the *National Review's* "cheese-eating surrender monkeys" had passed into the language, one of Jacques Chirac's old friends, still working in the service of his country, was musing on the reaction in Paris to events in America.

In the foreign ministry on the Quai d'Orsay, he said, they were alarmed that some congressman had removed "French fries" from the House menu on Capitol Hill, renaming them "freedom fries." They heard that in certain restaurants in New York—even New York!—French wine was being taken off the menu and replaced with wines from Oregon and *(quelle horreur!)* Pennsylvania. He smiled. "Things are so bad that I have heard that there is a terrible rumour running round the Quai that the President himself may even stop reading Marcel Proust." Laughter follows.

Nothing could sum up more neatly Bush's European problem. It may be that he has never felt it to be a problem in France or Germany, believing instead that there is an innate snobbery about America and a lack of understanding about its culture and purpose, which he can happily ignore. But with Blair it is different. He is the chosen one. According to someone who has watched them both at close quarters, one of the attractions of Blair for Bush is that he is not "a Euro-ninny." He stands alone. But behind him are many sceptics, many troubled friends of America, and many enemies.

An intriguing decision in the British Foreign Office suggests how shortsighted it would be to think of this as some passing cloud that the wind will take away in time. As a last act in the Washington embassy before retiring from the diplomatic service, Sir Christopher Meyer achieved a change of policy that he had been championing for some time. The Foreign Office has its own traditional training routines for recruits. They may be sent to learn one of the difficult languages—passing perhaps into the Arab sphere of operations, which has often been seen as the route to the top—and will have their careers moulded to give them a feel for different cultures. Before a foreign posting, they'll be immersed in the language and popular culture of the country to which they're bound. But if you're off to Washington, the view has always been that nothing is required. The language? They speak it, more or less. The history? Everyone knows it. Independence and the Constitution? Every educated person knows how to say, "When in the course of human events. . . ."

But what, Meyer asked, does "life, liberty and the pursuit of happiness" actually *mean* today? What does it say to most Americans? So he persuaded the mandarins of the Foreign Office to introduce a new policy. Those who're bound for the embassy in Washington or the consulates in Boston, Chicago, San Francisco, and elsewhere are now going to get some brief training in the fundamentals of the place that is America. There will be some lectures, and who knows, perhaps some history and literature.

The Foreign Office is a bureaucracy that moves ponderously. This change is significant. It reveals the extent to which Britain's closest ally is not necessarily becoming easier to understand but perhaps more difficult. Inescapably, George W. Bush is seen as one of the agents of that difficulty, even as he celebrates with Blair a partnership that has few modern rivals for its closeness.

If young diplomats are to be given the happy task of plunging into American literature before they begin to try to understand its politics maybe they will read *The Great Gatsby*. They'll follow F. Scott Fitzgerald into Gatsby's thrilling but empty world and contemplate the picture of a country driven by the excitement and inspiration of its past trying to reconcile the urgings of the America they know with the vanities that are the consequences of too much success.

They will probably not think of President Bush in Buckingham Palace being presented with the treasured memories of Buffalo Bill and life on the frontier. But they will perhaps reflect on Nick Carraway's words as he finishes his story—"So we beat on, boats against the current, borne back ceaselessly into the past."

# CHAPTER 6

# CRAZY FOR WAR

In the high summer of 2002, Blair appeared to his colleagues to have reconciled himself to war. He began to wear a distant look. He spoke of the possibility of failure at the United Nations and seemed convinced that only force would remove Saddam. There was much talk of coalitions and diplomacy, of resumed inspections in Iraq, and even of the discovery of a nuclear "smoking gun" that would let the crisis reach a natural climax and solution, but by this time Blair, like Bush, had turned his mind to war.

His private thoughts were often concealed in the noise of diplomacy, but they kept breaking through to the surface. In his last press conference before Parliament rose for the summer break in July, he had stressed his commitment to the United Nations as the forum where all must be decided, but when he was asked to give a promise that the House of Commons would be consulted properly before Britain went to war, he preferred simply to recall that he had sought a vote before committing troops to Afghanistan and to enter a heavy caveat. "I am not going to pin myself to any specific form of consultation."

None of his colleagues had any doubt what that meant. His

mind was already focused on decisions that could not be far away, whatever the UN negotiations produced. At this point, Blair was not even sure if the long effort to bring the Americans back to the UN table had succeeded. Bush was beginning to be aware, at last, of the political difficulties that were crowding in on Blair and his anxiety for the UN to provide justification if it came to war, but it was not yet certain that the Americans would turn to the Security Council. Bush was no fan of Kofi Annan, the secretary general, a fact that Downing Street grudgingly had to accept.

Downing Street now understood the ferocity of the opposition in Washington to the only policy that seemed to offer political cover for the Prime Minister—an agreement in the UN that if Saddam didn't comply with its own inspectors and end the trickery of twelve years, he could be removed by force. Blair knew that Cheney, Rumsfeld, Wolfowitz, and such administration insiders as Lewis Libby in Cheney's office and Elliott Abrams, Condi Rice's deputy in the National Security Agency, were opposed in principle to what they saw as American subjugation to the UN. Bush felt the pressure of those who wanted war at any cost, and Blair the weight of sentiment in his own government and party against a war on American terms.

The agent of compromise, who tried to relieve the pressure on both leaders, was Colin Powell. He had often seemed a weak secretary of state, whose influence in the Oval Office was compromised by others whose access to Bush was more intimate. His disdain for Rumsfeld was well known, and among conservatives he was identified as the remnant of an old diplomacy that they hoped had passed away, so he often appeared to be an adviser whose place in the inner circle was never guaranteed, despite the level of popularity he maintained with the public. Sometimes he was there; sometimes he wasn't. Powell, however, was prized by the British. He understood Blair's anxiety over needing the support of a broad coalition for war, because he shared it.

Blair's concern was his own freedom of action. Without UN sanction and the support of a coalition of the sort that had supported the Afghan campaign, he knew he would be hobbled.

He would be a leader surrounded by doubters, fighting public opinion and the press, and he had a politician's instinctive understanding of how difficult it would be to conduct a war like that. It wouldn't matter that he thought he was right if everyone else thought he was wrong. Powell's interest was different, but coincided with Blair's. He feared the loss of allies whose help he needed in the Middle East and on the Indian subcontinent, in NATO, and in the unstable outposts of the old Soviet empire. Blair spoke of his fear of an America acting alone in the world; so did Powell.

Powell shared these thoughts with Jack Straw. It was around this time that they became more than acquaintances as foreign ministers, and firm friends. They were speaking on the phone almost daily—on one day during the later UN negotiations, eight times—and they shared their frustrations. Powell was frank about his problems, extraordinarily so. Referring to the Cheney-Rumsfeld-Wolfowitz group in the administration, Powell did not feel it necessary to conceal his irritation and feeling of alienation from their view. He told Straw in one of their conversations that they were "fucking crazies."

That phrase catches the quality of the manoeuvrings of the summer of 2002. Powell knew that Bush believed that if the UN inspectors were accepted back by Iraq, their work might disrupt the timetable that a reluctant Pentagon was drawing up for a spring campaign. Their instinct would always be to ask for more time: it was a job that was never done. The President had made no irrevocable decision to go to war—until the orders were given, there was always the theoretical possibility that plans could be unscrambled—but he was settled in his mind. He would not allow the UN to impose delay, the technique that was almost its *raison d'être* as it tried to smooth out disputes and give combatants time to reconsider.

Blair was indeed desperate for time, not just because he clung to the hope that Saddam might succumb to the pressure of inspections and capitulate in some unlikely but not inconceivable way, but because it would be possible for him to justify war if he had the support of a UN-sponsored coalition and if—as between his frequent moments of despair he still hoped—they discovered evidence of weapons of mass destruction to prove that Saddam's threats were not rhetorical but real. So, gnawing away at the two leaders' resolution was a dangerous divergence of interest. While they appeared as one, drawing on each other's support as evidence of an unstoppable conviction that was beyond argument, they were still being pulled in different directions. Bush couldn't afford to delay; Blair couldn't afford not to.

There to exploit that fault line were Powell's "fucking crazies." It is an odd way for a secretary of state to refer to the vice president of the United States and his friends, but there is no doubt that Cheney was the most powerful of those who were warning Bush that the UN route was strewn with dangers and false turnings. Ideologically, Bush did not share the neoconservatives' near demonic characterization of the UN as an instrument of appeasement and a dusty monument to the static politics of the Cold War, but neither was he given to rhapsodies about its importance. Before he came to office he had hardly been a student of world affairs, and the debates about the future of the UN had not been the stuff of politics in Austin, Texas.

But around him were those who argued that with America as the unchallenged superpower, an organization established as a pillar of the post–World War II settlement could not be the arbiter of the reordering of power in the new century. Powell, of course, had his answer—that America acting alone would be a lightning rod for every rogue state and every terrorist network, and that the alienation of old allies would bring a profound weakening of its influence, whatever military force it might be able to bring to bear. In other words, the greater the isolation, the more the notion of a superpower with freedom of action was an illusion. But could he—and Blair—persuade Bush?

The struggle for influence that dominated the month leading up to the anniversary of 9/11, when Bush visited Ground Zero and went on to speak to the UN General Assembly, was therefore an ideological wrestling match inside the administration, with the

British offering tactical support to one of the combatants. Having persuaded Bush—they hoped—of the importance of the "internationalization" of the Iraq campaign for Blair, they were now helping Powell to turn that understanding into practical politics. It meant that when Bush went to address the UN, in the annual General Assembly session that fills New York with heads of state and their gridlocked motorcades, he had to signal America's reengagement with the UN in its argument with Iraq. For Blair, anything less would be a disaster.

His Cabinet was already creaking at the seams, and other European heads of government, with whom he had to do daily business, were gaily predicting that the cowboy Bush was determined to ride the range solo. Knowing it was likely that war would come in six months or so, Blair had to make sure that Bush made at least a gesture toward the multilateralism that eager critics from Paris to Moscow to Beijing were accusing him of having abandoned.

Powell's dinner with the President on August 5, 2002, at which he pressed the case for a constructive approach to the UN, has become one of the important chapters in the saga. It highlights the extent to which Powell had to engineer a private conclave with the President to make his case. He spoke to colleagues afterwards as if it had been a successful political manoeuvre; but for a secretary of state to be reduced to such tactics to get the President alone for a long talk was evidence of an inherent weakness that Blair did not overlook. He knew that Powell was a friend who would continue to work for an international coalition, which suited Britain, but he would never be the decisive influence in the White House.

Yet the dinner seemed to be a success. Word came back to London that Bush had bought Powell's argument for greater American engagement with its restless allies and believed his report that British support might crumble if Blair wasn't given a helping hand. The secretary of state put the case again at Crawford in the middle of the month. Bush and Blair spoke. Blair believed that the President might be more willing now to sound enthusiastic about the UN, whatever his private thoughts might be. But it was a battle far from won.

As if to remind the British of that, Cheney popped up just before Labor Day weekend, with Bush's speech less than two weeks away, to raise doubts about the efficacy of nuclear inspections. If the argument was that the inspectors would help to end Saddam's defiance of the UN, he said, it was simply wrong. Inspections would give no such assurance. In other words, they were a waste of time. The fact that all the members of the Security Council except the United States believed that containment had been a reasonable success—including Britain, despite Blair's growing pessimism—did not trouble Cheney. He wanted to make it known that the United States should not allow the UN to play for time. There was a war on terror to pursue, and like it or not, it led to Baghdad.

There was enough concern about the coming Bush speech for Blair to fly to Camp David for a meeting on September 7. He was now alarmed about the state of opinion in his Cabinet and in the country. They did not want war, but if there was to be one, it had to be sanctioned by the UN. Without that he would lose his foreign secretary, his UN ambassador, and a chunk of his Cabinet. He would not have been able to survive if he had tried to fight Saddam without going to the UN first. Thus, Blair was anxious for reassurance about Bush's intentions. He got it, but it was a tense meeting.

It was preceded by a piece of intelligence that epitomizes the way this struggle was fought. The night before the Camp David meeting, a Blair official who had been involved in the planning for the talks received an unexpected phone call. It came from a former American ambassador of high standing in the Clinton years who had no direct links with the Bush administration but who had a private intelligence network that brought news from its inner counsels. The message was simple: "Watch out. Cheney is going to be there." Again, the vice president appears as a vaudeville villain, the dark presence that casts a shadow. Blair was told to expect him to sit through his conversations with Bush, which usually have private phases with no one else around. Sure enough, when the huddle of ambassadors and advisers melted away to leave the President and Prime Minister alone, Cheney settled into a corner seat in the President's cabin with, as one British observer put it carefully, "that funny crooked smile on his face." Cheney is an amiable man in private, capable of political backslapping in the country club style, and he can appear emollient. But he pitches hard. The reason for his presence was clear to Blair. Bush mustn't give away too much.

Blair had one principal purpose, to convince Bush that it was in the American interest (as well as in his own at home) to fight Saddam in the halls of the UN before sending troops to the desert. He succeeded, but Bush also left Camp David with an assurance. There was no doubt that Blair was committed to support a war if it came. This was neither an agreement spelled out in simple words nor put on paper, but it was clear. Blair would not leave Bush's side.

From that moment Blair knew that he was committed to a war that might unseat him, would certainly convulse the Middle East and split the European Union. It might poison relations with Vladimir Putin, on whom he had expended so much energetic affection. It would cost lives. The truth of the Camp David summit is that it was an opportunity for Blair to step back, which he decided against. The reason was that he had no desire to. His conviction had hardened to a point where he accepted the logic of those who could not contemplate another deal with Saddam. Although the neoconservatives were arguing that the UN was not necessary, and Blair profoundly believed that it was, his mind was nonetheless made up. He hoped, of course, that a *deus ex machina* might roll onto the stage and change everything—a devastating admission from Saddam to the inspectors when they returned, even a collapse of the regime from within—but he doubted it. There would be war.

He was still a little way short of absolute certainty, but his mind had hardened. He believed the case for regime change had been made, although he knew that he would have to persuade his electorate, not to mention his Cabinet, that there was a threat sufficiently immediate to justify it. He had to do for them what he no longer had to do for himself—find a justification for the threat of invasion in the weapons of mass destruction that were still the object of the inspectors' fascination and bewilderment.

He left Camp David convinced that the months of diplomacy now to be played out in New York had to have one aim above all—the birth of a coalition to support military action if the inspectors were thwarted once again, as he believed they would be. It appears that he never seriously contemplated warning Bush that he could not support a war on any other terms. He argued that it would be very difficult for him if he could not call on the support of leaders other than Bush to justify war, but he did not say that he might find it impossible to fight.

The view in London was that one of the conditions he had laid down for supporting Bush when they met in Crawford in April had not been fulfilled—an enthusiastic American pursuit of an Israeli-Palestinian settlement—and it was, as one of his close advisers had always feared, a condition that hadn't become a condition. Instead, the focus was on UN engagement. If that could come, then Blair's support would be guaranteed. Indeed, his offer to Bush went further. He did not discuss what would happen if the UN effort failed, an omission that therefore convinced the Americans that he would stay the course. All that was required was a genuine commitment by Bush to a UN resolution. The Americans assumed that if they made the effort, Blair was a secure ally and they would be able to fight, as Bush desperately wanted, with a partner who could allow the United States to argue to the world that it was not acting as a superpower, arrogant and alone.

Blair therefore returned from Camp David having gained a promise, but having given Bush a virtual guarantee that was just as important. The White House believed that because he had not warned them that he would have to distance himself from Bush if there were no UN coalition, Blair had signed a contract that would not be broken.

Bush kept his side of the bargain. On September 12, he gave a

remarkable speech to the General Assembly, which caused astonishment in the ranks of ambassadors and heads of government
who filled the horseshoe chamber to hear him. He warned the UN
that it mustn't become a repository of empty words and had to
live up to the ambitions of its founders in being resolute in
enforcing its writ, but he managed at the same time to crank up a
degree of enthusiasm that had a startling effect. Even Arab ambassadors, prepared for a speech that they could dismiss as isolationist,
found themselves making statements to the television cameras
praising Bush for his internationalism. He had even announced
that the United States would rejoin UNESCO, the UN agency that
was the object of special derision on the American Right, and that
symbolic gesture helped to give tone to the speech. For a moment,
it was almost as if Bush felt at home at the UN.

The British delegation had to endure the speech in a state of
acute nervousness. As a result of State Department and British
pressure, a passage had been inserted promising American efforts
to get a Security Council resolution but had not appeared on the
teleprompter from which Bush read. Given the efforts of the
Pentagon and Cheney's office to make no commitment of that
sort, there were natural suspicions when the expected sentence
did not materialize. The agreement to commit the United States to
a resolution to put pressure on Saddam had only been settled a
couple of days before. There had been a difficult video conference
involving Powell in New York, Bush in Texas, and Cheney and
Rice in Washington in the last days of August, during which
Cheney once again made the case for resisting the blandishments
of the UN and its enthusiasts. He nearly won. Powell got the
commitment by a whisker.

When the expected sentence did not appear as they listened in
the General Assembly, the British delegation wondered if the
speech that they had been told on September 10 would indeed
commit the United States to a UN resolution had been sabotaged
again. Bush, however, ad-libbed a passage to make up for it. He
hardly had the skill that Clinton showed when in one of his State
of the Union addresses the teleprompter had been loaded with the

wrong speech and he had to wing it for several minutes, but Bush did manage to say that America would work with the Security Council for the necessary resolutions. Unfortunately, the plural "resolutions" was confusing, and his misstatement would return to complicate the argument that dominated the run-up to war, but at least he had thrown Blair the lifeline he wanted. The critics at home could be told that their doubts about Bush had been resolved. He was an internationalist after all. No UN resolution, no war.

If only it were so simple. The accommodation that Bush and Blair had reached could not cover the complications that were starting to ensnare them. They had agreed on a strategy that pitched their own relationship against the drift of thinking in their respective governments. The pulse of war was already beating strongly inside the Bush administration, with Rumsfeld seeming to have taken to heart the argument in Eliot Cohen's influential book of the moment, *Supreme Command*, which made the moral case for political mastery over the generals and argued that political leaders had a duty to remind the soldiers who gave the orders. A year after 9/11, all the caution about war that was distilled in Powell was outweighed by the confidence of Cheney and Rumsfeld, in particular, that there was no going back. And Blair was aware that in his own party, the balance was the other way around. His belief that war would be justified if Saddam continued to defy the UN was treated with scepticism and foreboding not only by a large number of Labour MPs but by some senior members of his government.

So, before he went to Camp David he promised to publish a dossier of evidence that would make the case against Saddam, a public argument that would convince the population at large that the danger from Iraq was serious enough for it to be disarmed by force if it refused to do so voluntarily. In a press conference in Sedgefield on September 3, he said: "If I was not to confront this issue now, and let us say that Iraq obtained either nuclear weapons capability, or developed ballistic missile potential with chemical or biological weapons and they used those weapons, and I thought back and could have done something about it then that would be something on my conscience." He invoked the examples of Kosovo and Afghanistan as proof of how an international coalition could be assembled on the side of right and said that the UN must be the means of dealing with the problem, not avoiding it. He told the Trades Union Congress a week later on September 10, "Let it be clear; should the will of the UN be ignored, action will follow."

Since his assurances in July that no action was imminent and his deliberately vague statement that "there are many issues to be considered before we are at the point of decision," his rhetoric had changed. Running through all his statements was the promise— the threat, as some of his colleagues saw it—that he was ready for war if it came. Nervous Cabinet ministers were assured that this was not as bloodthirsty as it seemed. There was no point in trying to force Saddam to comply with UN inspections without threats; the best chance of peace was in convincing Iraq that it was fruitless to resist the UN's will. But although Blair argued privately with his colleagues that there was no other way to force Saddam to compromise, they discerned in his speeches and answers a deeper purpose that seemed to have less to do with practical politics than with a settled conviction that war would come and would be justified.

In the first week of September, the BBC screened Michael Cockerell's documentary about the relationship between Britain and the United States which included a pre-recorded interview with Blair conducted five weeks before, on July 31. He was unequivocal. This was no knockabout performance at the dispatch box, nor an answer to a hurried question at an airport press conference. They were considered words. Cockerell asked if he was prepared to pay the "blood price" involved in confrontation with Saddam. As the question was asked, the Prime Minister nodded vigorously and said of the Americans: "[They] need to know—are you prepared to commit, are you prepared to be there and, when the shooting starts, are you prepared to be there?"

He was not simply threatening action because it might convince

Saddam to succumb peacefully; he said this because he believed it was right. In the same broadcast he said the relationship with the United States was a "cardinal belief." He put it like this: "The reason why we are with America in so many of these issues is because it is in our interests. We do think the same, we do feel the same and we have the same—I think—sense of belief that if there is a problem you've got to act on it." On the same night as his broadcast, an interview by Condoleezza Rice revealed the extent to which that promise from Blair would be tested. Asked about the strength of the administration's evidence for Iraq's possession of threatening weapons, she said: "We don't want the smoking gun to be a mushroom cloud." A few days later, Bush said in his weekly radio address that one of the reasons for his determination to confront Saddam was his knowledge that he had "illicitly sought to purchase the equipment needed to enrich uranium for a nuclear weapon."

He gave no source for this information, and it was just as well that he didn't. He was referring to the assertion passed via British intelligence to the CIA that an Iraqi official had, three years earlier, attempted to buy a kind of uranium ore known as "yellowcake" from the African state of Niger. Subsequent efforts to confirm the story failed. It became a piece of stray intelligence that had its moment in the sun and simply blew away, though it left a trail of embarrassing footprints behind it.

The rhetorical inflation in Washington continually caused Blair difficulty. While Bush celebrated his support as evidence that the United States had powerful friends abroad for the confrontation with Iraq, the ally who more than any of the others allowed him to make that claim was trying to avoid an apocalyptic tone, despite his tendency to resort to it himself. While Bush raised suspicions on the Right with his gesture to the UN and was under pressure to stand back from the diplomatic manoeuvering that was about to begin, Blair had to convince sceptics that he was willing to submit to the will of the UN, particularly if it became a struggle for supremacy between the Security Council and the President of the United States.

As he began the diplomacy that would, he hoped, produce a UN coalition strong enough to insist on nuclear inspections rigorous enough to give Saddam no means of escape, Blair still spoke of avoiding war. But his public words were heavy with the conviction that had settled on him in the days after 9/11—that the "war on terror" would spread beyond the borders of Afghanistan to Iraq. His commitment to a UN process was real, because it offered him the opportunity to make a political case that he could sell successfully. But his knowledge of the timetable in Washington and his growing understanding of the power of the pro-war faction in the administration meant that he realized from the start that diplomacy might fail and leave him alone with his decision. It was against that dark background that his officials prepared the dossier on the Iraqi threat that was meant to swing public opinion behind him.

But no document in the saga of war in Iraq caused Blair more political trouble, in particular its startling assertion that Iraq possessed some WMDs that could be prepared for use in forty-five minutes.

In a dossier which recycled much information which was already in the public domain, and was devoid of dramatic revelation, the forty-five minutes reference was naturally seized upon by every journalist who started to scan it to find the dramatic piece of evidence that would substantiate Blair's assertion in the introduction that Iraq posed a current threat. It therefore served its purpose at the moment of publication, but it became one of the most confusing and damaging sentences issued from Number 10 in Blair's era. Its origin became the subject of two long investigations and two years later it remained an emblem to Blair's critics of the way the case for war had been exaggerated. Across Whitehall, any reference to forty-five minutes became a kind of bad-taste joke, just as the word "dossier" came to represent to civil servants a special sort of public relations disaster.

The reference was to battlefield weapons and not to long-range missiles, and it came as a result of information passed to Downing Street by MI6 at the end of August in the last stages of the preparation of the dossier. Curiously, although it was prominent in the first accounts after its publication on September 24, the forty-five-minute claim had a time fuse attached: it was less of an instant sensation than a political time bomb. The argument about how the information in the dossier had been assembled, and about whether the intelligence services were unhappy about how their assessments were presented to the public, lay far ahead. In September, the dossier's main purpose was to allow Blair to make the case that there was an overwhelmingly practical reason to confront Saddam.

In the introduction to the document, Blair described the threat from Iraq as "serious and current." Parliament was recalled from its long summer recess to debate the government's assertion that current policy in Iraq was failing and could not be allowed to continue. Blair told the House of Commons: "His weapons of mass destruction programme is active, detailed and growing . . . The policy of containment is not working. The programme is not shut down. It is up and running." The threat would turn into a reality if the international community did not confront Saddam. No one could miss the message. Condi Rice was speaking of mushroom clouds, Blair of an active programme of WMD (though there was no claim of nuclear capability in the near future). Everyone was invited to contemplate the threat.

In one respect, Blair tried to keep some distance from Bush. It was still not his policy to speak of "regime change." Although it was an aim that had been adopted in Washington in the Clinton years (though without any enthusiasm for war in that administration) and Bush used the phrase quite naturally, Blair was still obliged by political pressures at home to make it clear that the aim was disarmament and not the removal of the government. One of the consequences was that he was required to make the case against Saddam's weapons programmes with maximum power. An argument that he was a bad man with a bloodstained history was not enough: Blair had to show beyond doubt that he was a threat.

As a result, the September dossier gathered together every scrap of information that was known about Saddam's weapons programmes and their history to suggest that the Prime Minister's alarm was based on hard facts. As the Hutton report revealed in 2004, the concern in Blair's office was to make sure that when the dossier was finalized by officials in the Cabinet office, working through the apparatus of the Joint Intelligence Committee (JIC), which oversees the intelligence and security services, it left no doubt in a reader's mind that Blair's fear of Iraq was rational. That was why, as the final draft was being prepared, the Prime Minister's chief of staff, Jonathan Powell, emailed the chairman of the JIC to express concern that the dossier was not clear enough about the "imminent threat" posed by Iraq. Nothing less would do.

Without establishing such a threat, Blair had no chance of persuading his party to take a path that might lead to war. And if he did so persuade them, they would still insist that the UN must be the travelling companion. Disarmament had to be the goal, and if inspectors were allowed to resume their work without hindrance, they would need time. The moral case for "regime change," on which the Bush administration was increasingly prepared to rest, was simply not enough for Washington's most loyal ally.

This difference with Washington reveals how profound were the worries in Blair's party about the push to war. Many had a strong ideological disposition against American preemptive action. A commitment to UN principles of collective security lay behind this view, but so did a deep suspicion about the motives of the United States. Blair might say, as he did in his Cockerell interview, that national interests on both sides of the Atlantic coincided in the Middle East, but many—perhaps most—parliamentarians disagreed.

There was restlessness inside the Cabinet. Despite Blair's deserved reputation as a prime minister who eschewed the long Cabinet debates encouraged by some of his predecessors and one who preferred to operate on his own as much as possible, his ministers were bound into decision-making at Number 10 in a way that would be quite foreign to a midranking Cabinet member in Washington. Whereas Bush called fewer than twenty Cabinet meetings in his first two years of office, Blair's senior ministers met every Thursday morning to make the government's principal decisions, prepare parliamentary strategy, and—in theory, at least—to discuss the direction of policy. Through its network of committees, the Cabinet is still the forum for policymaking (and the settlement of disputes) between government departments, however much the modern office of prime minister has become steadily more "presidential."

Cook, as a former foreign secretary, exercised significant power in the Cabinet. He had links to the left of the party, from which territory he had come, and despite his dismay at being removed from the Foreign Office after the 2001 election, he had managed to retain a mantle of loyalty that had not yet quite slipped off. He was not a member of the *salon des refusés* of sacked and never appointed ministers whose grumbles from the parliamentary back-benches were laced with bitterness and therefore lost much of their sting. As Leader of the Commons he dealt every day with Labour backbenchers and their concerns, and as the climactic phase of UN diplomacy began, he became the bellwether for the party's worry about war. Cook's sharp disdain for the Washington neoconservatives and his belief that Blair's Middle East policy was being sabotaged by Bush meant that he became the focus of Cabinet dissent.

At this stage, it was not organized. There was no plot against Blair, no coordinated effort to stage a Cabinet revolt. But week by week, Cook's interventions revealed the depth of his concern and in private a number of other ministers began to share it. His successor as foreign secretary, Straw, was Blair's principal lieuten-ant in trying to dispel this spreading cloud of alarm. Week by week, he would report that Colin Powell had convinced Bush of the importance of a UN process by which inspectors would return to Iraq. Then, Straw argued, war could be avoided. If weapons were found, Saddam would face such fierce international pressure through the UN that it would be impossible for him to resist. He would have no choice but to disarm. The alternative was either collapse from within, because the regime would have no more will to survive, or as a last resort an assault from a coalition so broadly based under UN authority that it could not be caricatured as an American imperialist army.

As the summer ended, Blair and Straw still made this argument with some optimism. Although fifty-six Labour MPs refused to support the government in the Commons when it discussed the dossier (and many others let their grumbles reach the ears of the party whips before they voted), the case for Saddam's commitment to a threatening nuclear programme appeared to have been made.

But September was also the month in which the shadows settled on the landscape in a pattern that would remain. Bush concluded at Camp David that Blair was a committed ally who would not draw back; Blair made the case for the dossier in such terms as to make it difficult for him to settle for anything but the disarmament of Iraq by whatever means necessary; in the Labour Party and the Cabinet itself, it began to be accepted that the depth of Blair's belief in the need to confront Saddam meant that he no longer thought UN support was necessary to justify war.

As if to demonstrate how difficult the politics of the next few months would be, the German elections on September 22 produced a victory for the Chancellor, Gerhard Schroeder, which had looked unlikely a couple of weeks earlier, when the polls had shown him sinking. His rescue came in large part from his decision to play the anti-American card in the last days of the campaign. With his foreign minister, Joschka Fischer, the leader of his Green Party coalition partners, he argued that Bush was a unilateralist who threatened to destabilize the whole Middle East for narrow-minded purposes. When Blair entertained Schroeder for dinner immediately after his election, they were honest about the gulf that was opening up between them. And they knew that on Iraq, Jacques Chirac in Paris was in line with Schroeder and not with Blair.

Although he was still a prime minister around whom everything seemed to turn, shuttling from Washington to the capitals of Europe and talking of the obligations to collective action, Blair was appearing a more solitary figure with each week that went by. One piece of telling commentary on his position came from an old friend and mentor, Roy Jenkins. Lord Jenkins of Hillhead was sometimes known as Blair's history tutor, and used to say that the Prime Minister had confessed to him that he wished he had read history instead of law at Oxford, a confession that Jenkins interpreted as an acknowledgement of a lack of historical awareness. He was now finding Blair's foreign policy something of a trial. In one of his last speeches in the House of Lords, that September, Jenkins said: "My view is that the Prime Minister, far from lacking conviction, has almost too much, particularly when dealing with the world beyond Britain. He is a little too Manichean for my perhaps now jaded taste, seeing matters in stark terms of good and evil, black and white." Who could argue that such attitudes were now the basis of Blair's policy? He had said so himself.

Looking back in May 2004, Blair tried to catch the hope that was still flitting through his mind at that period. "When you live inside these events, you get the nuance and sometimes the complexity of what is being said. When you put these things up in headlines or people, with the greatest respect, write books about them they look for something that is absolutely clear cut and simple and in headline terms.

"It is absolutely right that throughout the whole of 2002 the Americans were looking at and we were looking at what happens if there is no other way to deal with this issue other than military action. What is not true is that the Americans had decided to take military action come what may. That is not true. I happen to know that, from my own conversations with President Bush all the way through.

"Now, is it true that we were both extremely sceptical as to whether Iraq would back down? Yes, but I took the view—and this is why I was so disappointed that we didn't get a second resolution—that if the international community united and said to him—'look . . . you give this stuff up, you get your scientists properly interviewed, you shut down these programmes or else we're going to change the regime' . . . in my view if the international community had done that in a unified way, actually we might have even done it without a war."

The key members of the Security Council, apart from Britain and the United States, found this view unrealistic. If Saddam was being asked either to give up weapons or to prove he didn't have any, it would require time on the inspectors' part. Hans Blix, the former Swedish foreign minister who led the inspection team, said that the conundrum could not be solved without time. If there were no weapons that posed an immediate threat, it would be slow business to prove it; if there were, it would take time to identify and uncover them. UN time and U.S. time were out of sync. The Washington timetable would not allow the inspections to take the time Blix believed they needed.

Thus, unity on the Security Council was always unlikely. In London, the Foreign Office was doubtful about the French, an attitude that comes quite naturally. Chirac's ambassador was telling the British government plainly that they could not support a resolution that was the trigger for war. If the Americans chose to interpret a demand on Saddam as an ultimatum, with war as the consequence if it was not met, that was a matter for Washington: Paris would not agree to go to war. But inside Downing Street, they still hoped. As late as the first week of February, when Blair and Chirac met for a few hours at Le Touquet, one of Blair's principal aides referred to the French President being more "nuanced" in private than in public about war. He may have been, but any hope that he would reconcile himself to war was a product of hope and no more.

By the beginning of the year, Chirac had become aware of the depth of public feeling in France against war, fuelled by a traditional suspicion of American foreign policy and widespread dislike of Bush. When the French President dispatched an aircraft carrier—the *Charles de Gaulle*—to the Gulf, he was hit by a whirlwind of protest. Just as in Germany, where Schroeder had depended on distance from Washington to be re-elected, Chirac was trapped. He did not appear to be discomfited by the experience. At the end of January, Dominique de Villepin, who affected a superior air as foreign minister, assailed Powell at a Security Council meeting in terms that left the American secretary of state livid. Nothing, he said, justified military action. Chirac had not yet gone as far as that. Powell felt he had been patronized (he had) and insulted. Powell told the British that he couldn't abide Villepin, whom he considered hopelessly arrogant. In the immediate aftermath of the passage of UN Resolution 1441 in November, these feelings were already running strong.

Blair's relationship with Chirac has always had a roller-coaster character, plunging from a high point of agreement to the depths in an instant. In the months preceding Christmas 2002, it was going downwards very fast. Blair believed Chirac was reneging on the spirit of the resolution in refusing to use it to put maximum pressure on Saddam (instead of as an excuse to buy time), and Chirac came to believe that Blair had sold out to Bush in what he regarded as a humiliating way. He was also aware that damage to Blair in Europe could be useful to France.

In his first term, Blair had bounced around Europe as the new kid on the block and appeared to have the political force with him. Although his government would not commit itself to the single European currency—which France and Germany saw as the cementing of the political union they wanted from the Atlantic to the Urals—Blair was evincing an enthusiasm for the European Union that no Prime Minister had shown for a generation. He was young and fresh, and the veterans on the scene found themselves being shoved aside (Chirac had first served as Prime Minister under President Valéry Giscard d'Estaing in the mid-1970s when the much younger Blair was still a student). Although veterans were impressed by aspects of Britain's new enthusiasm for the European enterprise, it was not a comfortable feeling. In Iraq in 2002, Chirac saw Blair making what he considered to be a strategic blunder in putting his alliance with the United States above his commitment to the unity of Europe, and he recognized that it gave the Franco-German axis, which was the traditional driver of European integration, a chance to be strengthened again.

Blair was conscious of all these feelings in the autumn as he and the Americans (principally Powell) worked to get the votes for the UN draft that became Resolution 1441.

The prospect from Downing Street was gloomy, with only a few flashes of light. In Europe, where Blair was engaged in important negotiations about the eastward expansion of the European Union to embrace parts of the old Soviet bloc, his relationships were strained. In Washington, he was being drawn into a plan of attack that, week by week, was becoming inexorably part of the collective mind of the administration. His only hope was success at the UN in getting the inspectors back into Iraq and organizing Security Council support strong enough to bring Saddam's regime to a peaceful end. He was aware that even if Straw thought it might yet work, Bush didn't. His natural optimism was already draining away.

There was some relief when the last diplomatic coup of this phase of the Iraq crisis was engineered. In November, the Security Council passed Resolution 1441 unanimously. For Straw, in particular, this seemed a triumph. Even Syria, one of the rotating members, voted for a statement detailing Iraq's defiance of UN resolutions over twelve years and its efforts to frustrate weapons inspections. Iraq was now warned that if it was found to be "in material breach" of the resolution demanding compliance with the inspectors, there would be "serious consequences."

Understandably, the Foreign Office in London regarded this statement as a masterly (if unexpected) turning of the tables. They hoped that 1441 might yet be the mechanism for peaceful disarmament. Straw told the Cabinet that Blair's influence in Washington had helped Powell to get time from Bush for the necessary diplomacy and to gain the moral authority to press for a resolution that would make life impossible for Saddam.

But it was not so simple. Among those who voted for 1441, a number believed it could never be used as a justification for war. France and Russia, two of the permanent five members of the council, took that view. Villepin had managed to insert a telling "and" in the final draft, which France could use to argue that not only would Saddam have to be shown to have made a false declaration to the inspectors but he would also have to demonstrate a general failure to cooperate. He would have to fail twice before the "serious consequences." And France did not accept that "serious consequences" meant war. It would insist that another resolution would have to be passed before an invasion could take place.

Powell had started the negotiations on a resolution with the proposal that it should authorize the UN to take "all necessary means" to enforce its will. Those words were the usual code for war, and early on in the talks, Straw had persuaded him to drop them. The result was that the success in getting unanimity for 1441 was undermined by the inevitable vagueness of the threat. The ambiguity over "serious consequences" that produced unanimity was certain to undermine the agreement. The United States believed it could be used to justify war; France and Russia didn't; Britain hoped that it might, but couldn't be sure. While appearing to be united, the permanent five were divided.

The resolution settled nothing. It won some more time for Blair, but delay would only be useful if the unexpected happened to the regime in Iraq or if the inspectors uncovered a smoking gun with a speed they had never managed before. The creeping pace could not disguise the fact that it was ever more likely that Blair would be forced to support the United States by breaking with his other major allies.

The success in drafting Resolution 1441 was therefore an illusory victory. For weeks after the Security Council adopted the resolution in November and the inspectors returned to Iraq, Blair hoped that France would be able to accept its spirit. But that hope soon fizzled out. And without it, 1441 was revealed as a diplomatic cover for irreconcilable differences in policy. A gift of time at best; at worst, a pretence of agreement where none existed. At the first challenge from Saddam, that fragile cover would break.

It happened in December. In the course of three weeks, the inspectors began a new round of inspections, the Iraqis presented the UN with a 12,000-page report on their programmes for weapons of mass destruction—saying the country was now "empty" of such weapons—and the United States declared that Saddam was in "material breach" of 1441 by withholding information.

By Christmas, it was clear to Blair that he would be fortunate indeed if he persuaded Bush to try to negotiate a second resolution before resorting to war. It was what France demanded, what the Cabinet expected, what Blair would dearly like. But he knew how unlikely it was. Chirac's opposition to war was becoming clearer by the week, though Blair still clung to the fading hope that their friendship, in which he still believed in his cheerier moments, would help to produce a change of mind. He suspected it might be too late. In the United States, Rumsfeld's plans were already placing tens of thousands of troops in position for an invasion. But if a second resolution could be won, popular opposition to war in Britain might yet be turned around.

As the weeks went by, Blair's willingness to face war became obvious to his colleagues. In Cabinet debates—still rather short and unsatisfactory affairs—he revealed his pessimism about a peaceful solution, even as Straw was reporting on the ingenious efforts at the UN to construct a document so worded that it might serve as a second resolution—the one that would pick up where 1441 left off and provide a sounder basis for war by getting the UN itself to give Saddam his last chance.

Blair knew that Cheney and Rumsfeld were hoping to go to war in February. He was desperate to avoid that timetable. In telephone conversations with Bush in early January, he won some more time. The President was willing to wait, but not beyond early March. In Washington, Cheney was wearying of the familiar delay Blair had negotiated. Sitting with friends on his terrace one night, sipping a cocktail, he spoke of his frustration at the UN negotiations and the reason for them. "We are there for Blair. There's no other reason; no justification. We're told we have to do it." Cheney, who was still close to leading British Conservatives who had known him when he was defence secretary during the first Gulf War, had a much more jaundiced view of this Labour prime minister than Bush, who made his judgement solely on the basis of their personal dealings, without applying any ideological test. To Cheney, there was nothing to be alarmed about if Blair were defeated in Parliament: even though the Conservative Party was in a weak state, it might return to power. Bush, by contrast, was appalled at the idea that Blair might be forced out of office by the crisis, as David Manning was warning Condi Rice, his daily interlocutor, that he might.

So Bush gave Blair some time. But it was not enough to dispel the fear of Sir Christopher Meyer in the British embassy that the timetables for war and the second resolution could not be reconciled. The anti-war faction in the Security Council was so determined that it seemed there was no chance of winning an agreement that would authorize war in the event of Saddam's continued defiance in time to prevent the American war plan from being activated. The inspectors wanted more time; France and Russia wanted them to have it. They would not cooperate with Blair to get him off the hook on which he had been impaled by his friends in Washington, where time was the enemy.

It was painful, but Blair had by now made the choice. Addressing a conference of British ambassadors in the Foreign Office in the first week of January, he said: "The price of influence is that we do not leave the United States to face the tricky issues alone. By tricky, I mean the ones which people wish weren't there, don't want to deal with—and, if I can put it a little pejoratively, know the U.S. should confront, but want the luxury of criticizing them for it. So if the U.S. acts alone, they are unilateralist; but if they want allies, people shuffle to the back. International terrorism is one such issue." The ambassadors headed for the airport next day to fan out around the world sure of one thing. Blair would not wriggle out of war.

Meanwhile, the inspectors were talking in a way that was giving strength to his opponents. Blix told the Security Council two days after Blair's speech that his team had been in Iraq for two months "covering the country in ever-wider sweeps, and we haven't found any smoking guns." That same week a British opinion poll suggested that only 13 percent of the British public would support a war if it did not have specific UN authorization (the figure rose to 53 percent if the UN sanctioned an attack).

Blair, however, was not retreating but advancing. He said on January 14, "It is a matter of time, unless we act and take a stand, before terrorism and weapons of mass destruction come together." Whatever the inspectors said, he was convinced that the Iraq threat was there. He told the House of Commons that "the consequences of our weakness would haunt future generations" if Saddam wasn't disarmed. Nothing less would do.

Before the end of the month, 26,000 British troops were off to the Gulf, where more than 125,000 Americans were already deployed. Ministers in London began to realize that a force of that size was unlikely to return without seeing action. Such things just didn't happen. On the last day of January, Bush and Blair had their fog-shrouded summit at the White House, followed by the awkward press conference at which Bush declined to show any enthusiasm for a second resolution—which had been an objective of Blair's when he arrived—and where he managed to get Blair to subscribe to his "weeks, not months" ultimatum to Baghdad.

With the Iraqis insisting that they were cooperating, the Americans insisting that they weren't, and Blair warning that an historic step had to be taken against the proliferation of the still-missing WMD, the scene was set for deadlock, and war.

The job of trying to wrest something from the fire fell to the British ambassador to the UN, Sir Jeremy Greenstock. He was a formidable product of the Foreign Office—a ferociously clever, legally minded wordsmith and tactician with a poker face. He also had the style of a slightly old-fashioned schoolmaster of the austere variety, which is exactly what he had been, at Eton. Greenstock sailed into battle on Blair's behalf to try to construct a resolution that could provide the political cover for the Prime Minister if, as everyone expected, no peaceful disarmament was possible. February was a month of failure.

The French were becoming more entrenched in their opposition to a resolution. As they hardened, so did Bush. Blair admitted in a telephone call with Cook that week that Bush was "afraid of disappearing down the swamps and marshes of the Security Council process." Those swamps and marshes, however, were balmy swimming grounds for a majority of the Security Council. They did not see Iraq as an immediate threat and saw no reason to abandon the containment that they believed had worked. Powell tried to persuade them with a pile of evidence, including photographs of sites allegedly being prepared for weapons plants, but nothing changed. Within two days of his speech, France and Germany were asking for a twofold increase in the number of inspectors and more surveillance flights to make the point that they still believed in disarmament by stealth. All the while, Washington was becoming impatient.

Greenstock shuttled to and fro, trying to stitch together a resolution that could authorize war. His American counterpart, John Negroponte, offered almost nothing, while Greenstock and Straw back in London juggled with phrases that might open a path through the labyrinth. Negroponte was given little freedom of movement by the State Department, and in his public remarks offered not a scintilla of encouragement to those who wanted a second resolution. Greenstock was trying to buy just a little more time. The faint hopes of a regime implosion in Baghdad had long since evaporated, so now the effort was simply to construct a text that could be approved and that would allow Blair to go to war with the formal backing of the Security Council. But in his public statements, Blair seemed to have accepted that it would not be so.

He told his Scottish party conference in Glasgow on the second Saturday in February that there was a moral case for removing Saddam that was as powerful as the moral case against war. As he spoke, about a million people were marching through London in protest. The total across Europe was at least six times that figure. But Blair said: "I ask the marchers to understand this. I do not seek unpopularity as a badge of honour. But sometimes it is the price of leadership. And it is the cost of conviction."

In New York, Greenstock's efforts ran into the sand. In one memorable last try, he said he thought that he might have found a form of words that could achieve "traction." For a day and a night, this *bon mot* enjoyed a little notoriety and stirred some brief excitement. But no. There was no traction. The wheels were spinning in the mud, and about to fly off the wagon. The last days of February were preparations for war. Blair won a vote in the Commons supporting UN efforts to disarm Iraq by a big majority, but a protest amendment was backed by nearly 200 MPs (including 121 of Blair's own party), which Robin Cook reckoned was the biggest rebellion on such an issue since Gladstone tried his Home Rule for Ireland in the 1880s. The harder Blair argued the case for standing beside the United States—not treating it as "some alien power that operates against our interests"—the more he found himself accused of subservience to Bush.

As March arrived, Blair was still spending hours on the phone trying to persuade the clutch of countries serving their rotating turns on the Security Council to support a second resolution. He couldn't. Even when Blix reported to the council on March 7 that his inspectors suspected Iraq might be trying to produce new missiles, he added that disarmament would be bound to take months. Give him time, cried a majority of the Security Council. By now, the United States had asked Saddam to leave Iraq—"or else"—and although Bush had decided to authorize one more push for a resolution, in a sop to Blair, everyone at the UN knew that the endgame had begun.

On Sunday March 9, Bush phoned Blair to offer him the chance to keep British troops out of the invasion and Blair gave his instant response: "No thanks." The next day, Chirac took the unusual step for a member of the permanent five of saying that France would veto any second resolution. "Whatever happens, France will vote no." It was the end. Afterwards, British officials argued that Chirac had made life easier for Blair by behaving with such intransigence, but that was a Jesuitic rationalization after the fact. Blair was isolated and facing an awkward vote in Parliament before going to war. As if on cue, Donald Rumsfeld made things more difficult for him with a bumbling press conference in which he said that the Americans didn't necessarily need British troops in the field—a throwaway line that infuriated Downing Street because of Blair's emphatic reply to Bush's phone call two days earlier (which was only known to a few of his staff). Whether Rumsfeld was being mischievous or flat-footed, his remarks made life even more painful for Blair as he headed for a weekend summit in the Azores with Bush and the Spanish prime minister, José María Aznar. A suggestion that it should be held in London was quickly stifled in Downing Street, Blair's staff realizing that it might bring out an even bigger demonstration than the million-strong march a month before. On the way, he read Cook's resignation letter, which would be released the next day.

Bush's staff, still hazy about the niceties of parliamentary votes in Britain, was now in a tizzy about Blair's peril in the vote. A year later, Blair admitted that he realized he might fall from power as a result of it. Although the Conservatives were supporting the motion that would allow military action and he would not therefore face outright defeat, he had decided that he would have to consider resignation if a majority of his own party opposed him. His authority would have gone. He warned his family that he might be out of office within the week. As it was, a majority of Labour MPs who were not in the government voted against him, but the support of the others and those in the government who were obliged to back him or resign gave him a majority of the Labour votes cast. It was a close call.

But war was now inevitable within days. Bush made the unexpected preliminary broadcast saying that Saddam had forty-eight hours to leave the country or face an invasion. On Wednesday March 19, the White House got information (probably passed to the CIA by the Israelis) about the possible whereabouts of Saddam, and Bush decided, on information given to him by the director of the CIA, George Tenet, to launch a "decapitation" strike that the Americans believed had injured Saddam but left him alive and able to function. The following day, the troops began their assault.

Blair found himself fighting a war that the public did not want and that infuriated his party. Even with a UN resolution, he would have faced bitter opposition; without one, he was walking into a bleak political landscape where some of his friends shrank away, others hurried away from him, and many of the words of support came from Labour's old opponents on the Right.

Even the speed of the battlefield campaign, which led to the toppling of Saddam's iron statue in Baghdad on April 9 as a symbol of victory and relatively few coalition casualties compared to the forecast of massacres some critics had predicted, did not ease Blair's pain. He had sacrificed a great deal for Bush. Across Europe he was portrayed as a cross between a staring-eyed warmonger and a lapdog anxious to cuddle up to the American president. At home, his premiership had become identified completely with war and his moral convictions. Blair knew then that there was no way back to the relatively easy popularity he had enjoyed for most of his six years in power, no way of healing the rifts with friends and allies who had rallied to his New Labour cry and now felt estranged by an invasion ordered by a commander in chief in Washington.

His decisions to accept the inevitability of war whatever happened at the UN and to refuse to demand too much of Bush in return were to change the nature of his leadership. Bush had gained from Blair's support. It allowed him to present the war as an international effort, graced by a genuine coalition. As Powell had told him from the beginning, a coalition without Britain would not look like a coalition at all—Spain, Poland, and Australia would not be quite the same. And in Britain it was often forgotten, because of the natural obsession with homegrown opposition, that Bush's poll numbers were not at all healthy as he prepared for war. Blair gave him more than a few thousand troops. He gave him an extra layer of political credibility, without which the enterprise would have been even more risky for a president whose country was still divided about his capacity for wise leadership.

They therefore became a pair of war leaders bound together by unexpected obligations. Bush found in a Labour leader a partner who could help his popularity. Blair found in Bush a Republican who brought him some painful political problems but who gave him the opportunity to exercise the moral convictions that had for a few years been beginning to define his premiership in his own mind.

But who won in the race to deal with Saddam? It is hard to escape the conclusion that the hawks had achieved what they wanted. Their plans had been delayed for a few months, but in the end the UN could not play for time. In that respect, the Blair who had appeared to be an impediment—always droning on about the importance of the UN—had become their ally. He accepted the outline of the moral case on which they built their plans, and he was willing to abandon the UN when it became clear that a second resolution was impossible. Instead of running for cover, he faced the House of Commons and won.

Therefore, he helped in an enterprise that, at the moment of invasion, seemed to give the neoconservatives their proudest moment. Ken Adelman, one of the true believers, said famously that Iraq would prove "a cakewalk." Others spoke of the people rising joyously to greet the liberators, and a flood tide of democracy spreading across the Middle East. Before long, these wilder hopes would collapse in a heap. But as American and British troops entered Baghdad, the neocons could reflect that they had won. Nothing was allowed to stand between them and Saddam.

There was a piquant celebratory dinner at Cheney's official residence on Sunday April 13, 2003. Adelman and his wife returned from a trip to Paris to be there. The only other guests were Wolfowitz and Lewis Libby. The true believers gathered at the flame and toasted the President who, in the end, had gone their way.

Cheney's house on Massachusetts Avenue is next to another mansion and offices on the hill that comprise Washington's Embassy Row. Its centerpiece is a fine house by the English architect Edwin Lutyens, and it is the residence of the British ambassador. There is no record of a celebratory dinner there on that night.

If they had held one, it might have been for Colin Powell. They might have talked about the crazies, and about the sequence of events that would mark Blair for the rest of his time in public life and would pose for Britain a series of interlocking diplomatic and political problems that would test his government to its limits. On one thing only might they have agreed with the revellers next door. For Bush, Blair, and all of them, nothing would ever be the same again.

CHAPTER 7

# THE RIDDLE

# OF THE SANDS

Spies and soldiers were perplexed by the Iraq war from the beginning, and when the old regime had been toppled, the shadows deepened. The aftermath in 2003, like the lightning fall of Baghdad itself and the disappearance of Saddam's army, was confusing and unruly. The facts and assumptions that were the war's justification seemed to shimmer and disappear like a mirage in the desert heat, and the very ease with which its first objectives were achieved taunted the victors with new uncertainties. Iraq remained violent, mysterious and threatening.

The military threat that was the justification for war was transformed quickly into a political crisis for Bush and Blair, whose first cries of victory were carried quickly away on the wind. The weapons of mass destruction with which Saddam was purported to be threatening his neighbors and the wider world couldn't be found. The gratitude of the population that was supposed to flow from Operation Iraqi Freedom was laced with bitterness at the occupiers. A year after the fall of Saddam in April 2003, the casualty rate among coalition forces was still rising. Above all, the two leaders of the coalition found themselves ensnared by the politics of a war that was meant to make a clear divide between good and evil but instead pitched president and prime minister into a draining moral debate with their electorates.

Their predicament was rooted in the uncertainties and arguments that gripped London and Washington even as the last, weary diplomatic manoeuvres were played out at the United Nations. Intelligence agencies were divided and Cabinets strained. Bush and Blair were thrown back on each other as the factions fought for supremacy. The CIA thought the Pentagon planners were wrong, and the Middle East watchers in the State Department struggled against the neoconservative tide they saw seeping into the Oval Office; in London, the "permanent government" inside MI6 and in the Foreign Office sang its traditional cautious song, and the military chiefs of staff made it known that they were fearful of the consequences of war.

However, having surmounted the arguments erected by the more cautious of their advisers and political friends and the doubts of many of their intelligence and military staff, Blair and Bush were determined not to flinch. A confident public voice is the price a war leader must always pay, however quavering it may sound inside his own head. They were encouraged to sound doubly resolute by the awkward knowledge that parts of the case for war were ambiguous and problematical. There was much about which they could not be certain, and in the paradoxical way of politicians, it made them more anxious to make the case with confidence. Like a lawyer in court, Blair would reach for particularly eloquent phrases to cover the thinnest parts of his case. Though he knew how much professional caution was attached to intelligence assessments of Saddam's strength, he was so convinced of the need to confront it that he pitched his argument in terms of a moral duty rather than a practical response to a balance of risk. It was his natural style.

The greater the danger of defeat at the bar of public opinion, the more important it was to strip the case of its complexities. Bush could draw on the support of a friend in London who sounded more and more confident of the justice of his cause, and in turn Blair settled naturally into the slipstream of a president for whom there was no way back.

Their support for each other inevitably pushed forward the case for war. The personal obligations of loyalty they had exchanged now acted as defences against those who preferred caution and wanted to play for time.

Blair found himself promoting a moral case he had laid out in increasingly stark terms after 9/11, a case that sat in opposition to the nuances and reservations that are the stuff of the analysts and advisers who never want to be caught without an escape clause and avoid certainties as a matter of professional pride. The collision between his confidence and their caution was especially painful because of a dramatic change in the way Britain's security and intelligence agencies now operated. In the previous few years, the corner of a veil had been pulled back and the first shafts of light were beginning to illuminate the secret world. The Iraq crisis gave the public the most tantalizing glimpse so far of how the intelligence business dealt with political leaders, and how in turn they talked to the spies. Whatever its contribution to the health of democracy might have been, this insight was a mightily uncomfortable experience for the government and its clandestine servants. But it meant that the politics of war were accorded part of their proper context: even before Iraq had fallen, the role of intelligence was more widely understood—or at least discussed—than ever before.

The Bush-Blair partnership can't be separated from the intelligence debates that preceded the war and the arguments that followed it, because the inherited assumption at Downing Street and the White House is that the flow of information, analysis, and gossip back and forth from the secret parts of the governments is the bloodstream of the "special relationship." With the nuclear agreements between the two countries made after World War II (which are renewed by every British prime minister as one of the first acts of office), intelligence is the tie that binds. For this president and prime minister it also became a troubling political argument, because they found themselves having to deal with uncertainties that became public and, eventually, the stuff of the argument about whether the war had been justified.

No modern conflict has been fought against such a public argument about the intelligence assessments that are sent to the Oval Office and Downing Street. Even before the troops went in, there was a debate in Britain about the advice Blair was getting. He was obliged to set up two inquiries. The first, under the retired judge Lord Hutton, was established as a direct result of the death of Dr. David Kelly, the weapons scientist. It focused on the battle between the government and the BBC over the claim made during a live interview by a defence correspondent that the September 2002 dossier making the case against Iraq had been "sexed up" by Blair's officials at the last minute to make it more forceful. Hutton eventually came down on the government's side, and the specific claim was withdrawn, but his inquiry exposed hitherto secret details of how the Joint Intelligence Committee and the security and intelligence agencies worked. Despite a "verdict" in Blair's favour, the whole episode sapped the government. The second inquiry was established to examine the quality of intelligence itself. Blair asked Lord Butler of Brockwell, a former head of the civil service, to investigate the intelligence background to the war. His report would spare individuals from direct censure, though its analysis of the consequences of Blair's style of government was sharp and damaging. Collective political judgement had been sacrificed, Butler said, for decision-making which bypassed traditional Whitehall checks and balances, and he concluded that, as a consequence, intelligence had been asked to carry a weight that it could not bear. The controversies and uncertainties of the run-up to war were therefore embedded in the judgements that would be made about Blair when it was all over, and when he was looking forward to elections in Iraq. The confusions had played a great part in formulating the case for war, and in persuading Parliament and the public that there was no other way.

As if to emphasize the residue of confusion that still clung to the war, that transfer of power was preceded in May 2004 by the resignation of the director of the CIA, George Tenet, and the departure of his deputy, James Pavitt, which were taken as admissions of intelligence failures, despite official denials. Even as they went, the White House and the CIA were arguing with the Senate Intelligence Committee on Capitol Hill about how much of their investigation into the intelligence failures surrounding 9/11 should be declassified and shown to the public: the unravelling of what had once been secret seemed unstoppable.

In London, even more than in Washington, the intelligence debate was the more dramatic because of its novelty.

Until the early 1990s, the glorious official fiction had been maintained in Britain that there was no foreign intelligence service at all. Everyone knew it was there, but its motto *"Semper Occultus"* was its badge: always secret. MI6, James Bond's service and the progenitor of John le Carré's "Circus" of spies, had no formal existence. Although its history ran as a glittering thread through the story of Britain's twentieth-century foreign policy and the Cold War, it had no legal basis. Its financing was concealed in the budgets of other departments and its chief was protected from publicity by an informal agreement that meant his name was never meant to be published, though since the 1970s, every one of them has been named from time to time. The idea that a contemporary picture might be published in a newspaper would have struck any member of MI6 with horror. Every foreign embassy in London knew his name; any MP with a vague interest in foreign affairs could find it out; many journalists would know who he was (though almost nothing of his views or his competence). But an enveloping shroud covered his whole enterprise, to which prime ministers and foreign secretaries would only refer in oblique terms.

There is a discreet club in Knightsbridge where old spies and veterans of special forces units gather to gossip and trade memories of their days in the field. Most of them could not have imagined the change that was going to grip the service, and its sister, the security service MI5, at almost exactly the moment the Berlin Wall came down and the era that had dominated their lives—the Cold War—came to an end. Within a few years their headquarters became public buildings, pointed out by the tour guides on open-topped buses, the names of their chiefs were as well known as the director of the CIA, a parliamentary committee began (gingerly) to monitor their activities, and the government would refer directly to their advice in the Commons.

It was not generally welcome to the retired foot soldiers who had trailed Russian diplomats through London's parks, or who had lived through the memorable humiliation of the defection of Kim Philby in the 1960s. Then they had faced the ridicule that accompanied the revelation in the 1970s that the surveyor of the Queen's pictures, the art historian Sir Anthony Blunt, had been known for twenty years to have spied for the Russians when he was in MI5 during and after the war. But times were changing fast.

Installed in a brash ziggurat of a building by the Thames at Vauxhall Bridge, MI6 was ready to flirt with public attention. Almost directly across the river, MI5 was doing the same. Their historic rivalry has been maintained for decades, and when Major's government passed legislation to give them their legitimacy, rescuing them from the wrong side of the tracks, they began more openly to let tales of their activities seep out. Consequently, disputes that had once been the talk of certain gentlemen's clubs in St. James's and in the bowels of the Foreign Office and the Home Office found a wider audience. Some of the traditionalists would say that the Iraq imbroglio was the natural result of the openness that the Major government believed was necessary, and Blair exploited. The embarrassment was certainly increased by the public attention; but the disputes would have happened anyway.

It would be hard to exaggerate the shock of the change in culture. A generation before, recruits to MI6 were not only required to submit, priest-like, to a lifetime of anonymity (which for most of them is still the case) but also entered a world that had rituals and customs that seemed to mark it out as a kind of eccentric army regiment, resolute in its intimacy and confidence. It was known that the chief was always known as "C," after the founder of the service, Sir Mansfield Cumming, and by tradition wrote all his letters in the green ink that had been Sir Mansfield's trademark, but that was the least of it. In the 1950s, the intelligence officers who performed most of the important functions of the service numbered probably less than 300, and they reputedly had the collective air of a louche reunion at an Oxford college with plenty of booze, fast women, and eccentricity. Everyone knew everyone else, they'd moved through the same world of private school and Oxford or Cambridge, and many inhabited the byways of upper-middle-class or aristocratic society. They enjoyed affecting superiority over their rivals in MI5, whom they saw as a collection of retired policemen and their plodding satraps, lacking any of the glamour of the boys who would ply their trade in the bazaars of Beirut or the streets of Moscow.

One veteran recalled the introductory lecture in the mid-1950s, when recruits were played a vinyl recording on a wind-up gramophone. The voice of a hero of the service, who had a glass eye and a romantic reputation, told of one particularly hazardous rendezvous with an agent, during which he had to rescue himself from drowning with the help of a penknife and a rope. He had staggered back to safety dripping with blood and badly injured, but with the information he had gone to get. This was the kind of life, he said, that they must be prepared for. There would be danger, but the satisfaction of duty done. His crackly voice would emerge from the gramophone like a ghost's, urging his successors to bend themselves to their task with the vigour and flair of the heroes who had gone before. The senior men of the service would stand around in silent tribute as the voice rose and fell and died away. As a regiment treasures its battle honours and the tattered flags brought back from foreign fields, so MI6 protected and embellished the story of its own glories.

The past was ever-present, and it lent a certain style to proceedings. As late as the 1960s, officers heading abroad for duty would be instructed on how to have their jackets cut by the tailor to allow for the easy concealment of a gun.

Soon afterwards, much of this heady glamour began to disappear. MI6's principal headquarters became a dingy office block near Waterloo Station with draughty windows and the spare utilitarian corridors that defined the cut-rate public buildings of the 1960s. Even C had been dragged from his lair in a fine Georgian townhouse in Westminster, from behind the traditional green light on his door that signalled he was ready for a visitor, to sit atop this skyscraper and supervise a service that still had its triumphs but was consciously beginning to shed some of the stylish accoutrements that had seemed to its critics too much like determined amateurism. New recruits would not expect a future C to be striking matches on his wooden leg, or wearing a piratical eye patch, or treating his senior officers as if they were classical scholars dropping by for a dry sherry before Evensong. MI6 became more professional, less interested in the class of its officers, and an organization where eccentricity was tolerated only at the edges.

The C who supervised the gentle emergence into the public gaze, in the late 1980s, was Sir Colin MacColl, who was still capable of padding around his office in sandals and appearing to the uninitiated visitor to be some down-at-heel office functionary rather than the chief himself, but who installed MI6 in its spectacular new home, with the help of Margaret Thatcher, whose affection for the service resulted in increases in its budget that were the envy of other departments in Whitehall. She liked her spies.

There was a slight swagger in the move to a new home that, to the horror of some more traditional officers, the service allowed to be used as a prop in a James Bond movie. Dame Judi Dench, who had become Ian Fleming's M in the films, was invited to lunch. Alongside the culture of secrecy that still attended the identities of officers, their training, and every detail of their operational lives, this was an awkward flirtation with the public. It was as if after the Cold War, with the Communist phase of the Great Game over, MI6 could lift one of its veils in a deliberate tease.

If this was a sign of confidence, it was justified. The reputation of the service was high in Whitehall. When Robin Cook became foreign secretary on Labour's election in 1997, he engendered suspicion in MI6 because he had been a severe left-wing critic of the security and intelligence services in earlier days, and a strong supporter of a Freedom of Information Act, but he quickly made his peace. He appointed a popular C, Sir David Spedding, from inside the service and in his time in government spoke warmly of its achievements. His successor, Jack Straw (who as a prominent left-wing student in the 1970s had been a target of MI5 surveillance) was equally supportive. With the Balkan crises of the 1990s posing questions for foreign policymakers that had not been asked before, MI6 found itself in demand. From the moment he was elected, Blair was fascinated. Perhaps because they knew so little, as no ministers had served in senior positions in government before, Labour's senior figures were rather in awe of their own underworld.

Blair also understood the power of the secret network from the moment in the course of his first week in office when he was inculcated into the secrets of the UKUSA Treaty of 1948, which established the intelligence relationship with Washington, and then signed the papers giving him control of the nuclear missiles that were part of the defence arrangement with the United States. For any incoming prime minister, these arrangements become a matter of day-to-day importance that is often unrecognized by the general public. For example, the government's vast listening station in Cheltenham—GCHQ—is not only the hub of electronic intelligence for Whitehall but a vital part of the listening apparatus of the National Security Agency in Washington. That is why more than half the budget for GCHQ is paid for by American taxpayers, a fact about which British governments have been naturally reticent.

As with all their predecessors, the relationship between Bush and Blair was built on this practical foundation. The niceties of a shared language (more or less), the threads of family history that still span the Atlantic, and the memories of World War II are often portrayed as being the essence of the partnership: in practice, the hard facts of intelligence and defence are the links that pull the two governments together. They are bound together by their weapons, their satellites, and the tentacles of their intelligence networks.

One scene illustrates the primacy of this aspect of the relationship. On the day after 9/11, with the air corridors over the Atlantic shut to all commercial traffic and every commercial airport in the United States closed, one plane took off from Britain to head west. It contained an interesting trio of visitors to Washington—the chief of MI6, Sir Richard Dearlove; the deputy director general of MI5, Eliza Manningham-Buller (who would soon succeed to the top job); and the director of GCHQ, Sir Francis Richards. Once in Washington, they were driven straight to the headquarters of the CIA in Langley, Virginia, to see old friends and colleagues. After dinner and discussions, they returned to the British embassy and the next morning they were gone. (By curious coincidence, they gave a lift home to their old boss, John Major, who had been stranded in Washington on a business trip—like George H.W. Bush, James Baker III, and a number of other veterans of the first Bush administration, he is a board member of the Carlyle Group, whose secretive dealings in the Gulf states have attracted interest and, in some quarters, notoriety.)

Both Dearlove and Manningham-Buller had served time in the Washington embassy as liaison officers for their respective services with the CIA and the FBI in the 1990s and were now in day-to-day touch with their counterparts in the Bush administration. Their presence in the hours after 9/11 was evidence of much more than a professional concern, however. They were engaged in a kind of family conference.

The network is strong, and personal. In London, the CIA station chief, who presides over an establishment of several dozen officers in the embassy in Grosvenor Square, attends most of the weekly meetings of the JIC, and processes their material. There was also a particularly strong link between George Tenet and Richard Dearlove. Tenet passed through London at least half a dozen times a year on CIA business, and seldom did so without calling on MI6.

Dearlove, who retired as C in August 2004 after five years in the job, is a close friend.

It is, however, not a partnership of equals. As one former senior figure in the American embassy in London put it, "If you think of the two organizations as being the two ends of a dumbbell, one is a helluva lot heavier than the other . . . You couldn't say they balance each other." MI6 prides itself on the delicacy of its penetration of some places where the CIA has found it difficult—in parts of the Middle East, for example—but it is inevitably the junior partner. Even with the planned expansion that Blair has approved, it is still a service with only a little over 2,000 directly employed staff. In the collection of raw material, it cannot compete with the scale of the CIA operation worldwide.

"Every morning a huge pipe opens up in Whitehall and the stuff from the agency just pours out," said someone familiar with the exchange of day-to-day intelligence. "Tenet does it very well. It's impressive. Good pictures and good salesmanship. As Blair has discovered, it is hard to resist." A generation ago in Whitehall, the flow from the United States came down what MI6 quaintly called the "Lampson tube conduit," given its nickname after the vacuum tubes once used in department stores to carry money and receipts from the sales desk to the cashier and back again, with much rattling and whooshing as the little canisters whizzed up the pipe. It is not a bad picture of the way information passes from Washington to London and back again, though now the instant screens and the simplicity of videoconferencing mean that the process is less mysterious than before. It is as if they are in each other's offices the whole time.

When the inquiries began to look at the intelligence failings leading up to the war, one of their preoccupations was the extent to which this closed world reassured itself, with one service reinforcing the analysis of another. The more their political masters demanded clear answers, the easier it was to pool information and look for clarity, even when there was none.

No one in the intelligence world in London is in any doubt of the overweening influence of Washington in their lives: it is the air they breathe. Indeed, one of the most celebrated moments in the modern history of MI6 is often quoted in the service to make the point. In October 1962, when Sir Dick White was C, he called all his officers together in the screening room at their headquarters for a special announcement. It was to say that it had been MI6's work that had enabled President Kennedy to resolve the Cuban missile crisis peacefully and that the moment should be marked as one they must all remember. No one would ever know, he said, because that was both the nature of their trade and its penalty. But it was the success of the service in the Penkovsky operation that had allowed Kennedy to understand the weakness that lay behind the poker hand being held by the Soviet leader, Nikita Khrushchev.

Oleg Penkovsky was a young colonel in Soviet military intelligence who became an MI6 agent in 1960 and then began to open a vast cache of military secrets from Moscow. By the time of the missile crisis in October 1962, after a spectacular series of clandestine escapades in Moscow and London, he had provided enough information to allow MI6 to persuade the CIA—and, more important, Kennedy personally—that the Russians' bluff could be called. MI6 had proof that Khrushchev did not have the capacity to threaten the United States in the way that was assumed by the hawks in the administration and among those chiefs of staff who wanted to bomb Cuba, where American photographic reconnaissance had uncovered the preparation of launch sites. Kennedy's resolution of the crisis by means of a quarantine, giving the Soviets the opportunity to withdraw and save some face, was attributed in London directly to MI6 and its playing of the Penkovsky material. In Washington it was handled by the station chief in the embassy, Maurice Oldfield, who would in his time become C, carrying the legend of that operation with him.

The story of the Penkovsky case has been passed down through the years, and it is used as perhaps the most successful evidence of the way in which the relationship could turn on a British operation. But the exception proves the rule: it has almost always been the fate of MI6 to play second fiddle to the CIA. That was the history replayed in the run-up to the invasion of Iraq.

MI6 found itself pulled along by a tide that made it very uncomfortable. It flowed from Langley, but also from Downing Street. Blair's enthusiasm for MI6's professionalism, allied to his alarm about the growth of Islamic terrorism, meant that like some of his predecessors in office, he began to demand evidence from his spies that they found it impossible to provide.

Blair's Camp David meeting in September 2002, when he saw the National Security Agency satellite pictures purporting to reveal Saddam's advanced preparations for the production of weapons of mass destruction, had a profound effect on him. For the previous six years, he had become increasingly worried about the failure to disarm Iraq: though he was not yet persuaded that war was inevitable, he was well on the way. He certainly had no doubt that if he believed it was necessary to invade, he would give the order. The sight of photographs that seemed to illustrate clearly the extent to which Saddam had been busy since the inspectors left in 1998 was therefore startling and reassuring at the same time. They were alarming, but they seemed to confirm the lurking certainty in Blair's mind that weapons programmes were still active. In particular, they purported to show that mobile laboratories for the production of chemical weapons had been identified. In a country the size of France, how would inspectors be able to find them all? Despite his political problems at home and his anxiety over gaining UN authority, Blair was ready to be convinced.

But MI6 was not. The truth about satellite intelligence is that, with the exception of France, which has stayed outside the military structure of NATO, only the Americans produce high-definition pictures from space. London was receiving reconnaissance pictures from conventional aircraft, but the American shots were the ones that mattered. Bush was convinced by the CIA that they did indeed show that Saddam was progressing with his programmes: the threat was real. Back in London, the analysts were less sure.

Dearlove's service had played a cautious game in the course of the previous year. Institutionally, MI6 is in the business of preventing wars rather than stoking the fire. Its job is to defuse crises, not inflame them. So the rhetoric of the Washington hawks was subjected to rigorous analysis by those who provide the material that ends up, through the machinery of the Joint Intelligence Committee, in the "red book" that contains the Prime Minister's intelligence briefing. They knew, as the UN inspectors acknowledged, that known stocks of chemical and biological weapons from the 1980s and 1990s couldn't be accounted for. But they were not ready to argue that active programmes were about to produce weapons that would pose an immediate threat. As was their custom, they couldn't give a cast-iron guarantee either way: but their instinct was to be reassuring.

As Tenet himself put it in a speech at Georgetown University in early 2004, "In the intelligence business you are almost never completely wrong or completely right. That applies in full to the question of Saddam's weapons of mass destruction. And, like many of the toughest intelligence challenges, when the facts on Iraq are all in, we will be neither completely right nor completely wrong." It is useful for a spymaster to claim innocence about any of his predictions, of course, but there is obvious truth in what Tenet said. The atmosphere in late 2002, with Bush moving closer to war and Blair preparing himself for the decision that he knew might come, was ripe for the misunderstandings that come from the grey pictures and stories that are the currency of intelligence.

Those who wanted to make the case for war were convinced by images that showed trucks being moved in suspicious ways—as Tenet put it, "a pattern of activity designed to conceal movement of material from places where chemical weapons had been stored in the past." Those who were anxious to avoid a conflict that they believed might be a disastrous path into a Middle East quagmire tended to want more proof. There was little of it to be had.

As if to illustrate the perils of the trade, Blair published his first dossier on Iraq in September 2002 as part of his effort to convince public opinion of the danger posed by Saddam. It included the claim that would set off the miserable chain of events nine months later that pitted the government against the BBC in the most bitter argument anyone could remember between the broadcasters and Whitehall, provoked the suicide of David Kelly, and launched the Hutton report, which in turn revealed much about the background discussions before the war that Blair, his closest officials, the Ministry of Defence, and MI6 would much rather have kept to themselves. The assertion was simple: that Saddam was believed to have weapons of mass destruction that could be prepared for use in forty-five minutes.

No single sentence in a government document in this generation has caused such trouble for a prime minister. In May 2003, the *Today* programme carried an interview with its defence correspondent, Andrew Gilligan, in which he suggested the forty-five-minute claim had been inserted in the dossier at the last minute by Downing Street as part of an effort to "sex up" the intelligence. His exact words, uttered in the course of a live interview, just after 6 o'clock one Thursday morning were: ". . . Downing Street, our source says, ordered a week before publication . . . ordered it to be sexed up, to be made more exciting and ordered more facts to be . . . discovered."

The Prime Minister was livid. Since he had presented the dossier in good faith to the House of Commons, he said, he was being accused of being a liar. No more serious charge could be made. His communications director, Alastair Campbell, who was already engaged in an acrimonious argument with the BBC about coverage of the war, went into attack with relish.

The battle rolled on into the following year, and the sorry saga only came to an end after Kelly was revealed as one of Gilligan's sources and committed suicide. The consequent Hutton report largely backed the government, the BBC retracted the offending sentence, Gilligan resigned, and the chairman and director general, Gavyn Davies and Greg Dyke, quit soon afterwards in a collective, bloody falling on swords. It was an unhappy episode for all concerned, and it left deep wounds. But when it was all over, the forty-five-minute claim remained. How had it come to be made?

The fact had indeed been received from MI6 and became an example of how a careful intelligence assessment can explode when the context is fuzzy. The morning after the publication of the dossier, the front-page headline in the *Sun* read simply, "Brits 45 Minutes from Doom," a reference to Iraqi weapons thought to be capable of reaching British soldiers serving in Cyprus in the Mediterranean. The threat was claimed to be clear—that Saddam had weapons of terror that were a threat beyond his borders.

MI6 had said no such thing; nor had Blair. But in the context of a dossier that made the case for war on Iraq if voluntary disarmament didn't take place, this seemed the prime piece of evidence. It wasn't. Blair was hazy even a year later about whether it referred to battlefield weapons or not, although the original claim—from a single source who claimed to have direct knowledge from Saddam's circle—was specific. But when the troops went in six months later and failed to find evidence of the weapons, the forty-five-minute claim became the "evidence" that all the intelligence agencies on both sides of the Atlantic had got it wrong. The critics said they had peddled war on a false prospectus.

The Prime Minister's 2002 dossier had presented the case in political terms. Although the government largely won its argument against those who claimed that intelligence had been massaged to the point of distortion, the careful qualifications that are said to be the hallmark of Joint Intelligence Committee reports were flattened out for the public dossier. The case had to be made clearly, because it was meant to persuade people who might be sceptical that the Prime Minister was threatening Iraq on good grounds. That was why, in the last days before the dossier was published, Blair's chief of staff, Jonathan Powell, emailed the chairman of the JIC, John Scarlett, expressing his concern that the dossier didn't provide evidence of an imminent threat. Since the Prime Minister's foreword to the dossier was arguing that there was a "serious and current" threat, the evidence presented had to be black-and-white and not at all grey. Reading the dossier, the public had to be convinced that Blair's belief in the threat from Saddam was well founded.

The forty-five-minute claim sprang out as the piece of evidence that made that case most clearly. It had come, it now seems clear, through the organization of Iraqi exiles, the Iraqi National Accord (INA), led by Iyad Allawi. While the Pentagon still inclined toward Ahmed Chalabi's Iraqi National Congress (INC) and succeeded in keeping up the flow of government funds to it from Washington— $35 million before it was cut off in spring 2004—the INA was preferred by the State Department, the CIA, and MI6. That was why there was considerable satisfaction in the secret world when, in June 2004, Allawi was chosen by the Iraqi Governing Council to be prime minister of the interim government that took over technical control of the country on June 28, 2004. His spy may have been Lieutenant Colonel al-Dabbagh, who told the *Sunday Telegraph* in London and NBC that he had smuggled out the information via a Baghdad general working secretly for the INA. He said he had been told: "If war breaks out we can use them within forty-five minutes."

It is easy to understand how valuable this information appeared, when MI6 received it at the end of August 2002. The dossier had been worked on through the summer and was nearly ready. Such detail was priceless. The weapons said to be capable of being prepared for use in forty-five minutes weren't defined, leaving journalists (and especially headline writers) with the scope to use their imaginations, but the government made no great effort to correct some of the wilder claims. As chairman of the Joint Intelligence Committee, Scarlett put it succinctly to the Hutton inquiry: "It was a fleeting moment. And beyond that, of course, it is not my immediate responsibility to correct headlines." A previous chairman, Sir Rodric Braithwaite, later expressed disdain at that remark, which was shared by at least two others among Scarlett's predecessors. It was absurd, Sir Rodric told the Royal Institute of International Affairs in London, to say it was not his fault if he was misinterpreted: "One writes in order to be understood by one's audience. The JIC and Downing Street have only themselves to blame if the public failed to grasp what they were trying to say."

Nearly eighteen months later, Blair was taunted in the House of Commons for apparently not being clear about which weapons were being referred to in the dossier. Michael Howard said it had been nearly a year before Blair had asked his officials which weapons were being described. The revelation, however, was not that Blair had not known the precise details. It was that he didn't feel he needed to know—for the reason that he was already convinced in his own mind of the threat from Saddam. He needed no convincing in a dossier, nor any new evidence from MI6. The forty-five-minute dispute, therefore, is much more than an argument about wording or the extent to which the chairman of the JIC was persuaded by Downing Street to give special prominence to the claim. It is an insight into Blair's mind in September 2002.

He was already at a point at which he needed no more convincing of the threat from Iraq. He had to persuade others; but not himself.

From the time when he began to talk to Bush in their first meeting in 2001 about the threat from al-Qaeda and speak about the proliferation of weapons in rogue states, Blair had been moving to a position of certainty about the Iraqi threat. He cited Saddam's well-documented efforts to produce chemical and biological weapons, his gassing of Kurds in Hallabjah, and his years of deceit in answering UN demands for openness and cooperation. What could be more obvious? He was still at it. Such evidence was thin, but he stayed hopeful. As one familiar with the intelligence byways of Whitehall put it: "He was quite simply playing Mr. Micawber," the amiable but feckless character in Dickens's *David Copperfield* whose life is one long wait for "something to turn up" and produce happiness instead of misery. The forty-five-minute piece of intelligence seemed at the time to be a godsend.

But was it a gift that should have been accepted? The piece of intelligence which became the buttress of the forty-five-minute claim was said by MI6 to come from a new source so sensitive that it should not go through the usual Whitehall processes of analysis. It was not put before the analysts of the Defence Intelligence Staff. Such "compartmentalisation" isn't uncommon with

sensitive information, but the decision had far-reaching consequences. It resulted in the forty-five-minute claim being presented
in the dossier with greater certainty than the DIS staff would have
wished. Dr Brian Jones, who retired from a senior post in DIS
later in the year, complained to his superiors in writing at the time
about the way the claim was expressed, and after his retirement
he said that he had doubts about the likelihood of new information from one source at the stage changing the judgement in
the DIS about Saddam's possession of chemical weapons to the
kind of certainty which the dossier espoused.

His doubts about the strength of the intelligence appeared to
have been vindicated when MI6 later reported to the Joint Intelligence Committee that it was withdrawing the evidence: the
source was no longer regarded as sufficiently credible. But the
dossier had been published. The claim had been made, and used
to support the "serious and current" threat cited by the Prime
Minister in the Commons. Was there a threat of that kind? Dr
Jones said he did not believe that there was.

This one piece of evidence touched the heart of the Government's case. Though Blair made a much broader argument for the
confrontation with Saddam, and continued to pursue a UN solution for six months after the dossier was published, the veracity of
the dossier became vital to the Government's defence. Winning
the argument in the Hutton inquiry about whether the report had
been "sexed up" by Downing Street in the last days, Blair still had
to contend with the accusation that the dossier had stripped
careful intelligence assessments of their subtlety and caution.

Unfortunately for Downing Street, that was a suspicion that
Butler shared. In his report, he said: "Dr Jones was right to raise
concerns about the manner of expression of the forty-five minute
report in the dossier, given the vagueness of the underlying
intelligence."

He went on to say that his inquiry team did not accept MI6's
reasons for withholding this piece of evidence from DIS, and said
that the JIC should have been able to depend on expert analysis.
The report noted baldly, "In the event, the JIC had no reason to

know that that had not happened." In other words, the committee whose task it was to sift the intelligence harvest and distinguish the wheat from the chaff was not told formally that the piece of evidence which caused it to approve the strong wording of the dossier had not been processed in the normal way. The implication was—in Butler's mandarin-speak—that the JIC had not been given all the facts, though facts were meant to be its business.

Butler was clear about the consequences. "The fact that it was not shown to them (the DIS) resulted in a stronger assessment in the dossier in relation to Iraqi chemical weapons production than was justified by the available intelligence. It also deprived SIS (MI6) of key expertise that would have helped them to assess the reliability of their new source." That deprivation did not appear to disturb them. Instead, the Prime Minister gained. "We were told afterwards that this clinched it," says Dr Jones. As Blair had hoped, there was evidence to sustain the "serious and current threat" which was the engine of his policy.

But the evidence did not last. The following summer, MI6 sent word to the JIC that it was being withdrawn: the source was not reliable enough. But neither Blair nor defence secretary Geoff Hoon knew of the new doubts until Butler reported a year later. This vignette illustrates how much uncertainty flowed through the system, even as the dossier was making its case in emphatic terms. What appeared to be clear-cut was as hazy as ever.

The Butler report was a scathing analysis of the way evidence was prepared, assessed and assembled. The former Cabinet Secretary scolded the Cabinet for not demanding the papers which had been prepared for it but not circulated, regretted the lack of "collective political judgement" in Downing Street, and said that the intelligence that paved the way to war had been asked to carry an importance it simply did not warrant. It was patchy, spasmodic and flawed.

Dr Jones confirms how uncertain the analysts were. "We were not sure about these things. And because we were not sure I was surprised that this was part—perhaps the main part—of the case for war." He found it "quite staggering" that fundamental errors were taking place in the processing of intelligence, and said that the intelligence community simply did not believe that Iraq presented a major threat as described in the dossier.

The Butler account revealed how in 2002 the appetite for intelligence was in part a political desire for reassurance.

The machine was hungry and had to be fed. Even as the British government's dossier was being published in London, Tenet was gorging himself on another feast that would, in the end, prove uncomfortably indigestible for the U.S. administration. He was briefing the Senate Intelligence Committee in private session about Iraq weapons capability. He produced a startling fact. He now knew, he said, what might have been intended for use in the high-strength aluminum tubes that had been intercepted on the way to Iraq. The CIA could now say that between 1999 and 2001, Saddam had tried to buy 500 tons of uranium oxide from Niger, so-called yellowcake, which is used as fuel in nuclear reactors and is capable of being enriched to produce weapons-grade material for a nuclear bomb.

It was a sensational claim. A less detailed version made its way into Bush's State of the Union speech the following January; Colin Powell used it in a presentation at the United Nations; and without naming Niger, Blair's dossier made the same claim. It had come from MI6. But the documents on which the claims were based failed to stand up to examination. Mohammed El Baradei, the director general of the Atomic Energy Agency in Vienna, told the Security Council a month after the State of the Union reference that they were fakes. One of his officials said the forgeries were so bad that he could not believe that they had come from a serious intelligence agency. In London, one intelligence operative who saw them said: "They were dreadful. It was the Zinoviev letter all over again." That letter is notorious to students of British politics. It was intercepted by MI5 in 1924 and purported to come from the head of the Comintern in the Soviet Union; its text urged Communists in Britain to intensify their efforts to produce chaos and revolution. Leaked to the *Daily Mail* four days before the general election of that year, it is widely thought to have contributed to the defeat of the first Labour government, whose prime minister, Ramsay MacDonald, said he felt like "a man sewn into a sock and thrown into the sea." It's generally thought to be a crude fake.

The Niger yellowcake claim did not have such immediately dramatic consequences, but its appearance in a State of the Union speech and in Blair's dossier meant that when it could not be proved, it added to the feeling of crisis in the intelligence community. When the American administration dispatched Ambassador Joe Wilson to Niger to investigate and he returned to report that he could find no evidence to support it, he had to endure the spectacle of his wife's unconnected clandestine work for the CIA being revealed—a leak (and perhaps an attempted smear) that he was convinced came from a source inside the executive branch, and which led to a lengthy FBI investigation that was deeply embarrassing for the White House and particularly for those, like Dick Cheney, who were most convinced that such claims about Iraq were true.

For Blair, these mistakes were painful. Unlike Bush, he had not presented the case for challenging Iraq as a commitment to regime change. Like Clinton before him, Bush was empowered by the Iraqi Freedom Act of 1998 (which also authorized the funding of Chalabi's INC) to make the removal of Saddam a foreign policy priority, whether or not weapons of mass destruction could be found. Blair had no such luxury and was aware that if he argued the case in the same way as Bush, his Cabinet might well fall apart. Straw would certainly have resigned if the path to war hadn't led first to the United Nations and its inspectors, and it is hard to think of more than a handful of loyal Cabinet ministers who would have supported Blair if he had tried to go to war without some evidence of a military threat. It was the only case he could make.

Thus, he more than anyone needed the evidence. It was sketchy. The forty-five-minute claim referred to battlefield chemical weapons, not to anything that could threaten neighboring countries. The yellowcake sale could not be shown to have happened, and the documents that suggested that it had were so unconvincing that they couldn't be published. He was stuck with evidence of past misdemeanors by Saddam and the assumption that his behavior hadn't changed: a powerful enough pattern to make a political point, but a difficult justification for war.

Blair was personally convinced that weapons of mass destruction were in Iraq. He'd seen the National Security Agency photographs, and even when analysts in MI6 and the Defence Intelligence Staff in Whitehall told him they were not wholly convinced by the photographs, Blair was confident that proof would be found. Despite what one ex-chair of the JIC (Dame Pauline Neville-Jones) described as "turbulence" in the intelligence community at the time of the dossier, they were still encouraging Blair in the belief that sooner or later they would find "the smoking gun." Another ex-chair of the JIC said: "People from Six (MI6) were running around saying they'd just missed a truck with chemical weapons the other day, but not to worry—they'd produce one soon. There was no doubt that they believed it, and so did the Prime Minister." This version ignores some of the scepticism flowing around the intelligence committee at the time. There were serious doubts among some analysts about whether Blair's confidence that Saddam was making progress in weapons development could be *proved*, whatever they might believe. But politics was driving the machine, and its pace did not slacken.

Towards the end of 2002, with the UN process beginning to sink into the sand, the search for weapons became almost frantic. The inspectors were damning about Saddam's policy of concealment and lies, but they could not produce the hardware to prove what Blair believed. And meanwhile, the intelligence services on both sides of the Atlantic egged each other on.

An icy commentary on what happened was provided in a report on Mossad, the Israeli intelligence service with whom MI6 and the CIA were cooperating closely. The all-party foreign affairs committee of the Knesset, the Israeli parliament, reported in 2003 that the agencies reinforced each other's "exaggerated analyses" of Saddam's capability. "The uniform evaluation of the international intelligence bodies was implanted somewhat in a sort of magical circle, and in a way of reciprocal feedback, which for most cases was harmful rather then useful," a clumsy description of something simple. The committee concluded that the tendency to reassure each other that their suspicions were correct led to "exaggerated self-confidence and lack of scepticism among the international intelligence communities in the Western world." The chairman of the committee, Yuval Steinitz, said: "The Israeli services give information to the foreign services, who use it for their own purposes and pass it on and it comes back to the Israeli intelligence services. That is a circle of feedback that feeds on itself without any substance in the field."

The family was in a huddle, reassuring itself. In London and Washington, the belief that more evidence would be found was becoming a conviction, at least among the politicians. Although MI6 still had doubts about how conclusive the satellite intelligence seemed to be, according to sources who were in touch with the analysts, the organization was still reassuring Blair that it had no doubt of Saddam's continuing intention to manufacture chemical and biological weapons and to reach his goal of nuclear capability within a few years. When George Tenet made a presentation to Bush just after Christmas 2002, he saw his audience shifting uncomfortably in its seats as he showed his slides: they didn't find the evidence overwhelming. This is when, according to Bob Woodward, he resorted to the basketball court to excite Bush: "It's a slam-dunk case, Mr. President."

Was it? After the war, and a year of looking for weapons without success, Blair said: "Yes, absolutely. That was the clear intelligence and I say I think our intelligence people would still say they believe that to be right."

Asked whether the human intelligence had been wrong or whether conclusions had been drawn that weren't justified, he said: "What is true is that we haven't found them although when the work of the Iraq Survey Group [of inspectors] is published finally there will be a lot of questions that they say they can't answer. I think they will probably say—though this a matter for them—is that the strategic intent to carry on the manufacture, when the inspectors were out of the way, was still there and they've got very strong evidence of that. Now whether Saddam destroyed the physical product or not—that's the open question. The only thing that is odd is that if he did destroy it why not give chapter and verse about it."

Odd indeed. Blair couldn't quite believe that Saddam had abandoned his weapons without boasting about it to *someone* in order to win some grudging credit. And if he didn't destroy them, why did all the intelligence that seemed to point to their existence not bear fruit? Blair was still insisting, as the handover of sovereignty in Iraq approached in summer 2004, that weapons might be found—"I'm not yet prepared to close the book on that at all"—but he was awaiting the report of his first Cabinet secretary and head of the Civil Service, Lord Butler, investigating the intelligence background to the war, and knew that the expectation in Whitehall was that it would be critical of the way the evidence was sifted, prepared, and evaluated.

As in Washington, where Tenet's resignation coincided with embarrassing revelations about the lack of alarm at al-Qaeda's activities before 9/11 and the talk on Capitol Hill was of bungling at the CIA and inadequacy in the FBI, Whitehall was preparing for a critical report that would almost certainly lead to a reorganization of the intelligence and security agencies. It was also seething with intrigue about the struggle that surrounded the collection and presentation of intelligence before the war that had been exposed so publicly.

The central figure was John Scarlett. As chair of the JIC, he supervised the clearinghouse for all intelligence and the forum for debate (and argument) among the agencies. He was a spy's spy. Reared in MI6, his greatest undercover exploits had been in Moscow. In the early 1980s, as an intelligence officer in the British embassy, Scarlett ran the KGB superagent Oleg Gordievsky, whence came a stream of intelligence from the heart of the Kremlin to be used by Margaret Thatcher and Ronald Reagan in the period when the last of the lumbering old warhorses of the Soviet Union—Konstantin Chernenko and Yuri Andropov—were in power before the reforming Mikhail Gorbachev arrived. It was Scarlett who devised the elaborate "exfiltration" plan that Gordievsky used when he realized that the KGB had rumbled him. He was taken in a black box in the trunk of a diplomat's car on a long journey to Finland and thence to London. Back in Moscow in the 1990s, Scarlett arranged the defection of Vasili Mitrokhin, who had assembled a vast archive of documents when he was arranging their transfer to new KGB headquarters, providing the most detailed picture yet seen of how the Soviet foreign intelligence service conducted its operations. So Scarlett was an operator.

As JIC chairman, he supervised the sorting of intelligence from his old service for the Prime Minister and the rest of Whitehall and monitored relations with friendly intelligence services, principally American. The CIA station chief and the liaison officer in London for Washington's Defense Intelligence Agency are automatically allowed to attend most of the sessions of the JIC. They are family.

But Scarlett was also working with a prime minister who had become fascinated soon after he arrived in office by the emerging evidence of an unpredictable and threatening terrorist network and had therefore developed an early intimacy with his spooks. He wanted to know everything and spent a great deal of time studying the reports. When Dearlove became C in 1999, he found a prime minister who wanted to see a great deal of him. Dearlove was hardly likely to resist. As it happened, he had a good relationship with Blair. In one of their early encounters before he became C, he had arranged to give up a ticket for the opera in St. Petersburg where he was due to sit next to the mayor, Vladimir Putin, and turn it over to Blair, who found Putin rather more interesting than the opera and began what became a useful friendship. In his years as C, he spent a good deal of time travelling with the Prime Minister, which few of his predecessors had done. Blair's plane would touch down in Syria or Israel or India, and a little-recognized bespectacled figure would be somewhere in the gaggle of officials trailing behind him, soon slipping off to do his own business.

He once almost came unstuck in the United States, where flunkies at Camp David did not realize that, unlike the CIA director, he was meant to be a figure who never emerged into the public gaze. At one press conference they prepared a place card for him and put it on a table where it would be in full view of the arriving journalists, for whom it would have been a novel experience. A Number 10 official spotted it just in time and whisked the label away, while Dearlove headed for the airport as fast as he could. The innocent reporters didn't know he had been there.

Whoever was C depended on having a good relationship with Blair. Although Dearlove's day-to-day contact was with Straw in the Foreign Office, a man who shared his caution about the strength of the "evidence" in the American photographs that were being waved around in the White House, he saw a good deal of the Prime Minister. Throughout the autumn of 2002, he was reassuring about the ability of his service to find the evidence that would show Saddam was continuing to defy the UN. The British position was still that such evidence could be found. In Washington, Bush was under pressure from hard-liners who took a different view. Rather than proof against Saddam being needed, only proof from him that he no longer had weapons should prevent war. The fact that such "proof" was impossible was, for them, the justification for an invasion.

This was the position being resisted in the British Foreign Office, but it was one to which Blair was being drawn. The longer he searched for the smoking gun and smelled not a whiff of cordite, the more he convinced himself that Saddam's history and his bombastic defiance of the UN was enough. But MI6 and the other agencies knew that the Cabinet was wobbly and needed something stronger. The trouble was that in the Defence Intelligence Staff, where the technical assessments were made, there was little confidence that evidence of weapons of mass destruction would be found. Although they had no doubt of Saddam's intentions, nor of the programmes he had set up in the past, they could not guarantee to provide Blair with the clincher. This was frustrating to Dearlove, who was under pressure to put incontrovertible evidence on Blair's desk. His discomfort was exacerbated by Scarlett.

The former man from Moscow was seen in his old service as something of a defector—to Downing Street. Did not Alastair Campbell himself call him "a mate"? And he was ambitious. In the jockeying around Blair, he was an important player. At Downing Street, the most important foreign affairs adviser was Sir David Manning, and not far behind was Sir David Omand, former head of GCHQ and now Blair's security coordinator, who might have become C a few years before had illness not intervened when the vacancy arose. With Eliza Manningham-Buller proving a feisty director general of MI5 (though in the American Embassy she was less popular than Dearlove), there was an energetic juggling of courtiers. In this battle for influence, Scarlett was proving a formidable warrior. He controlled the daily intelligence briefing seen by Blair; he moderated the disputes between MI6 and MI5; he sat one rung higher than the heads of individual agencies; and (as was demonstrated in the preparation of the dossier, as revealed in the Hutton report) he had the facility to package raw intelligence in a way that found favour with his political masters.

It was his committee that built up the case Blair was to use for war. In so doing, he earned Blair's gratitude. When Dearlove's retirement was announced—after his normal allotted span of five years—he nominated as his replacement the senior MI6 officer he had appointed as his assistant the year before. He had been put in charge of coordinating MI6's Iraq reports (although he was one of the service's Chinese experts), and it did not work in his favour. The committee that considered the candidates (chaired by Omand) chose Scarlett. Inside MI6, this was unpopular, according to two well-informed sources. There was disgruntlement in the Foreign Office, the service's supervising department; and in the Defence Intelligence Staff (which feared it was about to be sucked up by MI6 in a classic Whitehall power grab), there was unease.

The settled view of those who were privy to the preparation of the Iraq evidence was that it was Scarlett's skill in persuading Blair of the weight of the pieces of disparate evidence that found him such favor. MI6 could argue that it was on the verge of completing the jigsaw, but it never quite managed to do it. By contrast, Scarlett seemed the alchemist who could produce the gold.

By the time he was appointed C, however, the intelligence assessments that had persuaded were the object of great scepticism. However convinced the Prime Minister was—"If you talk to people in our intelligence or American intelligence they will say that they believe the intelligence we got was essentially right"—others were not at all sure. That word "essentially" covers many a glitch. The yellowcake that was supposed to have been sold to Saddam seems to have been illusory; the threat from the weapons that could be prepared in forty-five minutes was limited to the battlefield; and the pictures of moving laboratories and supposed chemical and biological plants were never turned into solid objects. And one of Blair's closest advisers through the Iraq crisis said bluntly in 2004: "As for the stocks of anthrax which we thought he had, the fact is that we were plain wrong." David Kay, the chief arms inspector in Iraq, did tell the BBC in October 2003 that no one doubted that Saddam held stocks of weapons of mass destruction before 1991 and it could not be proved that he had disposed of them despite thirteen years of UN activity in the country. But three months later, he told National Public Radio in the United States: "I don't think they exist. I actually think the intelligence community owes the president an apology."

Blair said: "There are two things that you know. One is that he had them. The other is that we haven't found them." After a year of coalition troops in Iraq, battered by his party for his dedication to the war and to Bush, this defiant statement of the obvious might have led him to something close to despair. But it hadn't. "The only two alternatives are that they are either still there or that in an extraordinary act of self-destruction he decided to get rid of the weapons but refuse to tell the inspectors about it." He has concluded that of the two alternatives, the first is by far the most likely.

Ask him if he believes history will vindicate his belief that WMD were being developed in a way that was a threat and he says: "Yes. Absolutely." He is a man almost devoid of doubt.

"You've got to remember two things. First of all the intelligence was that when they realised the inspectors were coming back in there was going to be a strategy of concealment. We're not talking about a huge amount of stuff and you're talking about a country the size of France. It's not hard to conceal the stuff. And secondly, the security situation has been such that it has been very difficult to conduct these searches." The Iraq Survey Group, at the time he was speaking, had visited less than one-third of the likely munitions sites, he said.

But Blair's confidence conceals the turmoil that enveloped the transatlantic intelligence community as completely as he and Bush were cocooned in their certainty. The family that encompasses the eavesdroppers and picture analysts, the spies who befriend generals and bureaucrats, the technicians who try to follow the trail of equipment and arms, and the elders of the spook business who direct their operations has been strained and riven by arguments in the Iraq story.

The CIA was furious at the yellowcake mistake, which caused Bush to mislead Congress; MI6 was wary of the satellite evidence that persuaded Blair but not its own analysts; the Defence Intelligence Staff in London was unpersuaded by the claims that chemical weapons were still being made; the Foreign Office and the State Department were suspicious of the pieces of intelligence provided by the contacts of Chalabi, the Pentagon's man; the Pentagon was suspicious of the material coming from Allawi, because he was the CIA and MI6's man, and a rival to Chalabi for power. As Bush and Blair sent their ambassadors into a last round of fruitless negotiation at the UN, the intelligence assessment was a muddle. Bush could say at least that he was persuaded of the justification for war by Saddam's past and believed Resolution 1441 gave him legal power; Blair was in a much more difficult position, caught in the entrails of the intelligence argument. It was not settled before war began and seemed to become more complicated after Iraq fell.

Tenet argued that he couldn't have ignored the human intelligence from Iraq—most of it originating in Chalabi's organization—but he acknowledged in his Georgetown University speech that it was not conclusive. "We did not ourselves penetrate the inner sanctum. Our agents were on the periphery of WMD activity," he said. Were the British in a better position? There was the forty-five-minute revelation, which came from a fairly senior military source. But there was nothing more to put in the dossier. By early 2003, when Blair wanted more evidence to put in the public domain, his officials produced a series of assertions that included some plucked from a Ph.D. thesis more than a decade old, found on the Internet. It is hard to believe that if a startling piece of intelligence from a source inside Iraq had been available it would not have been made public. As Adlai Stevenson threw the photographs of embryonic Cuban missile sites on a table at the UN in 1962, so Blair or Bush would have loved to have made a public show of certainty. None was available.

Porter Goss, the former CIA case officer and Congressman who would be Bush's choice to succeed Tenet, said simply: "We had a lot of marginal information—but we really hadn't got the breakthrough to a really good source in the inner circle that could have tipped us off." The former vice chairman of the National Intelligence Council in Washington, Gregory Treverton, said: "The least appreciated part of the story so far is how little collection there was and how little new information there was, particularly developed by the U.S. So you had people with strong views based on what had been the case—Saddam's behavior before—making inferences in the presence of not very much information."

Those inferences were encouraged by the political imperatives that Bush and Blair had established in their thinking on Iraq. Something had to be done; the information had to be pieced together; the case had to be made. The reason for the turbulence in the intelligence community in London, and the battles in Washington that culminated in Tenet's resignation at a moment of maximum embarrassment for him and for the administration, was that intelligence had failed to satisfy a political need. The leaders were hungry. In Washington and London that desire led to turmoil in the intelligence agencies, which worried that they were being drawn into political arguments with the opponents of war in support of their leaders, instead of retaining their independence as analysts. In both countries, inquiries after Iraq fell turned up evidence of how deep the disquiet was.

The reason was that they couldn't pretend to their political masters that the intelligence was as clear as they would like. It was patchy, grey, and intermittent. Tenet said satellite photos showed "a pattern of activity" that suggested movement from previous weapons sites was being concealed; there was reconstruction of facilities that had once been used as dual-purpose weapons manufacturing sites; human sources were passing on information about Saddam's efforts to get material needed for weapons. It was all there, but it wasn't. Hans Blix and his inspectors found unexplained gaps in the inventory of known chemicals, but no evidence of weapons manufacture; evidence of old weapons, but no new ones; plenty of mystery, but no certainty.

Through this fog there moved some strange characters, especially Ahmed Chalabi. He was not trusted by the British government and was disliked by the CIA and the State Department, which had worked with him before. The CIA pulled the plug on a coup attempt that he had planned in Iraq in 1995, and Chalabi continued to blame them for the deaths of many of his men when Saddam invaded the Kurdish north the following year. So his intelligence became part of Washington's own power struggle, going to Rumsfeld's Office of Special Plans in the Pentagon (an outfit hated by the State Department and the CIA) and to Cheney's office. As rival material, Allawi's claims, which were funnelled to Washington via MI6, attracted just as much odium from the Chalabi-supporting hawks. The intelligence maze therefore absorbed the political strains over Iraq, and in turn the politics suffered from the complexity of the resulting puzzle.

With political leaders demanding evidence and agencies competing with each other to produce the most startling fact, it was inevitable that a ratchet effect would produce some exaggeration.

But the problem may be deeper and simpler: that the core of the intelligence assessment was simply wrong.

One burrower through the darker corridors of Whitehall put it like this. "It was a blunder made by all the intelligence agencies— France, Germany and Australia as well as Britain and the United States. If the Russians did the same, they're not saying."

There was every reason for Saddam to allow lies to spread about his state of readiness to attack or his progression toward nuclear capability. Still obsessed by Iran next door, it was important that he should appear to Teheran to be stronger than he was. It was also natural that in propping up a regime fuelled by a cult of personality as well as cold brutality, lies should be the currency on the street. When one senior Blair official, his face creased by the strains of the crisis, admitted, "We were probably just wrong," he was probably just right.

Blair moved naturally to a position of justification that was built on Saddam's past crimes, his penchant for aggression, and his undoubted ambition for deadly weapons, but it greatly increased Blair's political difficulties and isolation. He had to do so not only because his intelligence assessments promised evidence that they could not find but because the turmoil among his secret servants became public. For the first time, as a crisis developed and a war was fought, the details of the advice on the Prime Minister's desk began to seep out. The Hutton report opened a side door into the world of intelligence, and in Washington the anxieties and near panic that followed 9/11 meant that the CIA and FBI were subjected to more intense public scrutiny than ever before.

The innards of the relationship between the two capitals were exposed. While president and prime minister and their diplomats wrestled with a crisis of power—and tried to manage the persistent disputes in their own cabinets—the public began to understand some of the ambiguities and the ironies of a world of intelligence where the object is to produce clarity and simplicity but the assumption is that they can almost never be found.

Driven by their political masters to prove their worth, the spies squeeze their sources and magnify their pictures. They search for connections and listen for a whisper that may lead them home. They try to prevent war—it's usually their business—but sometimes they find themselves pulled into the morass. Then they find they have to take the blame.

No Prime Minister had revealed more about the workings of intelligence. Blair did so partly because Kelly's death compelled him to commission the Hutton Report. Because of its findings he was forced to ask Butler to delve into territory which had once been out of bounds to all but a select few, and to produce an intelligence road map for the public. But Blair had also been drawn to the idea that there was virtue in a degree of openness. In the Prime Minister's mind, his motives and actions would be more easily explained—and justified—if the public knew more of what he knew from his secret sources.

The trouble was that as the spooks themselves had been brought up to know, the intelligence settled nothing. After Hutton and Butler, Blair found himself even more on the defensive. To his critics, the case for war seemed to have been weakened, not strengthened. From Butler, he drew the comfort that his motives were not questioned—his former Cabinet Secretary concluded that he had acted in good faith in making the case laid out in the dossier and in his speeches to the Commons. But Butler did not conclude that the case itself was sound. The war might not have been fought on a pretence, but the evidence used by Blair for justification was less certain than those statements and speeches had suggested. The intelligence, he concluded, was flawed.

Never had the sinews of intelligence and war been revealed so clearly. Yet the clarity itself was an illusion. Wreaths of fog still clung to the dossier, the intelligence reports, the decisions made in Downing Street. The arguments were laid bare, but the war remained a puzzle.

# CHAPTER 8

# CONSEQUENCES

The speed of Saddam's fall gave Bush and Blair a few weeks of illusory optimism. It was as puzzling as the absence of weapons of mass destruction, a mystery that seemed to confound the thinking that had led them to Baghdad. No chemical or biological attacks, no last stand by the Revolutionary Guard to turn the streets of the capital into "the gates of hell" that Saddam had promised, no sign of the resistance of an army of nearly half a million men who were supposed to have trained to repel the American invader. There was only collapse, and evidence of a regime that had lost all its once fearsome strength. It was odd, but it mattered that it had been quick.

The simplicity of the coalition advance, however, was a headline that concealed the truth of the story. Donald Rumsfeld's refusal to take the advice of his chiefs of staff on the number of troops required was apparently justified by the quick fall of Baghdad: in time, it would be seen as a mistake that would cost lives and precious time. The implosion of the army and Saddam's apparatus encouraged the occupying coalition to disband the Ba'ath Party and the security forces, a decision always thought by

British officials to be an error, which duly became a painful complication when the time came to try to put together a new security apparatus without even the skeleton of an organization. Above all, the small number of coalition casualties (compared with the several thousand Iraqis who died in the advance on Baghdad) induced a false confidence in London and Washington. Although Bush and Blair gave routine warnings of difficult days ahead, they were clearly relieved at the speed and ease of the first phase of the campaign. That relief was premature.

When they met at Camp David in the last week of March 2003, Blair thought he could make progress with Bush on the UN. Perhaps Bush could be persuaded to show the enthusiasm for UN help in reconstruction that had proved so difficult in the run-up to war. He was happy to speak of a UN role in aid, but there was no progress on political involvement. Ten days later, in Northern Ireland, Blair tried again.

This time he had more success, though it caused consternation in the White House. The phrase that Downing Street wanted to hear would include, it hoped, the words "vital role." Condoleezza Rice was, as ever, the channel through which the worries of those administration officials who were not present could be relayed to Bush. And, as the *New York Times* reported afterwards, she was pressured directly from Cheney's office to resist these words, which seemed to the hawks to be an unravelling of everything they had achieved in managing an invasion without the specific UN authorization Blair had hoped to get. Bush, however, was elated. The war was going well. He believed he could see an end to the worst of it within a few weeks. At their last meeting, he had heaped praise on Blair—"We've learned that he's a man of courage, that he's a man of vision, and we're proud to have him as a friend"—and he was ready to help. Blair was struggling with a wave of public scepticism toward the war and was in the familiar position of needing the White House to show that he had been given something in return for his support for Bush. So the words "vital role" were uttered, nine times.

There would be a role for the UN, which was vital for Blair. But it was unspecified. This was hardly surprising. However, Bush had no notion of what the appropriate role might be. And a number of senior members of his administration were determined that there should be no role at all, apart from assistance in the distribution of aid.

At this stage, however, such questions were for the future. These war leaders were confident that they were about to claim victory soon.

Baghdad Airport was already in coalition hands, and within a day of their meeting at Hillsborough Castle outside Belfast came the moment that symbolized the end of Saddam—the pulling down of his statue in the middle of Baghdad. Its hollow metal legs pointed to the skies and it lay as a humiliating memento of the regime, though the leader himself was off on secret wanderings that would keep him out of American hands for months. By the end of April, Bush was ready to say that the war was over.

A banner saying "Mission Accomplished" was draped on the deck of the aircraft carrier USS *Abraham Lincoln* before Bush landed in the fighter plane he was allowed to pilot briefly, to declare that "major combat operations" were over, words that would echo around him as his re-election campaign began and the news from Iraq became a daily story of injury, death and incipient chaos.

Blair did not have Bush's luxury of a population that might be ready to believe good news from Iraq. He was also aware of the coolness of European leaders, who were already meeting to discuss a new European and Security Defence Union (without Blair) and the sour opposition of Putin, whom he visited in Moscow just before Bush's celebratory announcement. In his first press conference since the end of the war, Blair was asked the awkward question that would pursue him for the next year and more: "Where are the weapons of mass destruction?" Even at this stage, there was a weariness in his reply: "As I say every time I am asked, I remain confident that they will be found."

Although his defence of the war was already moving closer to the ground occupied by Bush in his enthusiasm for pure regime change, Blair was still stuck with the argument he had used to persuade a reluctant Cabinet and party to go to war with him: that the danger from Saddam was real and not theoretical, not a problem to be dealt with in a distant future. He needed the evidence, but none was appearing. Even as people saw pictures of a strangely calm Baghdad and heard that resistance seemed patchy and weak, they seemed to be unconvinced by the achievement. On May 12, Clare Short finally left Blair's Cabinet, accusing him of being "increasingly obsessed by his place in history."

It was a telling shaft. Short had lost a good deal of credibility on the Left by using a radio interview to criticize Blair during the most recent UN negotiations, but she had decided not to resign. Even to some of those who agreed with her most passionately about the war, it seemed an oddly indecisive rebellion. To accuse a prime minister of recklessness—it was a word she used several times—was so unusual for a Cabinet minister that no one could imagine that she would want to stay, and it was assumed she'd leave the next morning before she was fired. She didn't, and Blair decided against throwing her out on the spot, partly because he believed that martyrdom would help her to build up a campaign against him but also because he realized that if she was allowed to stay in the government (as he suspected she'd like to), she would appear to be a critic afraid to pay the price of her view. His calculation was right. Short found herself accused by ideological soul mates of clinging to office in an undignified fashion, and by the time she sent her letter of resignation weeks later, she had lost the advantage that she might have gained if she had walked out sooner. But her accusation that Blair was playing a longer game, with a strategy that went beyond Iraq, reflected an unease at the alliance he had made that was much deeper than an anxiety about day-to-day tactics in the streets of Baghdad or Basra.

Blair's troubles were a more accurate reflection of the post-conquest problems that would assail the two leaders than the public support that raised Bush's poll ratings in the immediate aftermath of the fall of Baghdad. Blair's experiences refuted the easy assumption that the hawks had been right and that Iraq could be transformed quickly and more peacefully than the United Nations, the European Union, the Democrats, and other assorted doubters could have imagined. Blair could not have appeared under a banner carrying the "Mission Accomplished" message, and if he had issued the deck of playing cards that American administrators soon produced in Iraq, carrying the pictures of the fifty-two most wanted heads of the regime, he would have been scorned by his colleagues, perhaps even laughed at by the public. Unlike Bush at this stage, he was already dealing with the consequences of the decisions they had made together.

The atmosphere was strange. In Baghdad, a certain unreal calm had settled. Easter weekend fell in April, a couple of weeks after Saddam scuttled away and his palaces were ransacked. Most of the explosions came from the regular destruction of arms dumps around the city or from minor firefights that were only brief bursts of noise in the night. In the streets, the market traders began to emerge gingerly to do business again. Most shops were still boarded up, and the poverty that had been partly the result of UN sanctions for years was obvious everywhere, but behind the fearfulness and suspicion that still held sway it was possible to sense a stirring of hope.

In Baghdad's small Catholic cathedral on Good Friday, 300 or so worshippers met for morning Mass. They were defiant, as they'd had to be for years, but they were daring to hope that life might start to find a normal pattern again. Borrowing phones from Western reporters, they tried to get through to relatives who had fled to Syria or the Gulf or Lebanon to say that all was well, or at least that they were alive. Their archbishop, tending a tiny flock that had struggled for years against state-run violence and intimidation, said that victory had to be more than the removal of Saddam: life had to begin to mean something again for people who had known three wars in twenty years, the pain of sanctions, and the heavy hand of a totalitarian regime. He was happy, but his eyes betrayed his refusal to be too hopeful.

The danger of optimism was, in those early days, greater than the danger from snipers or angry crowds. On the Shiite pilgrimage south to Kerbala, which began that weekend, it was possible to imagine for a moment that the transformation of the country had begun. Thousands upon thousands of pilgrims began the traditional barefooted march to two of the holiest mosques, to commemorate seventh-century martyrs whose deaths in Kerbala are still mourned today. The pilgrimage had never been formally banned in the Saddam years, but those who took part were marked men. Now they converged from every corner of the country, and the road south from Baghdad was crowded for four days with lines of pilgrims who sang together and stopped to hear sermons by the side of the road, clustering around huge pots of steaming rice and soup, where Western strangers were invited to join in the sustaining meal before the crowd took to the road again.

In Kerbala itself, where all the narrow streets seemed to lead to the golden domes of the mosques, there was a vast throng assembled. It numbered probably 2 million, and in the midst of the solemnity associated with the pilgrimage, there were high spirits. These Shiites did use the word *liberation*, and Western correspondents found themselves asked to send the good tidings back to Britain or America. The pilgrims thanked Allah for Bush and Blair.

The month after Saddam's fall provided genuine evidence of the sense of release and revealed considerable goodwill toward the occupying forces. But it was limited. Even then, only a few days after Saddam's departure, the thanks to the troops were accompanied by the hope—almost always—that they wouldn't be there for long. And there lay the contradiction that the coalition governments would find it impossible to resolve quickly.

The very speed of the transformation concealed the difficulties ahead. The expectations aroused when coalition troops attached the steel hawser to Saddam's statue or when they mingled happily on the fringes of the pilgrim throng in Kerbala could not be fulfilled. The idea that any of this would be easy—that water supplies could be restored in days, that the electricity system could be reconnected, that sewage would flow away out of sight again, that the banks might begin to print money that had some value—was doomed to be undermined.

You did not have to scrape the surface for long to glimpse the depth of the problem. Not far from the centre of Baghdad is a women's hospital where many of the city's children are born. Throughout the bombing that preceded the war, some of the midwives stayed at their posts, protecting their patients instead of going home to their own children. There was no light for most of the time, and their equipment was rudimentary. Proper sterilization of the instruments was impossible. They often had to deliver babies in the dark. After American troops arrived, three armoured cars were stationed outside the doors as protection. But none of the soldiers could speak a word of Arabic. They were fearful of snipers and suspicious of all the locals. The cultural distance from those they were meant to protect—from what?—was immense. They were kids from the Midwest who knew nothing of the place they'd been sent. There, at the moment of "liberation," the air was laced with suspicion and tension.

The situation was worsened by the awkward decision of Turkey to refuse to allow the American Fourth Infantry to enter Iraq across its border, which meant that the troops sent first into the streets of Baghdad were instead young marines who had raced up from the south and who had never been expected to do the job. As one of their officers said outside the hospital: "These guys are great at running up a beach, but not this." Even where it seemed as if a certain freedom was being granted, and guaranteed, it had its limits. Everyone knew that some of those who'd disappeared from Ba'ath headquarters in a dozen towns, or from the bleak prisons of Baghdad, or from government offices on the banks of the Tigris would be prepared to fight the invader, sooner or later. The calm would not last.

Yet it was persuasive enough to cause Washington to make more mistakes. The lack of the welcome parties for the liberators should have given a clue. In the Pentagon, it had been assumed that there would be scenes in Baghdad that harked back to the fall of the Berlin Wall. Perhaps there might even be flowers strewn in the street. There weren't. People were still scared, and they harboured long-standing suspicions of liberators who had been imposing debilitating sanctions through the UN for many years and whose bombers had patrolled their skies for a decade. Glad though most of them were to see the collapse of the regime and the departure of Saddam, they were not ready to do what Paul Wolfowitz especially had predicted—fill the streets and shower the incoming troops with thanks and kisses of welcome. Iraq had been a country alive with suspicion and mistrust for too long; and the weariness of war could not be swept away in a few days.

This was obvious from the start, but nonetheless the Pentagon still dismissed the CIA–State Department plan for postwar recon-struction. Rumsfeld had believed it unnecessary when it had landed on his desk a few months before the war. He saw no reason for it to be given credibility now, and since the early days of occupation were a matter of military tactics and not politics, he was able to hold sway. The consequences of his equally significant refusal to give the Joint Chiefs the troops they believed they required were also hidden at first: months would go by before the insurgents' attacks on American troops revealed the inability of the occupying force to cope with the resistance from Saddam loyalists and militants who'd come across the border from Syria and Turkey and Jordan, determined to take the fight to the Western enemy. The misjudgements were compounded by the strange choice of General Jay Garner as the first administrator of the Coalition Provisional Authority (CPA).

Garner was, in the view of a number of those who worked closely with him, a disaster. One senior British figure whose responsibilities meant that he spent much of his time in liaison with the Americans put it like this: "The trouble with Jay Garner was that he couldn't impose his personality on a sparsely populated bar, let alone a country." That comment illustrated the extent to which the British contingent felt that the orders from Washington had simply not taken into account the urgency and the complexity of the political task that reconstruction demanded. Garner, the retired soldier with evangelical zeal, seemed to be the "clash of civilization" made flesh. He revealed how difficult it was to appear a liberator without seeming an occupier, too.

When he was replaced by Paul Bremer, the atmosphere seemed at first to improve, but the problems got worse. Within a few weeks the fruits of victory had soured. The disbanded Iraqi forces would be dauntingly difficult to reconstruct in another form; the State Department's Arabists had argued for a careful transformation that would build on the structures that had served Iraq in the past, but they had been sidelined in Washington. Now, according to one member of the CPA, "they just sat weeping into their soup" at headquarters in Baghdad, watching policy dictated from Washington play into the hands of militants who were beginning to increase the number of attacks on coalition forces or those Iraqis who were starting to volunteer for service in the police or the army. It was only after Bush declared the end of major combat operations that serious damage began to be done to American troops; only after Bremer told the world, "Ladies and gentlemen, we got 'im!" and a hairy and wild-eyed Saddam was seen being pulled from his hiding hole did troops begin to suffer an alarming number of casualties. Despite the Pentagon's determination to avoid publicity, the depth of the troop losses began to become clear to the communities across America that had sent them. Week by week, the insurgents began to inflict enough damage to suggest to the Iraqis that the battle was far from over. It was patchy violence, but its impact was felt in the United States.

As reservists who'd expected to be coming home in three or six months were told they'd be staying, the seriousness of the struggle began to become clearer. Troops were bedding down for a long haul.

In Britain, Blair had never made the victory a popular affair as Bush had done. He was tormented by the failure to find the weapons he had believed would justify the invasion and prove his forebodings right. His hopes for proper UN involvement were undermined by the Baghdad bomb that killed twenty UN staff, including Sergio Vieira de Mello, one of Kofi Annan's closest colleagues and one of the handful of international diplomats who could have hoped to broker the deals with Sunni and Shia, between the competing egos of politicians now starting to circle each other in the first stages of government making. Blair never had the moment of release that Bush sensed when he stood on the *Abraham Lincoln*'s flight deck. But Bush's experience was the more misleading.

The politics of Blair's war had allowed him little relief. Before the vote in March 2003 when he asked the House of Commons to approve the principle of military action (which he won by 396 to 217), he had told his family, in all seriousness, that it might be the end of him. A year later, he acknowledged that a bigger Labour rebellion could have forced him out. "I thought it was possible. Yeah. It was always possible that it could happen." Opinion polls in Britain suggested that a solid majority opposed Blair through-out the war. Even had he won a new UN resolution with some specific authorization of war, he'd only have persuaded a few. In his own party, he was dangerously exposed. Bush had been right to become alarmed that Blair might not survive and to have the White House brief him on the niceties of parliamentary procedure, which had previously been a closed book to him. Yet though he understood the crude fact that Blair's premiership was threatened, he could not sit in Washington and understand the nature of Blair's crisis, which had engaged the entire British government.

Even on such a fundamental question as the legality of war, Blair found himself in trouble. After the passage of Resolution 1441, he suffered the embarrassment of the resignation from the Foreign Office of one of its senior legal advisers, Sarah Wilmshurst, on the devastatingly straightforward grounds that she had con-cluded that without another resolution authorizing military action if Saddam continued to defy UN instructions, war was illegal under international law. She saw no way around the obstacle and said so as she left. A year afterwards, she would not discuss the details of her discussions inside the government but said she was justified by the fact that most international lawyers believed that 1441 was not an adequate justification for the invasion. By contrast, in the United States, the question of legality never turned into a central challenge for Bush. The mere suggestion could be dismissed as a partisan attack by someone gearing up for the looming presidential campaign. But for Blair, it mattered.

When the attorney general, whose quasi-judicial responsibilities mean he is answerable to the courts as well as to the Prime Minister, was asked for his advice, he was, from Blair's point of view, troublingly ambiguous. He gave an opinion that made invasion legal under the authority of Resolution 1441, but there was an addendum that alarmed Blair. Lord Goldsmith's view was that in post-Saddam Iraq, coalition forces had authority to deal with security but nothing else. Only the UN had the authority to give instructions for the political reconstruction of the country. It was the attorney general's advice that made Blair so insistent at the meeting with Bush in Northern Ireland, as the short conquest came to its end, to get a statement affirming the centrality of the UN.

He didn't want it simply because it might look good, but because his Cabinet might be told that Britain was behaving illegally in Iraq if it was acting under American rather than UN auspices. The attorney general's warnings were never made public, and though it was insisted at Downing Street that his fundamental assurance of the legality of war was clear, no one was able to examine its fine print. A year later, it had still not surfaced.

The prevailing view among other European leaders was that the war was either illegal or a political blunder of such magnitude that the question of legality hardly mattered. However, there were exceptions. José María Aznar in Spain and Silvio Berlusconi in Italy did not represent the centre of gravity of the EU, and their very support further infuriated those in the Labour Party who believed Blair was wrong, because they seemed to be the evidence that he was drifting to the Right, not just in his alliance with Bush but in his choice of friends in Europe, too.

Not for a week, and scarcely even for a day, did Blair feel that pressure lift. Although a natural rally-round-the-leader response followed the dispatch of troops and their performance in Basra in appearing to maintain civil order without recourse to heavy-handedness was praised by many politicians and commentators on all sides of the argument, Blair was suffering over Iraq from the time he made it clear, in the latter part of 2002, that he agreed with Bush's analysis of the Saddam threat.

From then on, anything that tended to cast doubt on the seriousness of the threat or its imminence was used to demon-strate that he had made an error. When the government produced the second dossier in February 2003 to help bolster a case that was creaking at the seams, Blair was horribly embarrassed when it was revealed that parts of its "evidence" about Saddam's Iraq had been harvested by his communications director, Alastair Campbell, from a Ph.D. thesis written more than ten years earlier and discovered on the Internet. Having already had the humili-ation of the nonexistent Niger yellowcake "sale" to Saddam, and with the UN inspectors saying that they could settle the arguments about WMD if they were given more time, it was hard for Blair to appear to be confident that he was set on the right course.

But as so often with Blair in the past, appearances were misleading. However uncomfortable he might have seemed and whatever his worries about persuading his colleagues and the public of the justice of his cause, he had no internal doubts.

His convictions were settled when he passed up the last chance to change his mind a few weeks before the war. Hans Blix was asking for just a little more time; the Security Council was telling Blair that it was not ready to authorize war. Demonstrators were encamped outside Downing Street as a daily reminder of his rising unpopularity. His party was splintering and would have looked even more rattled if the Conservative opposition had been in a condition to mount sharp and sustained attacks. He knew that his military advisers were concerned about the consequences of a long campaign on an army that had many responsibilities and insufficient reserves. Although his intelligence services were encouraging, they could not be certain in their judgements about Iraq. Yet he didn't change his mind.

Speaking one year later, he was as certain as he had been just after 9/11 of the necessity of confrontation in Iraq. Indeed, the passage of time and the onset of difficulties and scepticism around him appeared to have made him even more determined. "It was obvious to me after September 11 that you had to see through the issue of WMD—how you dealt with it, how you couldn't let this fester any longer, that you had to go and get after it. The place to start was Iraq, for very obvious reasons, because of the history. But I was hopeful right up until the last moment that it would be possible to resolve it peacefully."

When Robin Cook and the other most prominent critics accused Blair of having made a decision to back Bush as a matter of principle, they were right. It was not a matter of juggling advantages and deciding how to make the deal. He was determined to do it. That explains, of course, his refusal or his failure—as even some of his intimate staff would put it—to increase his demands on Bush at those moments when those around him wanted to hear him be aggressive. At Crawford in April 2002, at Camp David six months later, at the White House the following January, and in dozens of phone calls in between, he had the opportunity to step back. But his fundamental commitment to the idea of disarming Saddam was so strong, so intimately bound up in the emotions he felt and the conclusions he reached on 9/11, that it wasn't going to wither away.

Blair is convinced this determination is his great strength; his critics are just as sure it is a weakness that clouds his judgement. Some of them explain it, inadequately, by reference to his religious faith, and others, even more implausibly, as his desire to act obstructionist toward the Labour Party with whom his love-hate relationship has been such a hard struggle and such a part of his political personality. The truth is not so simple.

As became clear in the year after the invasion, he had become convinced that he had stumbled on a truth about the world of the new century that many other leaders either didn't understand or wanted to deny. Having crossed the Rubicon to war in the Balkans and having spoken of a theory of pre-emptive intervention two years before 9/11 in his Chicago speech, he now felt himself to be a statesman with the right to talk of grand strategy. It was precisely what his critics complained about: he was willing to be Tony *contra mundum*, awkward and alone. They thought it was a denial of the history of the twentieth century, because it appeared to run against the grain of international consensus and the idea of a stronger and more flexible UN, released from its Cold War straitjacket. He believed the contrary, that it was the proper response to a world that hadn't woken up yet.

"When 9/11 happened it should have been a wake-up call to the world. Unfortunately it was only a wake-up call to America—and to us I think, and to some others. But everyone else has just shrugged their shoulders." When he says that, it is hard not to picture Chirac, who has the most eloquent Gallic shrug of all.

"I had already been becoming extremely worried about this proliferation of WMD. I had actually had a discussion with George Bush about it at our first meeting. But I could see this Islamic extremism—and there's no point in calling it something else, because that is what it is—a total perversion of the faith of Islam, but nonetheless it is like that—and I could see it in Palestine, in Chechnya, in Kashmir, in large parts of the Middle East, starting to distort attitudes and to bring about a very dangerous conjunction of terrorism and states that are utterly unstable and repressive. What 9/11 did to me was to bring what had been at the back of my mind, sort of gnawing away, right to the front."

So when the consequences of the war in Iraq began to become apparent, Blair fell back on a view that had not changed since 9/11. His statement that "the place to start was Iraq" because of its history with WMD is an insight into the strength of his feeling. Although he argued strongly that an Afghan campaign was justified after 9/11 and it was premature to go into Iraq, he was all but convinced that one day he would. The truth is that Blair was as much persuader as follower in confronting Saddam.

It was for that reason that he was not alarmed by neoconservative thinking. He may have been unhappy with Cheney's insistence on a quick invasion and even more by his disdain for the UN—that disturbed and irritated him—but he found no difficulty in accepting the logic of the case that an Iraq war might in the end transform the Arab world. He puts it cautiously but argues that a reasonably stable Iraq with something that could loosely be described as democracy would encourage the Iranian reformers and help to establish a pair of strong states in the region, from which others would have to draw lessons. The long-held ambition of an alternative centre of gravity in the Middle East for the West outside a rocky Saudi Arabia would be realized.

It was important to Blair to maintain the idea that he had identified Iraq as a danger that had to be met and that he wasn't a supine follower of Bush. First of all, he accepted that the removal of Saddam and the discovery of mass graves to prove his years of wrongdoing could not justify war on its own. Although he insisted that the test of the invasion was to ask Iraqis in the streets of Baghdad whether they would rather have Saddam back, he understood that the justification had to be broader. He had no difficulty in trying to construct one. All his important speeches touching on the Middle East since 9/11 had attempted to make the moral case for intervention, and to place practical difficulties in that context. Asked in May 2004 if he ever considered that he might be wrong, he said: "Yeah, of course. You've got to assess and reassess the whole time and I try to do that. But I think the reason why it is so important to do this is that although it's perfectly possible to be wrong about these things—I don't claim any mystical powers of certainty about it at all—but if I am wrong we may have removed some deeply oppressive regimes and I hope helped those countries to a better life. We may have taken action that you can look back and say—did you really need to do that? But if I'm right and we don't act, the consequences are absolutely catastrophic. So it's a balance of risk."

But in trying to finding that balance he acknowledged still that many people, including colleagues in government, weren't convinced. "We haven't persuaded people yet. There's no doubt in my mind about that. That's why people were so deeply opposed to Iraq. In the end what is their feeling? That we're just exaggerating this. Yes, you've got these terrorist groups and yes they're worse than other terrorist groups and yes you might have states that are trying to develop nuclear weapons, but we have nuclear weapons. Why are you so apocalyptic about it? That's the argument. I totally understand it."

The apocalyptic vision, however, has never faded. In the pall of smoke over New York, he has seemed to see new horrors. Over Christmas 2002, he was gripped by a fear that the confrontation between India and Pakistan over the disputed territory of Kashmir, which has caused three wars between them in sixty years, might provoke the long-feared nuclear exchange between Delhi and Islamabad. Although the Indian government at that time, dominated by Hindu nationalists, found ideological favor in Washington, it came dangerously close to an engagement with Pakistan that could trigger war. Blair nurtured particularly close links with the Pakistan leader, General Pervez Musharraf, but he feared that a mistake on either side could be the spark for a devastating war. "There was a time when I was talking to George Bush about it every single day on the phone at length and we finally put together a plan to cool it all down, and fortunately it has moved into a different sphere. That was a very, very serious situation." The public wasn't aware of how close Blair believes India and Pakistan came to nuclear war. To him, the crisis was evidence that his doctrine of pre-emption and "strength" in the Western alliance was justified in pursuit of those who developed or traded nuclear or chemical capability.

Many could not be convinced, however passionate the argument. The drift of intellectual argument in Britain seemed to swerve around the Prime Minister. He was often dismissed as a deluded figure, somehow stuck in the slipstream of an American president bent on imperial adventures in pursuit of oil or, worse, in a fundamentalist confrontation with Islam fuelled by a dislike of any culture that refused to be Americanized. So even as Blair insisted he was arguing a case that rested on moral high ground, he was accused of pursuing a policy that had a quite different character. It was in the nature of Bush that the more he tried to raise the moral tone, the more it sounded on the other side of the Atlantic as if he were being driven by a fundamentalist Christian zeal that made the public uncomfortable and those in Blair's Cabinet even more hostile than they already were. Blair was caught between his anxiety—almost desperation—to reach for a higher plane in arguing the case for the war, and the difficulty of persuading his colleagues and the wider public that Bush shared those ideals.

In the year after Saddam's fall, that problem was crystallized in Israel. Four months before the invasion, one of Blair's principal advisers confided: "You've got to understand that he has more sleepless nights about Israel-Palestine than about Iraq. He thinks there are only eighteen months left for a two-state solution and then that's it." The "it" hardly needed to be specified—a descent through the familiar spiral into something approaching a pan-Arab war against Israel that would, as one of its consequences, pit Europe against the United States and place the superpower in permanent opposition to the entire Muslim world, without any of the private understandings that mitigated the isolation brought on by policy in Iraq.

Blair's defence of Bush always includes a reminder that he was the first American president to make a formal commitment to a two-state solution in terms that were even more explicit than Clinton's. The publication of the "road map" for peace, however, had been a last-minute concession to Blair the week before war began, and it was much more a political payoff than a new strategy. Bush was reluctant, and the idea was scorned in the quarters of the administration where all that mattered was the push against Saddam and radical Islam.

In the Foreign Office, they saw no sign of the intimate involvement that had become commonplace in the Clinton years. Blair insisted that Bush was determined to press on, but each suicide bombing in Israel produced such feelings of revulsion in the United States that the presentation of the case for dialogue with a

Palestinian Authority that was clearly unable to control the attacks, even if it wanted to, was considered to be so politically unwise as to be almost laughable. With the approach of election year, during which American policy on the Middle East traditionally goes into purdah because of the assumed electoral consequences of a confrontation with Israel, the Foreign Office in London believed that in Washington the problem had been put on ice. Blair insisted on Bush's commitment, but the following cool commentary, made by an intimate deeply involved in Downing Street's foreign policy, summarizes the weakness of his position: "People speak of the special relationship with the United States. Not only is it misleading as far as Britain is concerned, it misses the truth. There is only one special relationship in Washington. That is with Israel, because it is the only foreign country that can affect domestic politics in America."

In London, the drift of thinking in the White House was alarming. One minister closely involved in Middle East discussions said bitterly of Condoleezza Rice's deputy, who was in charge of the flow of Middle East advice from the National Security Council: "The world would be a much happier place if Elliot Abrams wasn't in the White House."

Blair could not change the administration's thinking about Israel. His acceptance by many Americans was a consequence of his understanding of the depth of the 9/11 trauma, which was genuine, but his value was more as psychological counsellor than candid friend. He might argue at Camp David for more political pressure to be put on Israel to change its policies in the West Bank and Gaza, but he could hardly go public with his doubts about American objectives. Straw and Powell might exchange their gloomy analyses of Bush's nervousness at tangling with Israel— fuelled by Karl Rove and Dick Cheney in particular—but in public Blair was stuck. He could hope for some words to which he could cling, like the Rose Garden commitment to the "road map," but he could not expect a wholehearted involvement in a crisis that in Washington was so dangerous politically.

Many Americans find it difficult to appreciate the hostility of the political climate in Britain, let alone the rest of Europe, to the kind of rhetoric that characterizes the Washington debate. Such characters as Tom DeLay, the House Republican majority leader, find it quite natural to go to a conference of the American Israel Public Affairs Committee (AIPAC), the principal pro-Israel lobbying group, and refer to the West Bank as "Judea and Samaria" and recall looking down from the Golan Heights: "I did not see occupied territory, I saw Israel." Such sentiments were seldom heard in Britain, where although the debate between the factions was fierce, it was fought on much narrower ground. Ariel Sharon is almost as unpopular on the British Right as he is on the Left, because he is felt to have damaged Israel's cause in the public mind. There is much less appetite for defending him than there is in Washington.

Blair's misery was encapsulated almost exactly a year after Saddam's fall. Blair visited Bush at the end of April 2004. Sharon had passed through Washington a few days before, carrying with him his plan for unilateral withdrawal from Gaza and "disengagement" from the Palestinians. Blair was obliged to stand beside Bush in the Rose Garden at a press conference at which the President hailed Sharon's plan as a hopeful sign. Not a single one of Blair's advisers believed it was anything other than a potentially disastrous diversion from the "road map," and the Foreign Office saw it as a reversal of more than thirty years of policy because it invited the United States and Britain to accept a final deal with the Palestinians that would leave Israeli settlements in the occupied West Bank. No British government, including Margaret Thatcher's, would have accepted that proposal, since it undermined the cardinal belief that Israel must withdraw from most of the land occupied in 1967. Now Blair was in the position of accepting it or breaking with Bush on an important issue at a moment when violence was increasing in Iraq, the politics of reconstruction was proving difficult, and public opposition in both countries to the war was on the rise. He chose not to challenge Bush. Instead, he said Sharon's proposal was an "opportunity" and a challenge to the Palestinian leadership to which he hoped it would be able to rise.

He did not believe it could. Long since disillusioned with Yasser Arafat and unconvinced by the figures who juggled for authority as Arafat's star faded away, Blair was in despair about the Palestinians. But he was also infuriated by Israel's tactics in the occupied territories, which he thought counterproductive and designed to obstruct rather than to promote dialogue. He accepted the Foreign Office view that the radicalization of the Palestinian population was hastened by each Israeli incursion and that Sharon's response to terrorist bombings inside his country was being orchestrated in a way that made more attacks inevitable. Never since coming to power had he seen less chance of progress toward a final settlement than he did in the wake of the Iraq invasion. His hope was that as a democratic Iraq began to emerge, there would be progress towards a settlement between the Israelis and Palestinians. By mid-2004 that hope seemed in tatters.

But he found himself in a position where it was hard to admit it. Although his House of Commons statement on his return from Washington was notably tougher on Sharon than he had seemed in the words in the Rose Garden and in a BBC interview immediately afterwards, he did not seem a leader who had any freedom of movement. If Sharon could return home with Bush's support, it would count as victory. He still had to deal with those on the Right inside his government who succeeded in frustrating the policy, and curiously, Blair and other Europeans could take some satisfaction in that. But on the principles of progress in the occupied territories, Britain and the United States were divided.

Blair had made the "road map" one of his conditions for supporting Bush, just as he'd insisted that the United Nations must be central in the new Iraq. Although in June 2004 the Security Council approved the handover of sovereignty in the summer to the interim government that would prepare for elections six months later, it was a "vital role" that came along much later than Blair had hoped. And looking at the Israelis and the Palestinians, he could see little sign of the progress that had been, for him, part of the picture. The Americans hadn't re-engaged.

Blair's irritation with the political fact that the war was becoming ever more unpopular was greatly increased by his knowledge that he had not been enticed into it, but rather had believed in the cause to such an extent that he'd almost concluded it would be an act of moral cowardice to retreat. Hence his refusal of Bush's offer to let him give moral support without sending British troops to Iraq (which Jack Straw had floated as a possibility in a memo to Blair the week before the invasion), and hence his refusal to change his rhetoric, even when it was plainly falling on deaf ears: "I think in the end the one thing that you mustn't do in the international community when you are dealing with a security threat is to make a demand or an ultimatum and then not follow it through. The consequences are devastating."

But the consequences of follow-through were damaging, too. Blair found himself in the position of a leader waiting for justification that might never come, or come too late for his own political career. His party was taking an electoral battering as a result of a policy that was his, and considered in the popular mind to be his alone, and he was discovering that the relationships on which the day-to-day conduct of efficient government depend had been strained and, in some cases, broken. Much of the press had also turned against him.

On the first anniversary of the invasion, Blair seemed more a solitary figure than ever before. This was glaringly obvious in Britain. Even on the world stage, which had always had such allure, he discovered himself tied to a president whose foreign policy had strained traditional alliances more than any preceding U.S. president in recent memory. His former Washington ambassador, Sir Christopher Meyer, said in June 2004 that the Western alliance had been through its greatest crisis since World War II. Blair might have felt entitled to curse his luck.

How different it seemed from the memories that were conjured up of Ronald Reagan. Blair watched Margaret Thatcher give a filmed tribute at the funeral in the National Cathedral in Washington, in which she described Reagan as John Bunyan's Mr. Valiant for Truth, for whom the trumpets would sound on the other side. It had not always been so. Those who were present remember her incredulity and rage in October 1986 when she discovered that he was on the verge of agreeing to a zero-zero nuclear disarmament deal in Reykjavik with Gorbachev and how, as one admirer put it, "she simply reached for her handbag" to swing it in the direction of Washington. But Reagan's success in winning enough affection to secure a landslide re-election in 1984 had been a political act of great subtlety and skill. Through the dark revelations about his Central American policy and the consequences of the Iran-Contra double-dealing and deception, Reagan sank in international esteem, but he had the good luck to reap the rewards after he left office for the sudden collapse of communism, something that he'd been mocked for imagining through much of his presidency. It was a spectacular stroke of good fortune. Even if his loyalists were right in attributing the implosion to his steadfastness in office (and the placing of Tomahawk and Pershing II missiles in Europe, which Blair, like all ambitious young Labour politicians, had opposed), he was the beneficiary of internal convulsions in the Soviet Union that he could not have predicted and barely understood. Politics, as Bush and Blair have reason to know, is often unfair. But the contrast between the fond recollections of Reagan and Bush's travails were highlighted at Reagan's funeral. Even as his body was being flown home to be buried outside his presidential library in Simi Valley, California, the *Los Angeles Times* was reporting a poll that showed Bush trailing John Kerry nationwide as they prepared for the summer conventions and the autumn campaign.

The feel-good factor that had been Reagan's mysterious gift was not a secret that had been bequeathed to Bush. And Blair left the G8 summit on Sea Island, Georgia, to fly north for the state funeral knowing that a majority of the summiteers wanted Bush to lose the election. He was spared the necessity of revealing his own support—pleading the natural diplomatic excuse of having to work with whichever president was elected in November—and in private would talk about Labour's warm relations with Kerry's people and his own confidence that he'd work happily with him, just as he'd surprised everyone in winning Bush's affections so soon after his parting with Clinton. But he was aware how difficult it would be. Clinton himself told me in London that although he had sympathy for Blair's position, caught between Europe and the U.S., his terrible predicament had come about by his acceptance of Washington's refusal to give the weapons inspectors more time. Hence his isolation.

It was true, and Blair knew it. Iraq had estranged him from a large part of his own party. It had marked him out internationally as a bold leader, but one whose judgement had gone against the grain. He had thrown his lot in with Bush and in return appeared to have been given very little back. Therefore, it was reasoned, he must have done it because he believed in it. To the more cynical denizens of politics, that was even worse. It was an accurate reading. When some administration officials in Washington wondered behind their hands what Blair had got for his support for Bush (the unspoken answer being "not very much") and Blair's own Cabinet looked for the benefits of a relationship that was meant to safeguard the national interest, Blair was driven back to his vision of a future that rested on hope. The soaring ambition of the speech he made to his party conference in October 2001 was now reduced, in the public mind, to body bags in Iraq, the murders of people volunteering to be police officers or soldiers in the new democracy that was promised, and the regular bulletins from bin Laden in some cave near the Pakistan border promising retribution. They watched the Saudi regime starting to shake, looked at the costs in the United States and Britain of internal security arrangements that four years earlier would never have been contemplated, and asked Blair: was it worth it?

"My belief is that the right way to tackle this issue is seeing two sides of the agenda. If there is a weakness in our current approach it is that in my view you cannot deal with terrorism security as simply a security issue. You also have to deal with the more compassionate side of the issue—the suffering of people as a result of the Israeli-Palestinian issue, the poverty, the lack of interfaith understanding. All these things need to be part of the agenda as well. I personally think that we could make our case—and this is what I set out to the American Congress—but you need both parts of that agenda to make the thing work."

There is a hint there—only a hint—of frustration that the Bush administration only understood one side of the agenda. That was the view of Blair advisers who for months had wanted him to find a way of distancing himself from Bush. If he could not do it by causing a scene at some Washington press conference—and it was obvious why the opportunity for that had long since gone—he might at least start to speak in a different way about the future of the Middle East. Those Labour MPs who had strongly supported the war and were finding life difficult with party members in their constituencies had a flash of gallows humor when they began to speak in the Commons corridors of "Operation Distance" as the course they were pressing on their leader.

But one of the consequences that Blair did not regret at all was the transatlantic alliance, which had been as important a part of his strategy as his working out of the emotions of 9/11. "Only a complete fool in today's world with its interdependence and globalization would not rejoice at the fact that we are the key partner of the world's only superpower and we are a key player in the world's largest and most powerful political union [the European Union]," he said.

His justification for the Iraq war therefore rests on two pillars—his own moral sense that it was "right" because of Saddam's offences and his belief that Britain had to act as the bridge between the United States and Europe, a role that would bring influence and power. But despite the value Blair places on these relationships, some of his friends believe he has underestimated the value to Bush of his support. It is as if Blair is proud of the benefits he believes he has brought to Britain by the influence he has wielded, but even at the height of his popularity with the United States, he underestimated the value Bush placed on being able to point to a serious ally who could give the enterprise the genuine label of "coalition." As a means of preserving links with old alliance, even to old Europe, Blair was useful. He could prevent complete estrangement from the UN and act as a soothing emissary in some of those most sensitive parts of the Arab world.

Soon after Blair leaves office, historians will try to judge whether he could have exploited this advantage more effectively. Those who think the war was wrong—either because it would fracture some of the uneasy balances in the Arab world or because it was an unnecessary assault on a regime that would inevitably crumble under its own weight ere long—believe he sold British support too cheaply.

But the truth is that Blair was less interested in a display of power than in a policy that had become something close to an obsession. It was not irrational, nor spurred on to any great extent by either mysticism or religious zeal, but it was a decision about the nature of the post–Cold War world that drove him to reject conventional thinking.

By the time he went to war, Blair was possessed with a sense of mission. Just because he has the capacity to seem relaxed and to switch from a messianic tone on a public platform to next-door-neighbour informality, he is not half-hearted about the policy he has pursued since 9/11. He has dispelled his doubts. And he knows, whether events prove him right or wrong, he is stuck with it.

There are many scars. The procedures at Guantanamo Bay that bypassed the Geneva Conventions were impossible for him to defend fully. When you ask him whether he agrees with the judgement of the White House counsel, Alberto Gonzalez, that the Geneva Conventions are "quaint," he bridles. "Of course not. Neither do the Americans. They are extremely important."

It's embarrassing to him that four British citizens released from Guantanamo Bay after two years' captivity without access to legal advice arrived back home to hear the home secretary, David Blunkett, say they were not considered any kind of threat to national security and could go about their business. Blair says: "It has troubled me. It is an anomaly and you have to resolve it at some point. The only thing that is very, very hard is the fact that we have actually received information back from these people that is useful. But I agree. That's the reason we got four people back. And we're in negotiation about the others."

But those negotiations went on for more than eighteen months with no result. The attorney general, Lord Goldsmith, sounded extremely frustrated when he told the International Law Association in London in June 2004 that he believed the American proposal for military tribunals breached a fundamental principle and Britain couldn't accept it. Couldn't accept it, but had to. Blair's first attorney general, Lord Morris, said it was a relief at last to hear the British government say that human rights were indivisible. He regretted how long it had taken.

Blair himself had raised the subject with Bush on more than one occasion, trying to get a deal for the return of British citizens to jurisdiction at home. The Guantanamo prisoners were millstones around Blair's neck, and the revelations of abuse in Iraqi prisons were equally unsettling. He said he was appalled and ashamed. To his critics it was no more than should have been expected. But Blair, the prime minister who had talked of the "blood price" in defence of a principle, was unshakeable.

Blair's commitment took Britain into its most serious foreign policy crisis since Suez, which occurred when he was a boy of three. The Suez invasion had infuriated the Americans because it had been cooked up in secret with France and Israel and was seen to be a disaster before it happened. Yet for a generation afterward in British politics, its impact was divisive and poisonous. It was seen as a mixture of deceit and incompetence, and therefore as a stain on the government that had authorized it. The prime minister who had presided over the fiasco was Anthony Eden, the golden boy of British foreign policy since the late 1930s who was destroyed absolutely by Suez. He was out within months and spent the rest of his long life in the darkness of its shadow.

Blair's Iraq policy was a much more serious series of decisions than Eden's gambit, and it had more profound consequences. He concluded that the United States was right to initiate a "war on terror" after 9/11 and although he never believed the link between those events and Saddam, he was ready to conclude that an assault on Iraq was justified as part of the West's response to the threat of a confluence of interest between terrorist networks and rogue states. Most important of all, when the UN inspectors and a majority of the Security Council asked for more time, he said no. He preferred Bush's judgment to theirs—because it coincided to a remarkable extent with his own.

Blair was not drawn to Bush by a sense of necessity. He understood the value for Britain of the relationship, but he understood that there were alternatives. Instead, he concluded—against the advice of a number of his advisers—that he should commit himself absolutely to Bush's war if the United Nations could not organize a diplomatic settlement quickly or Saddam did not seem about to fall of his own accord. And when he had made that decision, he was immovable.

Bush's policy was therefore given a new strength by the evidence of Blair's passion for the cause. The Democrats were puzzled, the Labour Party was split and confused, the European Union was anguished. Russia was mystified and alarmed. But Blair was convinced that one day the consequences of his policy would vindicate him. "It's going to take a long time," he mused in his garden. "There also needs to be a strong reforming movement within Islam. I think there is a sign of it . . . but it would be enormously helpful if we were able to make progress on the Israel–Palestine issue. . . ." The sentence is left unfinished.

Over Iraq, he convulsed the politics of his own country. He also played a role in the creation of an American view of the world that was probably more significant than that of any other prime minister since Churchill, Thatcher included. Her ideological comfort for Reagan was welcome, and reciprocated, but not decisive. Without Blair, Bush might have found it difficult to pursue the policy that took him to Baghdad when it did and certainly would have found it much more difficult to try to persuade the world afterward that the goal of a democratic Iraq—once that distant mirage—might yet be close. Blair was much more than a bit player who walked on stage when required and left when his services were no longer needed.

He was central to the enterprise. But he was doomed to be the junior partner. That meant that when the Pentagon flexed its muscles over the State Department in the early days, he could not change the policy in Washington. Britain was disturbed by the decision to push aside Powell's plan for postwar reconstruction, by the process of "de-Ba'athification," which was meant to cleanse the place of Saddam's loyalists, and by the assumption by Garner and then Bremer that a scorched-earth policy would allow democracy to flood in to replace the totalitarianism of the past. As the military historian, and Conservative, John Keegan put it: "The neoconservative mistake was to suppose that, wherever tyranny ruled, democracy was its natural alternative." It would not happen as it had in Eastern Europe. Keegan said: "To think in such a way was to reveal a dangerously post-Marxist cast of mind. Marxists can think only in political terms. They accept, even if they despise, liberal and conservative opposition. What they cannot accept is that their opponents may be motivated by beliefs which are not political in any way at all."

The task proved much more difficult than the optimistic ideologues had believed. The country was in chaos. The ruined ministries offered no foundations for an effective administration. The dissolution of the Ba'ath Party and the Iraqi army meant that there were no remnants of order on which to build something new. The victors were surveying a chaotic landscape within which a weary population became steadily more antagonistic toward the occupiers and where insurgents and Saddam loyalists seemed to be finding it easier to attack coalition troops and "collaborating" Iraqis with impunity.

Day by day, violence got worse. Fewer than 100 coalition troops had died before Bush said that "major combat operations" were over. In the year following his declaration of victory in April 2003, nearly 600 Americans died.

Two days before the scheduled handover of power to the

interim administration on June 30, 2004, it was announced that the ceremony had already been conducted quietly and more or less privately. The decision was an acknowledgement that it might well be disrupted by violence. The formal proceedings occurred behind barricades with few witnesses, and there were no crowds. In Istanbul where he was attending a NATO summit, Bush got a note from Condi Rice telling him that power had been passed on. He scribbled on the note: "Let freedom reign!" and, in contrast to so many important documents in the saga, it was displayed for the cameras. Bush described the handover as a "proud, moral achievement," said evil had been defeated, and once again linked the fall of Saddam to 9/11. The war on terrorism was being conducted "where we are finding them instead of waiting for them to find us at home."

Blair, by his side, resisted such language. He was no longer talking of Armageddon, the apocalypse, or good and evil. None of his officials were in a celebratory mood.

Downing Street and the Foreign Office believed that American policy during the occupation had been counterproductive in stirring up the violence that a quick victory had been meant to suppress. The pictures of torture illuminated the gulf between the occupiers and the population most dramatically (the Red Cross having told Washington that it believed that 60–90 percent of those being held were innocent of any crime), but the feeling in London about the American efforts at "peace building" came near to despair. One of the most senior Foreign Office diplomats dealing with the Middle East described it privately just before the transfer of power as "a catastrophe from beginning to end."

Straw himself admitted publicly that much could have been done differently, and when it was put to him that the Cheney-Rumsfeld-Wolfowitz group had dictated the policy, he went so far as to say that surely no one would expect him to agree with those people. But Blair was not in a position to take such a step backward. Whether he liked it or not, he was now seen as an architect of the policy. Private arguments in the past counted for nothing; the outcome was his as much as it was Bush's. There was no escape from the consequences.

In Clinton's view, Blair had made an effort. "He tried to do three things—get rid of whatever weapons stocks there were, preserve the transatlantic relationship and the European Union and work through the UN." But it was too late. "When both sides in effect fell away from him—the US on one side and France and Germany on the other—he was left with the prospect of walking away from what he believed were WMD sites, or walking forward without the UN and Europe. It was a terrible dilemma for him."

His response to that dilemma was to accept the Washington view with which he had been in sympathy for so long. Having made the case that the threat was real and imminent, he found himself unwilling to turn away from war, nor from its consequences.

# CHAPTER 9

# THE LONER

The Blair smile is a disguise, because it suggests a gregarious character. One of his closest friends at the top of his government tells the truth of it like this: "Tony has always been a loner and we all know it."

This judgment seems curious, because Blair feeds on crowds, drawing political energy from their presence and apparently enjoying the feel of them. He is the first British prime minister able to wear jeans without looking uncomfortable, and he exudes relaxation rather than tension. All this, however, is only half the story. Blair has a solitary side, and his political style owes more to that part of his character than to the easygoing figure who was sculpted for the electorate. It has also caused most of his troubles.

His day-to-day exercise of power, his choice of friends, the ambiguities of his attitude to his party, his reactions at moments of crisis, the way he thinks about politics—all of it comes from a character that is protected by a flinty carapace and resists most intruders. Blair is explained by his individualism much more easily than by the outside forces that may sometimes seem to have made him what he is. As the years in office have gone by, these influences have become less important than the core personality. As Blair has aged into his fifties, becoming thinner, a touch greyer, and with a rougher physical edge, some of the soft padding that politicians have to acquire has been stripped away. His essential wiring has been revealed.

Without war in Iraq, this change would have been more subtle and slow. But he devoted so much time to explaining his thinking (and defending it from the scepticism that flowed around him in a rising tide), that war acted as an agent of transformation. Just as some increasingly nervous members of his Cabinet worried about his single-mindedness and his refusal to take even a short, symbolic step away from Bush, so he believed that his effort to convince the country of his policy was the most important political engagement of his time in office. He wanted to lay himself bare: that was the point.

It drove much of his party to distraction—"Tony's mission" made them uncomfortable precisely because of the messianic flavor it exuded—but it became the inescapable *idée fixe* of his leadership. A year after the invasion, he said that Iraq was "an historic opportunity" despite all the difficulties; he meant, too, that he believed it to be a historic test for leaders like him. Would they be bold enough to see it through? And against that challenge what else could matter?

No one doubted that his spirit of conviction was the essential Blair, and not some political device or invention. After seven years in power, and ten as the leader of his party, he had reached the plateau where his great political last battle was to be fought to a finish—not about the economy, or health care, or taxation, nor even about the "fairer society" that he had made the objective of his years in power, but about international order. It even superseded the European question, which he had once thought to represent as the "Great Task." A number of Cabinet colleagues (perhaps even a majority of the twenty-one) agreed with Robin Cook when he said that it was the wrong battle in the wrong place at the wrong time, and Downing Street felt chilly in spring 2004. "It's over," said one of his senior ministers around Easter.

"We don't know when or how, but he is coming towards the end."

The atmosphere seemed to feed on itself and become more fevered. The government slipped and slid into elementary mistakes as if its steering gear had gone haywire. Michael Howard began to draw blood across the floor of the Commons. Blair himself stumbled into an unnecessary dispute in reversing his opposition to the referendum on the new European Union constitution, which all at once made him look indecisive, split his Cabinet, delighted the Opposition, allowed the Euro-sceptic right-wing press to claim victory over a weak prime minister, and left the Labour Party in Parliament wallowing in a potent mixture of embarrassment and irritation.

As night follows day, such moments in politics inspire talk of a leadership crisis. For the first time, Blair's dogged enemies—who had once amounted to perhaps two dozen MPs in a parliamentary Labour Party of more than 400—were joined by many more who allowed thoughts previously kept private to start to circulate more widely in the places where political people gather: might it at last be time to think of the end of the Blair era and the succession? They were tired of moral certainty.

But it was the passport he carried abroad. Bush said after their summit in Crawford in April 2002: "The thing I admire about this prime minister is that he doesn't need a poll or a focus group to convince him of the difference between right and wrong." At home, the complaint about the government that was proving the opposition's sharpest weapon was the mirror image of this: that Blair and his party were obsessed with the witchcraft of the spin doctors and the machinery of focus groups and polls. Nothing was done for the right reasons, but only for the purpose of catching a passing bandwagon or a transient political mood. So Blair was simultaneously the conviction politician who set a course and stuck to it and the snake-oil salesman who always had a bottle of something new in his bag.

The best clue to the real Blair lies in the fact that there is truth in both these complaints. His willingness to go to war and stick to

Bush's side reveals his utter determination that he is right. And many of his government's own difficulties have come from the character trait that underpins that foreign policy: the willingness, even the anxiety, to exercise power in an individualistic way, with important decisions taken with the advice of a very small number of people and sometimes alone. His is a very personal premiership.

So, the contradictions that surrounded him as he passed the seventh anniversary of his first election are less puzzling than they first appear. His strength as it appeared in Washington and his problems as they began to multiply at home were all recognizably of his own making: his character and the way he conducted his politics had produced them, and he was now so marked by them that his friends as well as his enemies believed he wore a stain that would prove indelible.

Nor was Blair entirely unhappy at the roughed-up edges of his mature profile. He certainly regretted the European muddle, even apologizing to his Cabinet for the way he had handled it, and he was visibly unnerved by some of Howard's rapier thrusts, but he was quite content to be seen as the unbending warrior of Iraq, confident that in time his policy would be vindicated. One of the reasons was the comfort he felt in going against the grain of liberal opinion, which by the war's first anniversary had turned decisively against Blair. Asked this question by perhaps his closest friend in government over a lunch table: "Our people really hate us now, don't they?" there was only one honest answer: "Yes, they do." He was talking not so much about Labour MPs, discontented and rebellious though they were, but about the broader swathe of "our people" outside Parliament to whom Blair and the war had become unpalatable.

To the well-heeled, left-of-centre professionals who had enjoyed the arrival of a prime minister who would reflect their social concerns but thoughtfully spare them the class-war rhetoric of socialism and its taxes, Blair was now the fashion accessory that was put back in its box.

The distancing they engaged in, however, troubled them much more than it upset him. Instead of flailing around in search of lost support, he tried to explain again why he was set on his course; even when faced with gloomy accounts of falling party membership or some dire electoral prediction, he'd insist that his conviction couldn't be undermined by unpopularity; he might not have been revelling in the isolation that sometimes appeared to afflict him, but he seemed to friends to adopt a kind of grim contentment that he was paying the appropriate price for a policy that had come to mean everything to his premiership, almost as if the weary obligations of day-to-day politics had passed away. The greater the distance, the more important the conviction became.

He became remote. As if in response to the opening up of a divide, the Cabinet began to get more restive. The arguments began to find their way into the newspapers more often. David Blunkett threatened resignation in an ugly dispute with Jack Straw on the question of a National Identity Card; a number of ministers were furious at Blunkett's hard line on the touchy questions of immigration and asylum and plotted his removal; Charles Clarke, the education secretary, was so angry at Blair's decision to support a referendum on Europe that he couldn't bring himself to offer a few words of support of the policy to his local newspaper; Patricia Hewitt, the trade and industry secretary, was so disturbed by the consequences of the war that she began to act as a lightning rod for Cabinet worries and distanced herself from Blair. Above all, Gordon Brown maintained a brooding silence on the war except in answer to direct and unavoidable questions, when his words seemed to express dark resignation rather than enthusiasm.

They knew, too, that it was no bizarre change of character that had produced the troubles that were sending tremors through the government and disturbing the Labour Party to the point where it had became a sullen outfit held together by tribal loyalty and not much else. They were seeing the real Blair.

His political career was the most unusual at the upper echelons of modern British politics, and not simply because he became Prime Minister without having served in a previous government. He was remarkably immune to political influences as a child, and even when he was a student at Oxford in the mid-1970s, he played no part in the politics of the time. Members of his post-1960s generation seemed to have shed much of the swaggering excitement of that age, temporarily entering a rather quiescent phase, from which they would only be awakened by the Thatcher revolution of the 1980s. Blair conformed to that pattern. His Oxford friends weren't activists of any sort, and he left to read for his bar examinations with no political accoutrements to mark him out.

It was toward the end of the 1970s that he became an active member of the Labour Party, in the company of his friend Charlie Falconer, with whom he shared a flat. Falconer, cheery and usually smiling, is an exceptionally clever lawyer. He and Blair had a good time together, and it is characteristic of Blair that he decided toward the end of his first term in office that Falconer should join the government. By the simple expedient of making him a member of the upper house, the House of Lords, he was able to make him a minister. By the time Blair was settling down for the great Iraq crisis of the second term, Lord Falconer of Thoroton was lord chancellor—the ancient office Blair had decided to abolish as part of his constitutional reforms—and acting as a friend and confessor to a prime minister who was beginning to find that the gang with whom he'd surrounded himself in the first days in Downing Street had dispersed.

Alastair Campbell was gone, his departure sealed by the convulsions of the Hutton report, which revealed how the temperature of his battles with the BBC and Fleet Street had risen to become a fever. Peter Mandelson, the arch-insider, was off to Brussels as a euro-commissioner. A clutch of aides had gone, weary after years in power, and his circle began to shrink. His touch with the parliamentary party had never been sure, or intimate. Now it was awkward and distant. They grumbled about him; he grumbled about them. Everyone was getting on everyone else's nerves, and in that fractious atmosphere the old problem with Brown began to heave beneath the waves, the leviathan that was always ready to break the surface.

At the end of 2002, when he was struggling to assemble a majority for the latest phase of his National Health Service reforms, Blair saw many of the rebels one by one in his House of Commons office. One after another of the MPs argued against the reforms, but Blair would often say that he understood the argument, didn't agree with it, and would not be changing his mind. Quite a few got up and left after a few minutes, dismayed that they weren't given any chance to change the Prime Minister's mind. Blair argued that he was acting straightforwardly and honestly: he was committed to these changes and would not be blown off course. Month by month the distance increased.

The Conservatives were finding their feet again in opposition, and everywhere there were signs of frustration in the electorate. At least Gordon Brown could claim, with considerable justification, that he'd presided over a remarkable period of stability and growth—low inflation, low unemployment, and growth that in some years exceeded his forecast. But his very credibility and strength were another problem for Blair.

Brown, whose relationship with Blair had been the spinal chord of the government but also the source of much of its angst, was his great rival and had retained a stature that seemed unaffected by the war and its associated alarms. As far as the Chancellor was concerned, the "war on terror" was a question of paying the bills. He took little part in the national debate on security or on the issue of Iraq itself, limiting himself to formal expressions of support for the Prime Minister. There was no pretence that Blair and Brown were as one on the war. Brown became the natural rallying point for dissident MPs who saw in him the only alternative to Blair.

The government's longevity made the problem worse. Ministers were tired. Blair had been in power for seven years by May 2004 and suffered from an inevitable creeping ennui in the electorate. They were beginning to look beyond him, though they knew not to what.

Blair's governing style was a matter of character and something produced by the strange shape of his government as a kind of dual premiership. He was encouraged in his methods at Downing Street by the need to manage Brown's huge personality and dominance, and the simmering ambition that hadn't cooled in the years since Blair became leader. It demanded an exclusive Downing Street, built around private meetings and deals, and made it more difficult for Blair to deal openly with the machinery of government.

Anyway, Blair preferred to deal directly with his own teams of advisers. In foreign affairs, for example, Sir David Manning became an alternative source of power to the Foreign Office. The diplomats resented it but had to live with it. His role, as daily conduit to the White House, epitomized the Blair style. It led to the accusation that has been made against all modern British prime ministers but to none with as much justice as to Blair—presidentialism.

In Europe too, Blair discovered that the important decisions are almost always made in one-on-one conversations with other leaders. As with Europe, so with the world. After 9/11, he became his own Foreign Office and Ministry of Defence. He zipped across the continents, but he found his greatest satisfaction in the ability to construct a personal relationship with Bush.

An episode with Clinton in 2003 highlighted the way Blair had become a presidential figure. The former president had given Blair a helping hand onto the world stage. They had disagreements—on Kosovo, notably—and Blair felt some hurt toward the end of Clinton's second term when he believed he'd lost interest in Northern Ireland. But in general they were friends, and after the presidential election of 2000, they parted as close buddies who'd continue to see each other.

In the summer of the Iraq war, Blair was attending a conference in a country house north of London. He and the former president were going to have a colloquy by the fireside for all the distinguished guests, from both sides of the Atlantic. But Clinton was late. He had been playing golf at St. Andrews, and whether or not it was an argument with one of the fearsome bunkers on the Old Course, he was running well behind time. Blair was angry when he had to start alone, and his temper didn't improve when, in the middle of his remarks, everyone rushed outside at the sound of whirling helicopter blades to greet the former President. Those who were with him realized that he felt patronized. He was the Prime Minister and host; and Clinton was, anyway, an ex-president and no longer the real thing.

Clinton sensed the atmosphere and did his best to smooth it over. But the following evening they were both due at a dinner at Guildhall, and this time Clinton arrived first. He decided as a matter of diplomacy to be at the front entrance when the Prime Minister arrived last, as the more important guest. This time, Clinton made it clear that he was the has-been, and Blair was the leader in power. It was a small incident but telling for its insight into Blair's confidence. He did not see himself, as a British prime minister easily can, as a supplicant hoping to get some scraps from the Washington table. Instead he saw himself as a statesman in power. And, as he knew, so did Bush.

His party didn't like it. The more he revelled in the role, the more he found former supporters peeling away, dismayed by the war and disillusioned with the drift of policy at home, which many Labour MPs began to believe was veering rightwards. Blair, as usual, wasn't interested in ideological labels and just carried on. Increasingly, Blair led without the sound of the cheering behind him that had once followed him everywhere. By the summer of 2004, the atmosphere was sour and his position was hazardous.

Yet Blair enjoyed the space he had created around himself. He had no illusions about the consequences of war if he couldn't convince the country soon that there had been good reason to fear Saddam and that Iraq was going to rise from the ashes. He has said that he will only succeed if that happens: "We are justified provided we make the place better. Don't be under any doubt about that. The only thing you have an absolute duty to do if you remove the regime [is] you have to make the place better." He said he has never had doubts, only some dark moments going to war: "In a situation like this where it's life and death you do what you think is right and you give the country the leadership that you think is correct—and then you know the rest is in the lap of the gods."

Waiting for that judgment, Blair is alone. He will take the consequences if it is hostile, and his party will talk of the tragedy of Blair, how high ideals and achievements were undermined by war. As he began his longest summer, however, it was striking to see his belief that some day vindication would come.

At the end of April, he paid a quick visit to Washington. It was on the day Bush gave his unwelcome support to Sharon, with Blair at his side in the Rose Garden. The prime minister then drove to the British embassy for some interviews. Between them, he wandered onto the flagstone terrace. The diplomatic staff were there, drinking tea. Manning and Blair's chief of staff, Jonathan Powell, were huddled together. His Downing Street minders were preparing to get him to the airport. Blair broke away from the throng.

He stood alone for a few minutes on the stone terrace, sipping tea. No one approached him. He looked out towards the garden, some early cherry blossoms lighting up the scene. It was peaceful, colourful, and quiet. He wasn't disturbed. No one thought of coming close. After a few minutes he turned back, his thoughts in place. His staff fell in behind him, and off he went.

At such moments there were flashes of the solitude that clung to him, even when he appeared to be at the centre of a throng, as when he and Bush next met on a cliff top in Normandy, to remember the sixtieth anniversary of the D-Day landings on June 6, 1944 and the beginning of the end for Hitler.

World War II fighters and bombers dipped out of the haze and bent-backed veterans polished their medals for a last commemorative march, but these two leaders were not only looking back. They carried the weight of a future that they had decided to shape in their own way and that would mark them, and a new generation, as indelibly as the old infantrymen and GIs bore their scars of the campaign that began with the bloody rush ashore to those beaches stretching for fifty miles along the coast.

*Liberation* is a word used easily in Normandy, with no scintilla of embarrassment. There were no demonstrations against the commemoration of D-Day. Such a thing would be unimaginable. Gerhard Schroeder became the first German chancellor to feel able to travel to Normandy for the ceremonies, aware that the liberation of Germany itself as a consequence of the invasion was for him the most important of all. Vladimir Putin was there, too, another symbol of change. Chirac played host to queens and presidents and prime ministers, greeting Schroeder with a bear hug that to their two countries was a symbol of the most important European relationship of all, the enmity that once divided their peoples forgotten and transformed into a political alliance. It was a day for fine words and high sentiments under the red, white, and blue vapour trails of the French Mirage jets that swept in from the horizon and within sight of the cemeteries with their thick carpets of white crosses.

For everyone in France for D-Day, the reunion was a celebration of the dissolution of old rivalries and battles. They were united by a war long gone. But another divided them.

The alliance between Bush and Blair may be thought occasionally by each of them in a dreamy moment to be a renewal of the Churchill–Roosevelt pact after Pearl Harbor, but those are almost never the terms in which they express it. They seldom speak of it as a conscious reaffirmation of that deal. In their minds, it is a contemporary phenomenon, and the scene played out at Arromanches was a flickering movie from the past, grainy and fuzzy and from an era fast slipping away over the horizon.

Two of the leaders, Bush and Blair, stood apart. Their policy in Iraq was opposed by the most powerful of the other leaders there, and resented. Chirac, Schroeder, and Putin shared none of their belief in the benefits they thought would flow from Saddam's removal. Blair, in particular, was isolated. He'd spent seven years in power trying to embed Britain in Europe more firmly than his predecessors. Now, by his alliance with Bush, he was straining the relationships that he had once thought would allow him to make his mark as a New European.

Bush smiled his way from Rome to Paris as he travelled to Normandy, deliberately avoiding even oblique references to Iraq in a speech at the American war cemetary, but he knew that all but a tiny handful of the guests at Arromanches wished him ill in his re-election campaign. Spanish troops were on their way home from Iraq, the Poles were increasingly nervous, the Italian government battered by unpopularity that sprang directly from anti-war feeling. Putin was aloof. France and Germany oozed some self-satisfaction about being right about the depth of the quagmire. And Blair, though his commitment to the invasion was as strong as ever, was facing a nightmare set of midterm elections for local councils and the European Parliament, which duly produced for his party the lowest share of the vote it had ever achieved in an equivalent contest.

His old adversary Clare Short said his resignation was the only way to "correct" the government's failing, and the flow of political comment looked beyond his era to whatever might follow. Gordon Brown uttered words of support that were carefully chosen as ever to avoid any impression of overenthusiasm, and a view began to settle in British politics that Blair was approaching the end.

A simple question came from everyone's mouth: had Blair promised Brown a new deal, like the one that has dogged them for the ten years since Brown agreed to support Blair for the leadership in 1994? Ever since, Brown has believed in a promise that in the second term of government, Blair would step aside to let him have his chance. Blair insists that nothing so clear was ever agreed, and the dispute has bubbled and boiled between them and their camps of followers ever since. At the height of the Iraq crisis, they had to face it again.

Brown made a speech to the party conference in October 2003 that infuriated Blair. The chancellor said in his peroration that the government was at its best "when it was Labour," a deliberate piece of mockery of Blair's "New Labour" that was understood by everyone in the hall. In his anger, Blair said that week: "What's he up to? We're going to have to sort this out." Everyone knew what he was up to, of course.

Brown's ambition was encouraged by the party's agony over war and Blair's plunging popularity. On two important domestic policy matters—reforms in the National Health Service and university tuition fees—Blair was facing defeat in the Commons and had to get Brown's help in persuading enough rebellious MPs to save the government from humiliation. It came in time, but only just. In the last twenty-four hours before the university vote, Brown called the dogs off. Blair was angry that it took so much effort, and he knew that Brown was demanding a price for his silence on the war.

One of Brown's close friends outside the Commons told a backbencher who longed to see the end of Blair and who asked in February how long it would be: "I can tell you that the deal has been done. He will be out in the summer." No one in Downing Street would give credence to the idea of an agreement to go. Cabinet members like Straw insisted that Blair was committed to fighting the next election. But by the spring, everyone began to wonder.

Blair insisted to anyone who asked him that he had made no promise. It was what he had always said about the conversation which they had at Granita in 1994 that has passed into political folklore—which Brown interpreted as a guarantee of the succession and Blair refused to recognise as a negotiated deal. That had been an ambiguous affair, and here was a re-run, almost exactly ten years after. In the Brown camp, there was an expectation that the change might come before the general election expected in 2005; in Downing Street the response to the whispers was a traditional moan about "Gordon," the word almost always accompanied by a long sigh. The consequences were friction and misunderstanding.

Brown was preparing for the summer comprehensive spending review and was engaging in the private negotiations for which he was famous, keeping as much away from the eyes of Number 10 as he could. In response, Blair began to show more irritation with his Chancellor than his staff had seen for some time. The conference speech had not been forgotten. A new element entered the troubled equation. Blair began to speak of an ideological divide. He was pressing on with social reform. Education, the NHS, law and order to come . . . the Blair agenda was unapologetic in the face of criticism from the Left that he was running a New Right government. Blair spoke of the danger that a Brown Government might unravel his reforms. Almost for the first time, Blair began to imagine precisely what kind of society he wanted to leave behind him.

In that context, Brown was a threat. It meant that when Blair plunged into a difficult spring, their relationship was bound to get worse. It did.

On his return from his visit to the White House, preceded by a short family holiday in Bermuda, Blair announced that he had changed his mind about having a referendum on the new constitution for the European Union now being negotiated. He'd been under pressure from some members of the Cabinet to change his mind and while he was in Bermuda he decided, alone, that they were right. But it seemed a disastrous U-turn. He'd argued for months that it was a matter of principle that there shouldn't be a referendum, which the Conservatives wanted because they thought the result would be "no" and it would finish Blair. Now, he said, he had concluded that the people should be allowed to give their opinion. It split the Cabinet and—worse—made Blair seem to be running scared of polls that said the constitution was highly unpopular.

Charles Clarke accused Straw of having engineered the change and thereby of weakening the government. The foreign secretary denied it. Blair performed weakly in Parliament and looked a battered figure. He'd had to stand by Bush in Washington, listening to him praise Sharon for the Gaza disengagement, which Blair thought was a betrayal of the road map, and now Europe was sucking him down again.

That week, Straw wondered if the end might be coming. At least three other members of the Cabinet spoke about a leadership crisis. The corridors of the Commons were awash with wild rumour. Brown was talking to his supporters and asking them to stay calm: the message they took from the conversations was that all would be resolved soon. The parabola tracing Blair's descent since his decision to go to war seemed to be reaching its nadir.

He understood that some members of his Cabinet were already planning for life after his departure. He knew that perhaps half the parliamentary party would be happy to see him go, and that there was dwindling loyalty in the other half. He discussed it with one or two of his closest colleagues. He had had two objectives— to try to justify his Iraq policy by staying long enough for the vindication that he believed would come, but to avoid the Thatcher mistake of staying until the wolves were pawing at the door. "They're never going to drag me out of here with my fingernails scraping along the carpet," he said in May. But neither did he want to give his critics the victory of seeing him go before there were elections in Iraq.

The balance was painful. A number of his ministers feared that he was on the verge of resignation. He confessed to some of them that he was worried about the effect of the pressure on his family. At least twice in May and June, a group of Blair loyalists in the Cabinet felt it necessary to reassure him that he hadn't lost their support and should persevere. They denied emphatically that they had to talk him out of resignation, and Blair's spokesman dismissed the talk of an early departure as fantasy. But the whispers would not subside. At least two of Brown's friends continued to tell reporters privately that Blair had agreed to go before the end of the year. Even when his wife, Cherie, was quoted in the *Daily Telegraph* as having said he would "go on and on" (the phrase associated with Margaret Thatcher in her most defiant mood), Labour MPs who did not relish the idea of a Brown premiership were expressing their worries that Blair might wake up one morning, cry "Enough!" and walk into the sunset.

He was caught between his belief that Iraq might begin to find a kind of stability within a year or so and his frustration at the opposition to him, which he knew was beginning to sweep through the party. Brown's power seemed to increase. In the preparations for his three-year review of government spending—

the exercise that was to be the foundation of the general election campaign—he flexed his muscles. He restricted the amount of information that was shared between the Treasury and Downing Street, made clear to ministers that he was frustrated by the inability of Blair's officials to make up their minds on important matters, and turned the spending review into a demonstration of his own power. He saw himself setting the pattern for the next term of Labour government, while Blair was enmeshed in the consequences of war and struggling to repair a badly damaged image.

As they waited for Lord Butler's report on intelligence and Iraq to criticize the mechanisms that had led Blair to exaggerate the threat from Saddam, and as they contemplated the almost certain loss of scores of Labour parliamentary seats in the general election likely to come in 2005, Labour MPs were confused and fearful. They could not read Blair's mind and suspected that it swung between a determination to stay and a contemplation of the relief that departure from office might bring. That uncertainty caused the government to wobble. Ministers began to sound weary and unsure. Speeches were scanned for any reference that might suggest to the Kremlinologists that Blair was tilting one way or the other. Nothing was thought to be what it seemed.

Blair himself continued to insist that he looked forward to a third term in office, saying in a BBC interview, "I don't know how often I have to say it . . ." But he had to accept that his belief in vindication in Iraq was not shared by most of his colleagues, however much he might insist that the failures in intelligence and political misjudgements shouldn't be allowed to undermine the victory over Saddam. He said in Downing Street in May that he did expect to be proved right. "Yes, I do," he said without a moment's hesitation.

"What happens in a situation like this is that people end up losing all sense of perspective and history is then rewritten. The situation is this. There is absolutely no doubt that Saddam was a severe threat to the region and the wider world. There is no doubt even on David Kay's evidence that he was wholly in breach of UN resolutions. So it's a question of whether for the purposes of physical concealment that he destroyed the physical product or not.

"There is no doubt in my mind either that we would not have had the progress on WMD that we have had in respect of Libya, Iran, North Korea, the AQ Khan network [in Pakistan] unless it had become absolutely clear that we were prepared to take in the end—as a last resort—to take military action in order to enforce the international community's will."

The concession from Libya, agreeing to open its weapons programmes to inspection, had been a particular source of satisfaction for Blair. MI6 had run the operation that uncovered the extent of the WMD programs and persuaded the Gaddafi regime to do a deal. They uncovered programmes—"on a turkey farm," as Bush was fond of saying—about which the CIA knew nothing. The connection to Iraq of Libya's decision to co-operate was questionable—Gaddafi had huge economic reasons for seeking a rapprochement with the West—but it was nonetheless a British success that could be presented as one more victory in the "war on terror." Such breakthroughs were few. Blair went himself to Tripoli to celebrate the deal with Gaddafi.

Since 9/11, Bush had said that any country that harboured terrorists should be assumed to be hostile to the United States, yet everyone knew that if that designation were to be taken literally, many more countries than those listed as part of the "axis of evil" would be targeted. The policy required common sense; but the rhetoric was absolute in distinguishing between the "good" and the "bad." The consequences were always going to be messy. Blair had experience of this difficulty. At the start of his first term, Robin Cook had said he wanted a foreign policy "with an ethical dimension," an innocent-enough statement but one that invited the kind of scrutiny of arms deals and human rights records of distant allies that inevitably produced contradictions and embarrassments in droves.

How could Britain support the human rights record of its friend General Musharraf or ignore the performance of many of the

Middle East regimes with which it was felt necessary to do business? President Mubarak in Egypt was running a state of emergency that had been in place for more than two decades, and there was no sign of what Blair and Bush would call the kind of democracy they were promoting in Iraq. Cook's "ethical dimension" was subject to so many caveats and exceptions that it began to look like a cover-up instead of a searchlight. With his departure from the Foreign Office, the phrase was allowed to die.

The "axis of evil" revived the old problems, because it was subject to precisely these kinds of contradictions. Donald Rumsfeld himself, after all, had engaged in a cheery handshake with Saddam in the 1980s when he was working in the pharmaceutical industry and performing some service for Reagan as an unofficial envoy. But Bush asserted moral simplicities, and in public Blair concurred. In private, he might pursue active diplomacy with Iran, but at Bush's side he would agree that any state that harboured terrorists was an enemy.

Such ambiguities persuaded the sceptics that he had abdicated judgement, and he failed to convince them that fighting al-Qaeda meant confronting Saddam, too; he confused a public that believed that it was a policy directed from Washington; above all, the evidence that he said would demonstrate the imminence of the threat was nowhere to be found.

It was one of the greatest political failures of his premiership. In his early years he was a necromancer in politics, creating things previously unknown. Conservative voters voted Labour without closing their eyes. Rupert Murdoch praised a man of the Left. The opposition in Parliament was weak and flailing in its impotence. Blair had the power to write his own rules and shape his own time. But when he went into Iraq, he found himself accused of one trait that had never previously been pinned on him: weakness.

There may be two or three members of his Cabinet who believe that he was right not to distance himself from Bush, but no more. Straw has been loyal, but in the stream of memos that he sends to Blair at all hours of the day and night—"I'm a nerdy sort of person, and I'm always taking notes," he says—he rehearsed the options that would have allowed Blair to step back twice in the spring of 2002, when London became aware of the seriousness of Pentagon planning for Iraq and Blair understood how determined Bush had become; then at Camp David in September that year, Blair could have expressed his apprehension instead of assuring the United States that if there was a UN resolution giving some cover (even if it did not authorize war), he'd be there; and he could have insisted that the inspectors should have more time.

If Blair had followed one of the alternatives and distanced himself from Bush early on, he would have ruptured a relationship that had become all-important to him. He rationalized his decision by arguing that Rumsfeld and Cheney would then have found a reason to crank up their suspicions about the British ally. In private, he expressed his doubts about the Pentagon's plans for Iraq, the weakness for Chalabi, the regime at Guantanamo Bay, the performance of Garner and Bremer. In public, none of this emerged, Blair believing that his influence depended on arguments remaining private. His party, however, was impatient. It saw no results from this personal special relationship.

Blair's predicament was illuminated in spring 2004 by the strange case of Katharine Gun.

She was a translator at GCHQ, which has been the subject in the last few years of the greatest modern investment in intelligence gathering in Britain. She was a Mandarin specialist, presumably spending her days listening to interesting conversations sucked up by bugs and satellites in Beijing. During the climax of the UN negotiations on the second resolution, she came across something that was not in her normal line of work. She saw a request from the National Security Agency in Washington for "aggressive" bugging of UN diplomats. In the last push to see why the Security Council would not accede to Britain's request, it seemed that Bush had decided to leave no stone unturned. A request from the National Security Agency arrived at GCHQ asking for a "surge" in intelligence from the delegations of members of the Security Council. Such a request would not have been made without a political order from the White House.

It meant that the ambassadors of Chile and a number of African countries were to be bugged. Ms. Gun was outraged. She did not believe that intelligence gathering should be carried out in such ways, despite the assumption by all UN delegations that many countries bug each other regularly as they go about their business in New York. She told a journalist. Eventually, long after "major combat operations" were over, she came to trial charged with breaking her obligations under the Official Secrets Act. She was prepared to argue that she had acted in the public interest. It was a defence that was unlikely to succeed in court, but it would certainly produce some evidence that would be awkward for the government. The case was therefore dropped, just as it was about to open. Someone who was accused of serious offences was allowed to walk free, with government lawyers packing their bags and leaving the court. The explanation was simple. The prosecution was not worth the embarrassment.

Ms. Gun was ready to argue her case on moral grounds. She was a loyal member of the intelligence services but had a belief in the limits of the secret power of the state that would not allow her to acquiesce in a surveillance operation that she believed was wrong. Her view was as simple as Blair's, and similar: sometimes there were obligations that transcended the normal rules.

But her story had a twist that made it even more uncomfortable for the government. The former Mexican ambassador to the UN, Adolfo Anguilar Zinser, told the *Observer* in February 2004 that the information from the spying operation had been used to *prevent* a possible deal for a second resolution. In his account, American officials undermined an effort to produce consensus on the Security Council for a resolution by informing the Mexicans quickly that they knew what was being planned, and that it would not succeed. At the very same time, Blair was spending hours on the phone with members of the council, trying to reach a deal for a little more time for the inspectors in exchange for a resolution to authorize war if they failed. It may be that the intelligence he was using to try to produce an agreement was being used by the Americans to stop one. With each revelation, it seemed as if Blair's efforts had been doomed from the start and his faith in Bush misplaced.

Gun's case highlighted both Blair's strength and his weakness. He had succeeded in finding himself a place that was somehow outside politics, a vantage point on the landscape created by 9/11 that seemed to him to afford a uniquely sharp insight into the world unfolding at the start of the new century. It was a personal belief—he might even have used the word "crusade," had its connotations in the Middle East been less sensitive—that went deeper than the practical political judgement that the transatlantic link must be preserved. But it led him into a partnership he couldn't control.

Labour's middle-class supporters were divided by the war, its intellectual ballast drained. Blair's personality became the focus of politics, such was his fervour about the war on terror and Iraq, and it skewed the debates that the government would need to win to be re-elected. In Europe, once the glittering object of Blair's hopes for the second term, there was suspicion and outright hostility towards him. And in the Middle East, the morass in Israel and the occupied territories seemed deeper than ever. The deal with Bush had produced nothing much there.

The war brought nothing but trouble. It was the first to be fought as a result of intelligence, and when that proved uncertain and contradictory, its rationale began to collapse. Its benefits for the rest of the Middle East were less quickly obvious than the war's strongest proponents had expected—and the terror networks, whose involvement with rogue states had been one of the justifications for war, seemed even more threatening than before. The radicalization of many young Muslims increased.

All this came from an alliance with Bush that gave the President a valuable international component to his policy. He could point to a voice from "old Europe," embedded in the UN and the networks of influence that had run the world before the Cold War

and survived it, and extract from that support a degree of justification. It reassured those Americans fearful of a superpower
adventure with no legitimacy abroad, and it turned the war into
an agreement rather than a spasm of revenge for 9/11. Without
Blair, Bush's credibility would have been more difficult to sustain
at home.

For those in the Labour Party, that was the most troubling
realization of all. It was not the choice of war alone that disturbed
them, but the choice of partner.

Blair therefore turned what he had hoped to be an affirmation
of the historic friendship between the countries into a divisive
argument. As the leaders became closer, the worries about Washington policy became deeper and the cruder kind of anti-Americanism more prevalent. He had placed his office at the disposal of
the United States, not in the sense that he abdicated a feeling for
the British interest or that he was so dazzled by the power of the
presidency that he lost the power of speech, but because he
believed that he was the only European leader who could anchor
Bush's policies outside the United States. The price of that judgement was high.

If John Kerry were to displace Bush in November, he knew that
the damage would be immense at home (and the Conservatives
knew it—a number of them around Michael Howard were hoping
for a Kerry win because of the effect on Blair). He would be left
open to the charge that he was the last serious remnant in the
Western world of the Bush cheerleaders' chorus and would have
to go through the contortions of creating a third presidential
friendship from a standing start.

And if Bush won again, who knew what lay ahead? The "axis
of evil" would still be there. On the morning after Labour's
disastrous performance in the European elections in May, Cook
took to the airwaves to say that Blair's best hope of recovering his
party's position was to say, with respect to such campaigns as the
Iraq invasion, "Never again."

But Blair would never say never. Even in his troubles, he
enjoyed the feeling that just as he had taken on his party in

ideological battles from the moment of his election as leader, he was challenging history. In this he shares the neocons' impatience with conventional wisdom: he has the same urge to challenge it.

Blair, despite the familiarity people on every continent now have with him, is in some ways a deliberately remote figure. In taking Britain to war in the Middle East, he challenged the assumptions that had been one of the strongest threads in British foreign policy for nearly all his lifetime. When fifty-two former diplomats wrote an open letter to him expressing their pain at the Iraq invasion and chiding him over what they believed was a neglect of the central question of Israel and the territories, no one believed that it was anything other than a *cri de coeur* from inside the Foreign Office. The old boys were speaking for those who still served but were condemned to public silence. Their view of Blair was as the prime minister who was striking out on his own, with his personal foreign affairs advisers in Downing Street and a diplomatic style that owed too much to his personality and instinct for the liking of the old guard. And as for Bush . . . It would be hard to find anyone in the quiet recesses of the Travellers' Club in Pall Mall, where the Foreign Office eats and drinks and gossips, who would have much to say for him. But their alliance has been the inescapable fact for policymakers for four years.

Cook weighed in again: "Britain now finds itself yoked to a White House approach to the Middle Eastern region that is not the product of any knowledge of its complexity or understanding of its culture, but the result of the simplistic and fundamentalist ideology of the neoconservatives who influence Bush. Both the Middle East and UK are victims of the faith-based foreign policy pursued by the Bush administration."

Blair became Prime Minister at a moment when Britain was still, to its own surprise, struggling with a half-understood legacy of Empire. By the time he was born, that era was drawing to a close, and as Union flags were being lowered for the last time across Africa and Asia in a long, slow sunset, an argument over modern Britain's national interest was about to begin.

Blair had no choice but to take on the argument over European integration that had divided the two main British parties for a generation, though he came to power with few grand ideas about the world order. He wasn't schooled in the ways of international affairs and was driven primarily by the imperatives of domestic policy rather than any global ambitions. But his character and his personal instincts drew him toward the world stage. So did Bill Clinton, whom he soon found to be a soul mate of sorts.

Each had a certain love of the sweeping statement and the gleaming horizon. That trait unhinges many politicians and leaves them presiding over the wreckage of dreams, but by the time Blair began his second term in 2001, he was persuaded that following his nose had served him well. Having been accused of warmongering in the Balkans, he would point to Milosevic in the dock in The Hague as proof that he'd been right to urge the bombing campaigns and the threat of troops against the Serbs. The result was that he was susceptible to the call from America when it came.

The causes were accidental—the hairsbreadth election of Bush, the timing of the attacks on New York and Washington. The response, however, turned those spins of the wheel into a pattern. Blair ran with his luck and made it seem a course that had been preordained, much as a Roman general might look at the augur's arrangement of chicken bones and see in them the spur to action for which he had been waiting, the justification by fate for the fight that lay ahead.

Those who worry about Blair's penchant for the moral crusade are right in identifying the tendency but often wrong in attributing it solely to his religious beliefs. Although strong, they are more confused than critics imagine, and he does not draw from them a set of guidelines for politics—only a feeling of obligation. It is true that it was that obligation as much as an understanding of the power of the transatlantic alliance that drew him to Bush after 9/11.

He found that he needed reassurance for beliefs about the threats of the new century, and found them in Washington. He also found a president who, to his surprise, turned out to be decisive in ways that his caricature concealed. The picture of Bush that is emerging from the Iraq story is—right or wrong—of a president who was steely-eyed and determined. But Blair's choice sent a shudder through the European political establishment and horrified many friends who never thought they would be pulled into an American war by a Labour prime minister. It had become impossible not to feel strongly about Blair. His policy was the dividing line in politics, pulling his friends and his enemies in all directions.

And in the United States, he enjoyed his accolades. Congress feted him, various polls showed his popularity higher than Bush's, and a Mr. Jon Danvers of West Falmouth, Massachusetts, established a website at www.thankyoutony.com, which collected observations on the British prime minister, however glutinous, with the promise that they would all be forwarded to Downing Street.

Nothing quite like it had been seen before. It was probably just as well that when he appeared before both Houses of Congress in July 2002, he didn't make the same joke as the great journalist and broadcaster Alistair Cooke, who, when he was accorded the same honour in the 1970s, said he'd had a dream in which he forgot what he was going to say and blurted out, "And so, ladies and gentlemen, I accept your nomination for president of the United States." If Blair had tried that one, someone might have taken him seriously.

He is level-headed, and he understands the consequences of the historic choice he made. In joining Bush at a moment when Europe was leery of his presidency, he was doing much more than trying to be the bridge between the old world and the new. He was trying to make himself indispensable to both continents, the only man who could carry the subtle messages from Washington to Brussels and back again. But the consequence was to turn himself into what the novelist John le Carré calls in his haunting phrase "the minstrel for the American cause," singing the song wherever he went, even when the audience was sullen or hostile.

Blair is naturally resentful of any suggestion that he has aban-

doned the national interest in his alliance with Bush and points to
the interest all Europe must have in an America anchored in the
world and not whirling dangerously in its own orbit. He can detail
the differences he has with Bush—on climate change, a profound
one—and make the case for the influence he has been able to
bring to bear on Israel and on the UN because of his special access.
The question for his colleagues, however, is which of the two
benefitted more: Blair or Bush? They have concluded that the
answer lies in Washington.

Clinton himself has sympathy for Blair's predicament as he tried
to swing the balance by exercising influence with Bush, but
though he was eloquent about the difficulty of Blair's position as
the putative bridge-builder, Clinton himself had wanted more
time. He had agreed with Hans Blix in early 2003 that it was
worth stretching the inspection timetable. A few more weeks and
who knew what might be established. "I think he should have
been allowed to finish the job. I think that's where the big mistake
on the part of the United States was," says Clinton.

It was that determination to draw the UN process to a close that
pitched Blair into war. He couldn't get security council agreement
on a new resolution that would have been a trigger for war in
exchange for a little more inspection time, so he delivered on his
promise to Bush. Blix himself spoke to Blair at the end of February
2003 in an effort to persuade him to part with Bush on the
timetable: he pointed out that several hundred sites visited by the
inspectors and identified for them by MI6 had turned up nothing.
Blix, who had no illusions about Saddam's past ambitions, now
believed that the intelligence was flawed and that there might be
nothing there. But Blair could not be moved. The promise of
"weeks not months" made at the White House in January would
be honoured.

His choice left him isolated among colleagues, many of whom
believed that his loyalty to Bush had produced rewards that were
very meagre indeed. They might be loyal—might even urge him
to resist any suggestion that he might give way to Brown before
the election, as a number of them did—but would remain con-

vinced that there were moments when he could have distanced himself from Washington, to the benefit of his government and his party, and chose not to.

In that respect, Blair failed. The defence of his convictions meant that he was trapped in support of a worldview that seemed to contradict directly his policies toward Iran and Libya, his objectives for Israel and the Palestinians, and his belief in the primacy of the United Nations. The leader who had spoken after 9/11 of a call to international action, and a global war on both poverty and terrorism, appeared to be the agent of a policy that divided the world into good and evil, right and wrong. He had become a divider at home and abroad.

There are no calendars for prime ministerial lives. Some are short, some long. Some fall from power—three of the last eight have left office without an election—and the parliamentary system, even when there is a huge government majority, is an unpredictable and wilful beast. A year after he invaded Iraq, Blair knew that he was nearing the end of his time. It might last a year or two, taking him beyond what he could still hope would be a third winning election if attention turned away from the world's troubles; or it might end sooner. But Blair's unquestioned mastery of British politics was over. Iraq would be his epitaph. Even if his batteries recharged themselves, as they have often done before, and even if he did something extraordinary before he went—like winning a referendum on the European constitution—he would remain the prime minister who fought a war that may divide peoples and governments for a generation or more. He would leave a Middle East in flux and a Western alliance in NATO that wonders after Iraq whether the old obligations of multinational partnership will ever be taken seriously again.

He would also leave behind a transatlantic relationship electrified. The shock has isolated him at home and made it more difficult for him to achieve his aims in other spheres. Instead of giving him strength, it has weakened him. He still does not think it was a mistake, because he believes in the cause as much as he did after 9/11. But the alliance he wanted to preserve has changed and damaged him.

That alliance has also changed America. Although Blair did not use the full influence he may have had in trying to prevent war, perhaps because inside he doubted how great its weight was and underestimated the momentary power he had, he was a prime minister who helped to define a presidency. He articulated fears and promised support, encouraging a policy that shaped an era. There was nothing neutral about Blair. Without him there might still have been war, but it would have been different. This prime minister who knew America only slightly, whose closest American friends were presidents, became a figure who escaped for a while from the grey processions of leaders who cross the seas to Washington and, for a time, was cherished.

His absorption into America's crisis was unpredictable but profound. Drawn into a "war on terror" that he allowed to encompass war in Iraq as well as the struggle with the terrorist networks that had begun to obsess him, he made a choice. When colleagues like Brown and Straw wanted him to step aside from Bush, he refused. When his party wanted to hear him speak against the regime at Guantanamo Bay, he was guarded in his criticism. When he learned of Clinton's mystification at the depth of his alliance with Bush, it made no difference to him. He understood that the decision to go to war was an irrevocable break for him, more serious than his commitment of troops to the Balkans or the bombing and sanctions in Iraq that had gone before. There was no retreat.

Accidents had helped to bring him to this point, but it was his own character that would not let him turn back. For Blair, the age of terrorism became the age of moral politics. That judgment was his own, not the conviction of his government or party and one that appeared to disturb a substantial number of those who had voted for him. It was authentic, but dangerous. His alliance with Bush seemed to produce meagre rewards for his government, and plenty of odium. Ever the politician who breaks the rules, Blair put that relationship above almost any other, despite the troubles it brought him.

He turned it from a practical friendship that could keep America and Europe together into a moral assertion about the politics of his age, one that separated him from the political culture from which he sprang.

With Bush, he began to write a narrative for the new century, a story line that challenged history and the conventions of the international alliances he inherited as prime minister. His tragedy was that although he believed that one day he would be proved right, he might never be forgiven for it.

CHAPTER 10

# A QUESTION
# OF TRUST

Opponents of the war withheld forgiveness from Blair, but it was a deeper lack of faith from the electorate at home that worried him more. Even as his relationship with Bush became more routine and more natural in his mind, and he reassured himself that he should not regret the invasion as it slipped into the past, the tendrils of creeping problems at home began to ensnare him.

Victory over Saddam ushered in a long period in which he lost the ability to command the political stage in the way he had once found straightforward. Bush's unpopularity grew, support for the war declined and the family quarrels and weary rivalries inside a tired government began to pull it apart. Everywhere he turned there was trouble. For the first time since coming to power, he appeared to struggle to keep control.

One word above all seemed to haunt him. Just as he and his party had succeeded in attaching the label "sleaze" to the Major government in the mid-1990s when it was lurching towards the end, making it indelible, so he found that "trust" became the word he couldn't shake off. Everything seemed touched by it—war and Bush, Europe and the referendum, taxes and public services, his relationship with Brown. No longer was he going to be judged on whether or not he delivered on his promises simply by a measurement of the number of hospital operations done or exams passed or jobs created, but by whether he meant what he said.

For a prime minister whose second term was dominated by a breach with his party on a question of principle—and, as he saw it, morality—this was especially frustrating. It was also energy-sapping. For the year leading up to the elections in Iraq he found his every political move dogged by the accusation that he was engaged in some form of double-dealing and the suspicion that nothing could ever be what it seemed. As Margaret Thatcher had become a model of inflexibility, John Major the leader who'd lost command of his party and, in a previous era, Harold Wilson the prime minister who was driven above all by a love of political manoeuvre, Blair at home became the reverse of the image he had created in the United States where he was thought to be an open book. He was the prime minister who was always thought to be up to something, even when he wasn't.

There were many reasons, some which flowed from the jumble of unfinished business that is bound to accumulate in government cupboards after nearly eight years in power and some from mistakes which revealed how tired and distracted his administration was threatening to become, not least because of the weight put on it by war and by the unresolved strains between its principal figures next door to each other in Downing Street. The problems surfaced in almost everything the government tried to do.

On such second-division questions as House of Lords reform and fox hunting, for example, Blair found himself in a terrible tangle. The failure to think through the consequences of the first stages of changes to the Lords (the easier ones) resulted in the Lord Chancellor, Lord Falconer, fighting a series of wearying battles with his own backbenchers as well as with the Opposition parties and a powerful group of crossbenchers, none of them so easily caricatured as creatures of the hereditary principle now that the Upper House consisted overwhelmingly of appointed peers. A Lord Chancellor who has to spend hours on the woolsack conducting a debate about what title he should hold in future, or even if he should exist, and whether he should wear a full-bottomed wig, is a minister who has a problem.

The Cabinet was not agreed on what kind of House of Lords it wanted: wholly appointed, wholly elected or something in between and, if a hybrid, how it should be divided among elected members and those appointed by some new sleaze-free committee. Though it was never an issue that would sway the electorate in a campaign, or even keep them talking in the pub for longer than half-time in a football match, it epitomized an unmistakable quality of uncertainty in government that was coming to cling to ministers like an unpleasant odour that wouldn't blow away. The peculiar machinations of the fox-hunting debate had the same effect.

Blair was particularly irritated that it was he who had recommitted Labour to a ban in England and Wales in an unscripted and off-the-cuff remark on *Question Time* on BBC television, setting in train events which would produce parliamentary chaos and a good deal of public ridicule. By the end, Blair himself was trying in vain to extricate himself from the consequences of his words by promoting a compromise long after the pro- and anti-forces had settled on a fight to the death, and he absented himself from the Commons for the last votes in what was universally assumed to be an effort to protect himself from further embarrassment.

In pursuit of the hounds and in defence of the fox, the government was forced to reach deep into its armoury for the bluntest instrument of all, the Parliament Act, to subdue the rebellious Lords and "save" its legislation to ban hunting with dogs—though most members of the Cabinet had long since lost any enthusiasm for it, not to mention the post-1997 new breed of Labour MPs in rural areas who feared annihilation at the hands of pro-hunting groups and the umbrella Countryside Alliance, which had largely succeeded in turning the argument into a debate about individual freedom. After parliamentary antics which Gilbert and Sullivan would have enjoyed, the ban became law, only for the government to try a last desperate manoeuvre to prevent it coming into force before the general election campaign.

Nothing revealed the frayed nerves in Downing Street more clearly than the decision in early 2005 that the Attorney General shouldn't oppose an injunction sought by the Countryside Alliance to delay the ban pending a ruling on its constitutionality. In the normal course of events, the Attorney would be expected to argue for implementation of the law. This suggested panic. The government was stuck with a piece of legislation its supporters still insisted had strong popular appeal, but which had turned into a parliamentary demonstration of how Blair's government, its huge majority notwithstanding, had lost its sure-footedness and had begun to stumble over obstacles which should have caused it little difficulty.

Inescapably, such muddles and about-turns seemed to be symptoms of a deeper malaise. In the fourth year of the second term, the Labour Party was in a period of anxious self-analysis. The approach of an election has that effect. Blair's MPs were increasingly grateful for the weakness of the Opposition—the depleted Conservative benches still found it difficult to sustain long bursts of damaging fire—because they realized how edgy their government was. There were almost weekly examples. Why, for instance, did Blair use one question time in January 2005 to express some support for a change in the law to redefine a householder's right to resist an intruder by force? The Lord Chancellor had already dismissed a Conservative private member's bill to do the same thing as unnecessary and a gimmick, and soon after Blair's intervention his Home Secretary announced that the government didn't support a change after all. Again, Blair seemed to have been unnecessarily jumpy. Why? His backbenchers were used to Downing Street's sensitivity to popular tabloid campaigns which might leave the government looking "weak" but they suspected that such episodes revealed a lack of political street-wisdom that was more worrying. Was the Prime Minister who had turned his second term into a demonstration of resolution in war starting to lose his touch?

The pressure of the war was immense. The number of Labour MPs who were willing privately to defend the strategy was shrinking fast, and public scepticism was growing. As measured by the polling organization Populus in its regular surveys for *The Times*, in the seventeen months from June 2003 to November 2004 opinion reversed itself. In the summer, a couple of months after the fall of Saddam, 58 per cent said they believed military action had been "the right thing to do" and 34 per cent disagreed. With two months to go before the Iraq elections, at the end of 2004, the figures were almost exactly the other way round—only 31 per cent supported military action and 57 per cent described it as "wrong".

This was a serious loss of public confidence. Blair was running an unpopular war, and one which he was seen to have promoted and organized with Bush. The Iraq invasion wasn't one which was an inescapable response to Saddam, but Blair's choice. With the Hutton and Butler reports identifying the depth of the unease in Whitehall, no one could be in any doubt about the Prime Minister's personal responsibility. He could never claim he had been forced into it; it was he who had been the persuader when others expressed worries.

He was no longer riding a tide of public support, and conversion to the cause of a referendum on a constitution for the European Union gave him a similar problem. A huge majority in any opinion poll taken on the subject expressed either deep hostility or suspicion of the project and only a small percentage—sometimes in single figures—positive enthusiasm. If he was to win a referendum in the first year of a third term a huge shift in opinion would have to occur, and Blair's ability to lead such a campaign was greatly impaired by the damage inflicted on him by the war. Much as he might complain in private that he had been bounced into the decision by Jack Straw—and he continued to do so months after the announcement of his change of heart—it was a policy which was his, another commitment which seemed overwhelmingly personal.

Yet despite all this, as he approached his third election as leader he was not a prime minister who seemed to be heading for defeat. He was not in the position of Jim Callaghan in 1979 or John

Major in 1997 who had both expected to lose, nor even the Major of 1992 who had to turn round a campaign that many thought would go against him. Blair was able to maintain a steady lead over the Conservatives despite his troubles, and found the opposition an unexpected source of solace in dark moments. Only rarely did Labour slip behind in the straightforward measurement of voter preferences, and when asked month-by-month which party they believed would win the coming election, a majority of voters said consistently that they expected Blair to remain prime minister when it was all over. Even those who disliked him intensely (and that number was rising) still saw him as a winner.

He remained, therefore, a most unusual prime minister for one who had been in office for nearly eight years. He was not a leader defined by his head-to-head contests with Michael Howard at question time, nor by opinion poll see-saws, but by the way he was preparing for a third term most electors believed he would win. Though the victory could not be taken for granted—the worries in the Labour Party about abstentions and defections were acute—the mind of the government collectively turned to how Blair would deal with the accumulation of difficulties that were making his life so difficult: how a third term would be *different*.

He therefore tried to manage the trick that was pulled off successfully by Margaret Thatcher in advance of her third election campaign in 1987, of presenting an image of a government re-inventing itself. Just as she had been able to portray her government as one that had to argue with itself about how best to proceed—because the Labour opposition of the day could be described, credibly, as not yet ready for government—Blair began to prepare for the election by emphasizing his determination to continue his struggle with elements in his party which were resistant to change, particularly in the public services. A phrase began to do the rounds in late 2004—"the manifesto will be so New Labour that it will make your eyes water". It was Blair's own.

Not only did he want to impart some energy to the campaign by demonstrating that the government was thinking of new policies (even as it was having problems handling some of the consequences of old ones), he was drawn naturally to the pulsing problem which had been the story of the last few years: his tussle with Brown. While Thatcher had used her struggle with the "wets" and "fainthearts" with great relish to burnish her reputation as an Iron Lady, Blair became combative with his chancellor more by accident. But as the end of the second term approached, it was a real struggle.

The conference speech from Brown which had caused Blair to conclude they must directly confront their differences was no passing moment of disagreement. A year later, the feelings which had stirred in that conference week in Blackpool were still raw. It turned out to be what Blair had sensed at the time: an episode that stretched their relationship to the point where it became an almost daily irritation to them both.

In the year after Brown's challenge at the 2003 conference, Blair sensed for the first time an ideological division between them which was beginning to grow. There had been differences all along—notably on how to couch the government attitude to the Euro—but only at this stage of the second term did Blair begin to believe that his commitment to public-service reforms involving market mechanisms were being threatened by Brown. It was not a particularly clear-cut division. Brown, after all, had been the evangelist for private–public partnerships which had mystified and disturbed the Left, and his obsession with the fiscal disciplines which he had carried into the Treasury with him like a set of commandments had allowed him to find a common language with Blair on economic policy. They were able to utter in unison the New Labour mantra that social reform could be produced by sound financial management, the central claim on which Blairism was based.

But in the disputes on university top-up fees and foundation hospitals in 2004 lay the seeds of an anxiety which grew in Blair's mind throughout the year. Was Brown now charting a quite different course, the one he would follow when he became—as he was sure he would—the successor in Downing Street?

By now, so much had been written about the relationship that it was a public affair. It was understood by everyone in the Labour Party and almost anyone with a passing interest in politics that their difficulty sprang largely from the closeness which had once enveloped them in the dark days of the 1980s and in the progress towards the first victory in 1997. It was because they knew each other so well that it was so painful. Even when Mandelson broke with Brown in 1994 and their friendship exploded in bitterness, the overarching family quality of the dealings around Blair was preserved. There were rows and sulks, and periods of silence, but calm was usually restored and the alliance preserved.

As had always been inevitable, however, time took its toll. Brown became the longest-serving chancellor since David Lloyd-George and had good reason to ponder on one of the old Liberal's favourite aphorisms—"there is no friendship at the top". With the passing of the years, the irritations began to weary them both and Brown's anxiety to succeed to the premiership began to gnaw at him. Those around him knew the symptoms and told the story around Whitehall and Westminster. However much Brown denied it, the picture being painted by his friends was of a frustrated man whose patience was ready to snap. Cartoonists saw him as a giant in a cave bursting to get out, the lumbering figure whose footprints marked the landscape, the restless spirit at the heart of government. The caricature stuck, because it caught the truth.

Though it would be misleading to picture Brown and Blair as crude ideological rivals, given their joint absorption in seven years of government, the differences which were becoming more obvious to Blair were also troubling Brown. Blair would say "we rub along" when he was asked how his relations with Brown stood, but he might as well have said "we rub each other up the wrong way". They did, and more often than before. It was almost as if they had begun to look for reasons to disagree.

Blair would speak of those eyes watering at the coming manifesto, Brown about redistribution of wealth and social justice; Blair about the importance of market disciplines in the public sector, Brown about the moral responsibility for dealing with child poverty. Neither would disagree in public with the objectives of the other, but each seemed condemned at this mature stage of their relationship to want to point up the differences of emphasis, or the differences in their priorities. Sometimes, almost without noticing it, they would use language that distinguished them from each other: it began to be something close to a compulsion.

This was a development that was encouraged by their bag-carriers and cheerleaders who fed the gossip mill with relish. It had become a habit which was now impossible to break. Quite early in the second term one close Blair adviser described them as "two extraordinary men—possibly great men—but of course you have to realize that one of them is mad". Such crude descriptions were common. Brown would be portrayed as the Iron Chancellor with the tragic flaw (ambition) and in the Brown camp Blair would be presented as a prime minister who reacted to his war-driven unpopularity by closeting himself even more closely with advisers regarded frankly in the Treasury as enemies—principal among them Lord Birt, Andrew Adonis and Roger Liddle (before he left to become *chef de cabinet* in Mandelson's commissioner's office in Brussels). With each twist of their own personal argument, the rivalries between their loyalists became fiercer and a vicious spiral drove them on.

Blair, consumed by war and the consequent need to recover his popularity to retain command of the political middle ground, became more anxious to define himself and in doing so tried to rekindle an idea of "Blairism" which would sharpen his public character once again, allowing him to stand out in the smoke of battle. Brown, still believing he had been given good reason to expect the succession at the end of the second term, was thinking his own thoughts: about child poverty, the constitution and public services. When the *Sunday Telegraph* journalist Robert Peston published his *Brown's Britain* at the beginning of 2005 it was seen by everybody in Whitehall as an account of the Chancellor's personal manifesto. Although it caused Brown some embarrassment, and completed the demonization in Number 10 of his long-time adviser Ed Balls because of his cooperation with Peston, the book was revealing about the efforts in the Brown camp to produce a coherent approach to government. In Blair's office, it was seen as an alternative manifesto.

That view was, of course, correct. To Brown, strategic policy thinking is a natural activity. He does it all the time. Although his serious policy differences with Blair have often been exaggerated—the difficulty in rubbing along has almost always been personal—by this stage of the second term he was embarked on a rethink about Labour's future. In character, therefore, the exercise was similar to Blair's but was beginning to point in a different direction. In particular, he began to look for a model for public services that tilted Labour away from the market thinking which, he thought, was getting too much of a grip.

This process was a product of the length of time they had spent in government and also of their weariness after years of up-and-down relations. Blair was tired of treading on eggshells in his conversations with Brown; the Chancellor was fed up with the tantalizing sight of a door to Number 10 which seemed to disappear in the mist just as it was about to open.

A typical product was Brown's speech to a new pressure group, Compass, in October 2004 when he laid out his ideas of a "public sphere" which should be Labour's natural concern and its home territory. In the course of the speech he acknowledged the frustration of Labour supporters who had expected more from their government, warmed to his own theme of the challenge of poverty at home and abroad, and expressed impatience about reform of the Lords (the policy area in which Blair and his closest Cabinet friend Lord Falconer appeared bogged down). On markets and public services, he was clear.

"There is such a thing as progressive politics achieved by people coming together for the common good to do what needs to be done but which cannot be achieved just by markets, however dynamic; cannot be achieved by charity, however philanthropic; cannot be achieved by individuals on their own, however well-meaning; can only be achieved in a public realm where people think of themselves not as consumers but as neighbours and citizens."

This was directed not only at Blair himself, but at the member of the Cabinet who was now established as the polar opposite of Brown—Alan Milburn, installed in the portmanteau office of Chancellor of the Duchy of Lancaster to supervise preparations for the general election, the job which had been Brown's in 2001 and 1997. The snub by Blair was public, since there could be no other interpretation of the reappointment of Milburn (who had left the Cabinet as health secretary, he said, to have a rest from the strains of front-line politics). He was not simply Blair's loyal sidekick (a Tonto to the Prime Minister's Lone Ranger, as Matthew d'Ancona of the *Sunday Telegraph* called him) but a stick with which to poke Brown. They had not lost the suspicions and irritations that had sprung up between them at the time of the foundation-hospitals row, and in Brown's state of near-permanent frustration with Blair, Milburn's arrival at the Prime Minister's side with daily access to his office was an affront. Milburn was no less interested in interpreting it in that way.

If Brown was already talking of public-service reform in a way that distinguished him from Blair, Milburn's role in managing the election manifesto was going to encourage the Chancellor to be even more frank. With each move on the chessboard, the game seemed to become clearer. The two friends and rivals were approaching the end game.

The period between the break at the end of 2003 and the pre-election preparations eighteen months later was the most difficult they had experienced together. Brown was set on a course that seemed to be a preparation for power, Blair on an effort to breathe some energy back into a premiership which sometimes seemed to be exhausted by war. It was on Iraq and not on the differences between Blair and Brown that the Labour Party was in turmoil, but such were the feelings of antipathy to Blair stirred up by Iraq and his alliance with Bush that the new fissures became part of the riven landscape that was the Brown–Blair story. It was as simple as this: if you were against Blair, you knew who the alternative was.

The curiosity of this stage in their rivalry was that it did not turn on the war, the very question on which Blair's leadership was being questioned in the country. It was true that Brown was sparing in his comments on the subject, and tended to offer opinions only when asked in interviews if he still supported the Prime Minister's policy (when the answer was always "yes"). Indeed, no figure of remotely equivalent stature in modern British government had said less about such a dominating subject than Brown. Yet he decided not to break with Blair on the war.

He made his position clear in Cabinet at the climactic moment in the run-up to war, when Robin Cook resigned after the failure of the negotiations to get a second UN resolution. At the meeting immediately after Cook's departure, Brown took the unusual step of intervening immediately from his seat directly across from Blair, just after the Prime Minister spoke. It was his custom to wait before offering his thoughts (often with his head down, scribbling). On this occasion he took the floor the moment Blair had finished. Cook had been wrong to go; the effort at the UN had been a good try and it was a pity it had failed, but the principle of military action to disarm Saddam was still justified.

This was no accidental contribution, a friendly piece of support when Blair needed it. Brown was making a calculated statement of his position. He would not try to split the government over Iraq, though it was something which he had had good reason to believe might force Blair from office. Brown had no interest in inheriting the premiership in such circumstances with the government in crisis. It might mean an election in dangerous circumstances; it would certainly plunge him into a foreign-affairs crisis with the United States of a sort that did not attract him at all and which would be a difficult start to a premiership. In any case, his friends reassured him, the Blair promise of succession became more of a certainty as a result of Iraq. A prime minister embarking on such a mission, in Bush's footsteps, was likely to have a shorter shelf-life than might otherwise have been the case. Therefore loyalty, without too much public enthusiasm for war, was Brown's wisest course.

The effect on Blair of the next eighteen months of war and botched reconstruction in Iraq did indeed match the predictions of those who expected trouble and unpopularity for him and his government. As Straw and others had suspected in early 2004, Blair had thought of resignation for the first time in the whirlwind of unpopularity that surrounded him. It was his unhappiest period in office. By the summer he had emerged from that patch, but with much of his party firmly aligned against the war (few Labour MPs in private being willing to make the case for it with genuine enthusiasm) he was suffering the consequences of another Great Misunderstanding of the sort that had punctuated his relationship with Brown for most of its two decades.

It had an eerie echo of the conversation they'd had in 1994 in settling the question of the party leadership, with Brown agreeing to step aside in return for formidable powers as chancellor if the election was won. Over the years, the implication that Blair would voluntarily stand aside if Labour had a prolonged period in office had become the talisman for Brown's supporters, and a promise. In Blair's mind it had never been any such thing. The recollections of the two men hardened over the years and could not be reconciled. Now, with war at the gates, they managed to engineer another promise-that-never-was.

Throughout the early stages of war in Iraq, Blair's colleagues had begun to see his premiership entering its last phase. He was tired, and even his characteristic ability to bounce back after a game of tennis or a short holiday couldn't conceal the effect of the pressure. He was thin and lined and preoccupied with the business of a reconstruction in Iraq which was going wrong. His irritation at Garner and then Bremer, and the Pentagon behind them, couldn't be publicly revealed, but he was aware of how the apparently easy victory in April 2003 had turned into a struggle which would be expensive in every way—in money, lives and political capital.

Around the time of Brown's "best when we are Labour speech"

in October 2003 the chancellor was denied by Blair the seat on Labour's national executive which he'd had since they came to power and seemed automatic. That passage of arms, on top of the feelings which were bubbling up between them once again, was enough to persuade Prescott, with Blair's active encouragement, to try to effect some kind of reconciliation. Like everyone else around them, the deputy prime minister thought that the effect on the government might be disastrous if they couldn't resume the day-to-day relations which had seen them through previous difficulties. In early November, he hosted a dinner at his grace-and-favour flat in Admiralty House in Whitehall, a hundred yards from Downing Street.

The claims by Brown's cohorts that Blair was planning his resignation, which rattled round Westminster in the following spring, had their genesis at this table. Straw and others—particularly the health secretary John Reid, whose ambitions to frustrate Brown by edging him out of the succession were beginning to grow—watched Blair wobble, and worried. But from Brown's camp came a different story—that resignation was the plan.

In disentangling fiction and fact in these encounters between the two, the problem is the intimacy of their understanding of each other. They have almost become mind readers. So much is unspoken. They are said by those who may be in a position to know to be reduced more often to frustrated shouts and displays of anger than used to be the case, but a great deal still passes between them under the surface. It is a stream which can carry many misunderstandings along with it.

When Blair and Brown sat at Prescott's table, they were both angry. Brown was stung by his exclusion from the NEC, which he had thought useful, he pointed out publicly, as a base from which to run the previous two election campaigns (perhaps he was having a premonition of the change which Blair finally made with the appointment of Milburn). Blair was furious about the conference speech and wanted to "have it out". Yet they cannot agree on what then happened. Blair denies ever having said that he would resign in the coming year; but in the request to Brown to help him through what would be a difficult patch, and the reference again to the eventual succession coming to the chancellor, Brown was encouraged to believe that it was in his mind. In his circle, it became the source of the belief a year later that once again Blair had gone back on a promise.

With such a background of mistrust, it was not surprising Brown found it awkward to deny convincingly the accusation attributed to him in Peston's book, that he had said he could never again trust anything Blair said.

The two years of the Iraq crisis, the strains of a relationship which had perhaps patched up too often, and the natural difficulties of a mature government which could no longer blame problems on its predecessors all began to feed on each other and the common ingredient, on which Michael Howard and the Conservatives could feast with glee, was trust.

Blair's chancellor didn't trust him, they said. The people didn't trust him on Iraq: where were the weapons of mass destruction? Promises on public services had been broken. Why should anyone believe Blair again? As a prelude to the election campaign which Blair was planning for spring 2005 this was about as unwelcome a political theme as could be imagined.

As if to emphasize the way in which Blair's premiership was now being shaken by winds from every quarter, an utterly unexpected blast unnerved him at the very moment when he was trying to steady the relationship with Brown in time for the election campaign and looking forward to Iraqi elections as giving some positive evidence of achievement in that country. David Blunkett's resignation as home secretary because of the complications of a love affair was one of the unlikeliest events with which Blair had ever had to cope—the fall of the minister who'd been probably his most unbending ally on the war as the result of an affair with the publisher of the *Spectator*, home of the young fogeys and intellectual playground of the Right. The picture was of a government to which almost anything might happen.

When Blunkett's affair with an unnamed married woman was first revealed in (almost inevitably) the *News of the World* in August

2004, it seemed as if he might survive. Even when the *Sun* followed up with her name and her pregnancy was revealed, he was in no mood to walk the plank, and no one seemed to want to push him forward. For everyone who disapproved of the relationship with Kimberley Fortier there seemed to be someone who expressed sympathy for Blunkett—divorced, blind and evidently lonely. Indeed, he was the recipient of more favourable coverage in the press than any political figure caught in a similar predicament in recent times. The Conservatives did not rush to condemn and there was much talk of private lives being private and a change in the social climate since some of John Major's colleagues had been destroyed as ministers for their sexual peccadilloes. The respite, however, was short.

In November, Blunkett was revealed to have started a legal action to establish his paternity of his lover's first child. At almost the same time, it was alleged in one of the titbits which were being fed to the newspapers about the affair that he had fast-tracked an application from his lover's nanny for an indefinite right to remain in Britain. Within a day, the Home Office permanent secretary had had to establish an independent inquiry under Sir Alan Budd, a former Treasury mandarin and government adviser, who began a series of interviews and a trawl of the email records in Blunkett's private office. The sky turned dark.

Already he was accused of involvement in the speedy arrangements made for the nanny by the notoriously slow immigration office, for getting her a train ticket on his House of Commons spouse's pass and of bringing two Home Office officials to a lawyers' meeting connected with his paternity action. The distinction between private and public lives which Blair had cited in Blunkett's defence was now hopelessly blurred. He had less than three weeks left in office.

The Budd inquiry began to uncover a muddle in his ministerial private office, the Conservatives began to smell blood in the water and, to cap it all, spicy extracts were published from an on-the-record interview he had given to the journalist Stephen Pollard who was writing a biography with which Blunkett had agreed to cooperate. His comments on Cabinet colleagues were ripe—Prescott was thin-skinned, Straw had left the Home Office in a mess, Patricia Hewitt had no strategic grasp, Tessa Jowell was weak, Charles Clarke had gone soft and Blair was tolerating more from a cantankerous Brown than he ought to. With these observations, Blunkett sealed his own fate. Straw, in particular, was livid. He wanted him out. Others began to cut the mooring ropes that were keeping the home secretary steady and he began to float away.

Any findings of possible wrongdoing would now finish him, and they did. Sir Alan found an email which showed that the nanny's application had been fast-tracked, though he could not establish direct involvement by the home secretary. Claiming he had done nothing wrong, but that questions about his integrity were damaging the government, Blunkett resigned the day after Sir Alan told him privately what he had found.

The information had been known in Blair's office for a few days before Blunkett himself was told by Sir Alan—and realized on the instant that he was sunk—so the Prime Minister spent the weekend at Chequers in the knowledge that he was almost certainly about to lose his home secretary, though at this stage Blunkett still thought he might struggle through. Blair had defended him throughout (and even said after the resignation that he left office without a stain on his character) and was therefore badly wounded by his departure. Howard was able to make merry in the Commons with Blunkett's tart observations on members of the Cabinet and Blair no longer looked like the Prime Minister who seemed to have the ability to dodge every obstacle in his path, but rather one who was tumbling into trouble as a matter of habit.

The news from Iraq was bad, the world knew that his relations with Brown were difficult and sometimes wretched, his Cabinet seemed to be calling each other names and his home secretary, in charge of the home front of the "war on terror", had been brought down by an affair with a socialite of the Right who was now revealed to have had at least two lovers in addition to Blunkett and her husband. Blair had presented himself, particularly in the

Iraq campaign, as someone whose convictions and purpose were always clear and who was therefore a straightforward leader. That image was now gone.

The coming election presented a new unexpected challenge. Blair would have to reinvent himself.

His problems demanded it. Muddling along with Brown was more awkward than ever and Labour MPs were stirring restively. They were angry at the playing out in public of the Cabinet's family squabbles—insisting that prime minister and chancellor come to a weekly meeting of the parliamentary party for a collective lecture on good behaviour—and they were becoming more disturbed by Blunkett's legacy at the Home Office, a regime which involved unlimited detention without charge for foreign terrorist suspects which was the subject of an excoriating critique from the Law Lords (by an 8 to 1 majority) who concluded that it was incompatible with the government's human rights obligations which Blair had once boasted of having incorporated in domestic law. In Iraq, despite an impressive turnout in the election at the end of January 2005, the violence against American and British forces was not diminishing, and brave talk of an "exit strategy" being conceived in London and Washington seemed optimistic.

Blair's life was complicated at every turn. Even if he won a spring or summer election with a comfortable working majority, which is what his pollsters were predicting at the turn of the year, he would have to deal with the Brown problem in some fashion. It seemed to be reaching a climax. And he had committed himself to a European referendum, probably within a year of the election, which still looked a loser. Nervous ministers had long been avoiding the subject in public, and Blair himself had shown only sporadic bursts of enthusiasm, despite his private commitment to the constitution which he believed (not unfairly) had been drafted in a way much more helpful to Britain than had once seemed likely. He knew he might not be able to survive a referendum defeat.

The Prime Minister who faced these difficulties was one who had been weakened, above all, by the campaign that had dominated nearly the whole of his second term. The overwhelmingly public view was that the Iraq war had been fought on a false prospectus. Some critics accused Blair of lying about weapons of mass destruction; but many did not, preferring to accept his argument that he had never said anything he did not believe at the time. The effect was the same.

Whether or not Blair had believed it, the "truth" of Saddam's imminent threat had turned out to be something quite different. In December 2004, the Bush administration admitted quietly that it expected to find no weapons of mass destruction. In London and Washington it was accepted that the hunt was over, though Blair had continued to express his belief that something would be found in the end. This was bad enough, because it undermined the judgement on which Blair had pinned his decision to go to war, but as the the arguments about UN resolutions and intelligence judgements began to slip far enough into the past to be subjected to cool judgement the scale of the error seemed to grow.

The dark shadow of the September dossier of 2002 refused to lift. The four inquiries into it—by Hutton, Butler and two Commons select committees—revealed how mistaken it had been. Hutton was the most forgiving, giving the benefit of his doubt to the intelligence officials who had come up with the forty-five-minute claim, but the document was now the most discredited publication of the Blair era (with the possible exception of the later, long-buried dossier mugged up from the old PhD thesis which was discounted almost as soon as it had been published). Blair's problem was not simply that it was the lingering evidence of an intelligence miscalculation, but that it seemed to speak of a style of leadership which he had come to represent. And if the way the intelligence had been sifted and tested was any guide, government seemed to have become a ramshackle business even when it came to war.

Not only had the government argued a case for invasion on evidence which turned out to be partly false, and inadequately scrutinized on its way through the Whitehall system, but it was revealed to have shown little interest in making sure that the "facts" which were the dossier's raison d'etre were accurately presented.

Geoff Hoon, the defence secretary, admitted as much in testimony to Lord Hutton which remained on the record as evidence of the way in which the government was willing to allow an impression to settle in the public mind, even when it knew it was misleading. Speaking as a defence secretary who remarked frequently on the gravity of the decision to go to war, and boasted of the care with which sensitive intelligence was handled, Hoon told Lord Hutton he saw no reason to correct the impression given in the press that the weapons which could be deployed in forty-five minutes were rather more fearsome than the tactical battlefield weapons which MI6 believed Saddam had.

Acknowledging that he knew that a number of press reports had misrepresented the intelligence, he was asked in the course of the inquiry why no corrective statement had been issued. He replied: "I do not know."

Asked by counsel for the inquiry whether he had "an absolute duty" to correct the mistaken interpretations of the dossier, he replied: "No, I do not."

Asked where in the dossier it was made clear that only battlefield munitions were covered by the forty-five-minute claim, he appeared to give an offhand answer: "I do not have it to hand, and I do not know whether it was made clear."

These words reverberated long after the first public debate on the publication of Hutton had subsided, because they encapsulated the government's predicament. Blair's ministers, after all, had been schooled for years in the arts of public persuasion. Under Alastair Campbell, it was meant to be the skill that distinguished them from previous governments. Rebuttal units and special advisers had proliferated across Whitehall, and press officers with sharp political purposes began to replace the civil service information officers who were the backbone of the system. The government believed it had a way with the press. When it was accused of being in thrall to "spin" as a way of justifying itself it argued that it was merely telling its own story as best it could.

Now Hoon was admitting that misleading "spin" was useful: he had no interest in correcting mistakes if they were helpful to the government. He did not know if the dossier had been clear or not in presenting the claim which seemed, on its publication, to be one of the most compelling reasons to believe that Saddam was a threat. It was not only on the opposition benches that his attitude was described as arrogant. Such exchanges left many Labour MPs dispirited and angry. How were they to defend the government against accusations that it had lied when the secretary of state for defence insisted to a judge that he had no duty to ensure the public justification for going to war was presented accurately?

The significance of these feelings spread beyond the debate on Iraq. The issue was one of trust, and it touched everything. Labour might be maintaining a more or less consistent lead over the Conservatives, but was it believed? Blair went to war as a matter of conviction, but found that just when he expected the Iraq election to herald an era in which he would be able to persuade the electorate that he'd been right he was dogged by the accusation that the moral case he had made was based on flimsy evidence and misleading arguments. And, said his opponents, if you couldn't trust him on war . . .

So Blair's challenge at the start of 2005 was to clothe himself anew. He must appear different. The task wasn't one being carried out in an atmosphere of crisis—he never lost his confidence that the election would be won—but in preparing himself for a third term he'd be confronting the problems that had destabilized his government. His answer as he prepared to argue his case to the country was one which brought together his attitude to the machinery of government itself, the experience he was going through with Bush, his attitude to the European Union and his relationship with Brown. The end of the second term became for the Prime Minister much more than a stepping-stone to a third and last period of government, it became a period of transformation. It was one with which he would challenge his party yet again and one which carried with it the danger that he would finally exhaust the broad support he'd need to govern, especially if his majority shrank and his many Labour enemies prepared for the kill.

But after his dark moments in 2004 and the government's scrapes and fumbles of the winter, he told those around him that he was more determined than ever to press on.

The figure who would emerge, if he succeeded, would be a Blair moulded by war instead of being stained by it. There would be no apology for Iraq, and no recantation of the New Labour message with which he said he was going to tackle the perennial problem of public-service reform. The second term with all its domestic problems would pass away and something of the spirit of the early days would return. That, at least, was the plan.

It involved confrontation—with much of his party and with his chancellor. In thinking about how to refashion his premiership for a third term, Blair had to contemplate the possibility that he might lose Brown—either because their partnership finally ruptured and he found himself having to ask for the chancellor's resignation or because he would offer Brown a new post which he would refuse and choose to depart instead. That permanent breach was not inevitable, but it was a possibility that Blair knew was growing.

He also knew that around the Cabinet table there was scepticism about whether he could recover from his Iraq battering. Clarke in the Home Office would be more of his own man than Blunkett, Straw was a little more distant from Number 10 than he had been and was closer to Brown than before, Prescott was talking about the party going through a period of geological change and younger ministers on their way up were being careful not to tie themselves too closely to a prime minister who had let it be known clearly that his plan was to stand down just before the end of a third term.

Having announced that he wouldn't fight a fourth election, Blair had to accept that the consequence would be a gradual softening of the power he could exert while the natural forces of politics began to work on all his potential successors.

His answer to that problem was typically Blairite. First, he would continue the efforts he had made to establish a prime minister's department in all but name which would complete the process he had encouraged since 1997 of turning his Downing Street office into something more like an executive centre of government. He continued to believe that it would make government better, even when one of his former Cabinet secretaries, Lord Butler, gave an extraordinarily frank interview to the *Spectator* in which he said that Cabinet government as practised by Blair tended to produce bad decisions.

His agreement with critics like Cook, who had long complained of a lack of openness in Cabinet and a decision-making machine that took too little account of the need to build political alliances, spoke of a sense of alarm among some of the patricians of the civil service, almost all of them now retired. They believed that the Prime Minister's suspicion of collective decision-making would make government worse, not better. They suspected Blair believed the opposite, and they were right.

Even the diplomatic Sir Richard Wilson, Lord Butler's successor in the Cabinet Office, offered a hint of his own misgivings. He told a British Academy seminar in July 2004:

"Different prime ministers have different ways of doing business and there is no 'right' way of running a government. It is quite possible to reconcile due process with an informal style. But the risk is that informality may slide into something more fluid and unstructured, where advice and dissent may either not always be offered or else may not be heard.

"This is certainly a matter which engages collective responsibility. Prime ministers are only as powerful as their colleagues allow them to be."

These words have the air of a warning: if ministers want a government that manages a parliamentary majority with skill and devises policies that are wise as well as eye-catching they have to shape it themselves. Otherwise, they will find themselves swallowed up by a Downing Street machine that has been getting steadily stronger for the last thirty years. Blair has been quite frank with colleagues about his wish to speed up that process, and his chief of staff, Jonathan Powell is open about their plans. Friends in Washington report Powell as saying of the White House system: "We're going to have a go at this. Let's see how we get on." No one would accuse Powell to trying to invent a presidency. His ambitions were more modest, but they did envision a strengthened central core to the Whitehall bureaucracy and it became an important Blair objective.

There was evidence of this in the apparent closeness to the Prime Minister of Lord Birt, an adviser who managed to retain a lair in Downing Street when lesser figures in the policy unit were shunted out of the building to distant offices. As director general of the BBC, Birt had been famous—and notorious—for his engineer's fascination with management mechanisms and systems of bureaucratic control. In Downing Street his advice began to concentrate on the machinery of government, for example in reworking the role of the Treasury across Whitehall—a reform which would, of course, have the happy effect of curbing the day-to-day influence of any chancellor who was becoming too powerful.

This was part of Blair's prospectus for himself. It sat alongside a commitment to intensify his own attitude to Labour's position on the political spectrum. He describes it typically as "progressive" and not "Left" and is perfectly happy to confront veteran critics like Roy Hattersley who became so disillusioned that he accused him in print of taking the party to the Right of the territory once occupied by Margaret Thatcher. With the sounding board of Blunkett gone (at least temporarily) Blair was recommitting himself to the robust rhetoric of the "choice agenda" which had become the centrepiece of his ideas for the public service. The more Brown talked of the "public sphere" and Labour historic commitment to the common good, the more Blair would talk of choice.

These attitudes could be yanked together with a bit of Jesuitical argument, and made to seem reflections of a common approach, but not with much conviction. As the run-up to the general election began they were speaking in political dialects so different that they sometimes appeared to be two separate languages. Moreover, each seemed to be enjoying the experience.

This was the truth of Blair in year eight of government. He had set a course, and was determined to see through at least three years of a third term. He believed it would enable him to entrench market reforms in the public services which would be irreversible, and to complete improvements in education and the NHS which would be visible in a way that much of the second-term changes were not. At the same time—and this objective was as important for him as any other—he believed he could restore some of the sharpness of profile which had been dulled by the war. It was partly a recovery plan for himself—a restoration of the political vitality which he knew he had lost—and, just as importantly, a challenge to his rival.

In his mind, all the strands of the previous four or five years came together. His convictions after 11 September 2001 would be strengthened by an Iraq policy that was about to bear fruit; he'd recover the momentum which his government lost in its legislative and administrative bungles of the third term; his friendship with Bush would produce progress in the Middle East which sceptics had thought unlikely during his presidency; he'd re-establish his leadership of a government which at times had seemed divided and uncertain; Downing Street. would become, at last, an executive centre of government. That was how it seemed to him as he looked towards the spring and the election planned for May.

But from another perspective this was Blair the dreamer playing with fantasies. When the 2004 rumours of a possible resignation began to circulate, and the Brown camp put out stories of a deal to pass on the premiership, they weren't believed because there was real evidence for them—but simply because they rang true. They did not seem a surprise. Many Labour MPs—perhaps a majority of the party—had become convinced that the Iraq damage, though not immediately fatal, was a kind of infection that would continue to sap Blair's strength. They might rally themselves for an election campaign—it is what politics teaches you to do—but they would not do it in the expectation of a full term under Blair's leadership, whatever he might say in public. They would certainly prepare themselves for a parliament in which at best they would have a substantially reduced majority, and in which there would therefore be the prospect of exercising more influence on ministers and on Downing Street. And many of them would use that power to challenge some of the thinking around Blair, with the likely support of Brown.

Blair's hopes seemed to them to be unfounded. Either way, the pre-election landscape did not offer Prime Minister Blair a clear vista into the third term. It would be a struggle.

His personality, however, was now more sharply defined than at any time in government. His attitude to party and colleagues, and to the world outside, was clearer in his own mind than it had ever been. That change had been brought on, above all, by his experience in Iraq, the fifth occasion in which he had sent British troops into battle. It was the strange encounter with George W. Bush and with the American way of war that moulded the Blair who hoped to serve a third term. He had been blooded in a conflict which his party did not want and which had lost him many friends. He had defended a president some of whose attitudes he found mystifying and whose friends sometimes alarmed him and, in the course of their alliance after 2001, Blair had taken to another stage the process that began with his election as Labour leader in 1994.

The instinct to go against the grain, the lure of the world stage, a sense of mission in a time of disorder and flux, an impatience with any thinking that seemed to flow from one ideological source, an instinct for the politics of personal persuasion—all these were traits in Blair which established themselves fully only in his second term of government and were now the sinews of his political character. He believed they prepared him for the third, just as the sceptics inside and outside his government thought they might bring on more of the problems which had so disturbed them after the first flush of excitement they experienced in 1997 has passed.

Blair's determination as he approached the election meant he was prepared for a fight. In particular, he was ready for the confrontation which must come with his chancellor. And so was Brown.

Each knew that the days of rubbing along were nearly over. Brown might remain at the Treasury, left to count the days until Blair's promised departure before the end of the third term, but he would be dealing with a darker economic outlook and spending plans that might prove too ambitious. It would be a relationship that would be bound to become more difficult with Blair, whose determination to think his own way into the future was becoming as strong as Brown's own, though without the rigorous discipline that was the chancellor's forte. They might have to consider the alternatives.

Blair had been urged for some time to challenge Brown directly with an offer of the Foreign Office, one he might be expected to refuse, even if it meant going to the back benches. It was a course that would be fraught with danger for the Prime Minister. Even if he could portray Brown as a sulky refusenik for turning down one of the great offices of state, a defrocked chancellor on the back benches with Brown's political talents and network of friends would prove a formidable enemy. And it would then be war.

But might Brown accept a move? The assumption has always been that he would not. Despite his passion for the problems of the developing world—emphasized in his African tour in early 2005—the world of diplomacy has never attracted him. He would be obliged to be a cheerleader for the European referendum which, though he insists that the commitment remains strong, he has never wanted to be. It would almost certainly prove an uncomfortable berth and his friends believed he would not accept it. Leaving British politics to go to the World Bank, for example, might even be preferable (and Brown has been courted by the likes of Bill Gates of Microsoft who saw him as an international figure). But his tribal instincts in the Labour Party, which Blair has never shared, would make it difficult for him to uproot himself.

So as they approached the election, they seemed stuck. Bla
was making it clear that he wouldn't do a deal to get out after
year of the third term—after the referendum, win or lose—an
was planning a manifesto that would define Blairism largely i
terms of public-service reforms of a kind that would sit easily wit
a right-of-centre government anywhere in Europe. Brown, mear
while, was thinking how he might fashion a premiership, give
the chance, and how he would put his own stamp on it.

In that atmosphere there was little to do except get through th
election with the minimum damage. The future could almo
certainly not be resolved finally between them until the vote
were in.

At stake for Blair was his legacy. As a prime minister wh
would always have "Iraq" engraved on his heart, he wante
something more to leave behind. There might be progress i
Israel–Palestine, he might even hope for some wondrous conve:
sion of the masses at home over the European constitution. Bu
whatever it was, he wanted it to be his alone. He had decided 1
try to solve the problem of trust by trusting himself.

In the years since 9/11, Blair had changed. His energy ha
come from abroad, particularly from his alliance with the Amer
cans. There was plenty of pain associated with it in the war whic
was its consequence, but in turning his leadership into a questio
of conviction Blair found himself. It is a personality that disturbe
some of his closest colleagues and government, and repelle
others, but there was nothing fake about it. The character wa
real. His attitudes to government at home, and his own ambitior
for a third term, would have been quite different without h
transformation into a leader who was shaped by war, for it seize
his emotions and dominated his thinking.

Perhaps it even convinced him that he held his fate in his ow
hands—that the maelstrom of Iraq and the crises of confidence i
his party and government could be calmed with the power of tha
experience. But if he believed that, it would be an illusion. Th
two-term Blair was a leaner and tougher political figure than th
one everyone knew before 9/11 but the accidents of history hadn

given him the alchemist's power to change things around him, at home or abroad.

American presidents have often found that at the start of the second term the freedom that comes with knowing there will never be another election to be fought is counterbalanced by a natural shrinking of power. The moment of maximum influence is past, and the ability to shape politics begins to fade. There are opportunities to be seized, but they are few and time starts to fly. Blair, like the President with whom he made war and who had fought his last election, was now subject to that natural law by which the political leader must live.

For all his conviction and the vigour he had rediscovered, the struggle would not become easier but more wearying all the time.

# A Note on Sources

Quotations from Tony Blair, unless attributed to public statements, come from an interview with the author on May 26, 2004, conducted on the record at 10 Downing Street. Quotations from others, unless their public sources are indicated, are from conversations or interviews with the author, for example in the cases of Bill Clinton, Hans Blix, Howard Dean and John le Carré. References to the books listed below are made clear in the text with a credit to the author. A number of remarks are attributed to individuals without the source being named, in order to protect confidences. In each case, I have private information that is definitive. Inevitably, I have drawn on many conversations with those in politics and government over several years in making the judgments in this book.

Blix, Hans. *Disarming Iraq: The Search for Weapons of Mass Destruction.* London: Bloomsbury, 2004.

Blumenthal, Sidney. *The Clinton Wars: An Insider's Account of the White House Years.* New York: Viking, 2003.

Clarke, Richard A. *Against All Enemies: Inside America's War on Terror.* New York: Free Press, 2004.

Cook, Robin. *Point of Departure.* London: Simon and Schuster, 2003.

Cooper, Robert. *The Breaking of Nations: Order and Chaos in the 21st Century.* London: Atlantic Books, 2004.

Gould, Philip. *Unfinished Revolution: How the Modernisers Saved the Labour Party.* London: Little, Brown, 1998.

Hennessy, Peter. *The Prime Minister: The Office and Its Holders Since 1945.* London: Allen Lane, 2000.

Kagan, Robert. *Paradise and Power: America and Europe in the New World Order.* London: Atlantic Books, 2003.

Kampfner, John. *Blair's Wars.* London: Free Press, 2003.

Keegan, John. *The Iraq War.* London: Hutchinson, 2004.

Major, John. *The Autobiography.* London: HarperCollins, 1999.

Naughtie, James. *The Rivals: Blair and Brown—The Intimate Story of a Political Marriage.* London: Fourth Estate, 2001.

Peston, Robert. *Brown's Britain.* London: Short Books, 2005.

Pimlott, Ben. *Harold Wilson.* London: HarperCollins, 1992.

Pollard, Stephen. *David Blunkett.* London: Hodder and Stoughton, 2004.

Riddell, Peter. *Hug Them Close: Blair, Clinton, Bush, and the "Special Relationship."* London: Politico's Publishing, 2003.

Stephens, Philip. *Blair: The Making of a World Leader.* New York: Viking, 2004.

Stothard, Peter. *Thirty Days: A Month at the Heart of Blair's War.* London: HarperCollins, 2003.

Woodward, Bob. *Bush at War.* New York: Simon and Schuster, 2003.

—*Plan of Attack.* New York: Simon and Schuster, 2004.

SOME RELEVANT SPEECHES BY TONY BLAIR

Economic Club of Chicago, April 24, 1999

NATO Fiftieth Anniversary, Washington, March 8, 1999

World Economic Forum, Davos, Switzerland, January 18, 2000

Labour Party Conference, September 25, 2001

Lord Mayor's Banquet, London, November 12, 2001

George H.W. Bush Presidential Library, Texas, April 7, 2002

Foreign and Commonwealth Office Conference, London, January 7,
  2003
Iraq Debate, House of Commons, London, March 18, 2003
Address to the Nation, March 20, 2003
Both Houses of Congress, Washington, D.C., July 7, 2003
Lord Mayor's Banquet, London, November 10, 2003
Sedgefield Labour Party, County Durham, March 5, 2004

# INDEX